Learning Through Life 1

Culture and Processes of Adult Learning

Learning Through Life

The other volume in this series is:

Adult Learners, Education and Training
Edited by Richard Edwards, Sandy Sieminski and David Zeldin

This reader is one of two that have been prepared as part of the Open University Undergraduate course, *Learning Through Life: Education and Training Beyond School.*

It is one part of an integrated teaching system and the selection is therefore related to other material available to students. It is designed to evoke the critical understanding of students. Opinions expressed in it are not necessarily those of the course team or of the University.

If you would like to study this course, please write to the Central Enquiry Service, PO Box 200, The Open University, Walton Hall, Milton Keynes, MK7 6YZ. A copy of *Studying with the Open University* is available from the same address.

Learning Through Life 1

Culture and Processes of Adult Learning

A Reader

Edited by
Mary Thorpe, Richard Edwards and
Ann Hanson

London and New York
in association with
The Open University

First published 1993
by Routledge
11 New Fetter Lane, London EC4P 4EE

Simultaneously published in the USA and Canada
by Routledge
29 West 35th Street, New York, NY 10001

Reprinted 1995, 1997

Typeset in Times by Intype, London
Printed and bound in Great Britain by
Mackays of Chatham PLC, Chatham, Kent

British Library Cataloguing in Publication Data
A catalogue record for this book is available from the British Library

Library of Congress Cataloguing in Publication Data
A catalogue record for this book is available from the Library of Congress

ISBN 0-415-08981-6

For Verna Rosen, 1933–92

Contents

Part 3 Learners' experience and facilitating learning

Figures

Tables

Acknowledgements

For permission to reproduce the materials in this volume, acknowledgement is due to the following sources: Chapter 1, ' "Really useful knowledge", 1790–1850' (edited version), Johnson, R. (1988) in Lovett, T. (ed.) *Radical Approaches to Adult Education: A Reader*, London, Routledge; Chapter 2, 'Feminist challenges to curriculum design' (edited version), Parsons, S. F. in *Studies in the Education of Adults*, vol. 22, no. 1. pp. 49–58 (reprinted with the permission of the National Institute of Adult Continuing Education, © NIACE); Chapter 3, 'Competency and the pedagogy of labour', (edited version) Field, J. in *Studies in the Education of Adults*, vol. 23, no. 1, pp. 41–52 (reprinted with the permission of the National Institute of Adult Continuing Education, © NIACE); Chapter 4, 'Chile, Santiago: breaking the culture of silence' (edited version), Archer, D. and Costello, P. (1990) in *Literacy and the Power: The Latin American Background* (reprinted with the permission of the publishers, Earthscan); Chapter 6, 'Education for adults', (edited version), Squires, G. (1987) in *The Curriculum Beyond School* (reprinted with the permission of the publishers, Edward Arnold); Chapter 8, 'Adult development' (edited version), Tennant, M. (1988) in *Psychology and Adult Learning*, London, Routledge; Chapter 9, 'The process of experiential learning' (edited version), Kolb, D.A. (1984) in *Experiential Learning* (reprinted with the permission of Prentice Hall, Englewood Cliffs, New Jersey); Chapter 10, 'Access: towards education or miseducation?' (edited version), Weil, S.W. (1989) in Fulton, O. (ed.) *Access and Institutional Change* (reprinted with the permission of the publishers, Open University Press); Chapter 12, 'Teaching learning: redefining the teacher's role' (edited version), Gremmo, M-J. and Abé, D. (1985) in Riley, P. (ed.) *Discourse and Learning* (reprinted with the permission of the publishers, Longman); Chapter 14, 'The interpersonal relationship in the facilitation of learning' (edited version), Rogers, C.R. (1967) in *Freedom to Learn for the 80s* (reprinted with the permission of the Association for Supervision and Curriculum Development, © 1967 by ASCD, NEA. All rights reserved); Chapter 15, 'The utilization of learning objectives: a behavioural approach' (edited version), Curzon, L.B. (1990) in *Teaching in Further Education, An Outline of Principles and Practice* (4th edn) (reprinted with the permission of the publishers, Cassell); Chapter 16, 'What is skill and how is it acquired?' (edited version), Sloboda, J. (1986) in *The Skilful Mind* (reprinted with the permission of the publishers, Open University Press).

While every reasonable effort has been made to clear copyright permissions with the holders of materials reproduced here, there are still some instances where we have been unable to contact the copyright holder. In this volume it proved impossible to gain permission for Chapter 7.

Introduction

Mary Thorpe, Richard Edwards and Ann Hanson

This Reader brings together major contributions to the exploration of the nature and significance of the learning that happens beyond school. This is adult learning, although some readers may identify more with a type of provision such as continuing education and training, access, vocational education and training (VET), further and higher education, nurse education and human resource development (HRD). The list could be even longer, for as Squires so clearly outlines (see Chapter 6), the rapid growth in this field over the last decade, and its increasing diversity of context and curriculum, means that our field can properly be considered to be any educational or training activity engaged in by adults, whether formal, non-formal or informal.

The selection of chapters has been governed by our aim, which is twofold. First, it is to explore the significance of learning both to those who undertake it and to society more generally, and second to consider how learning happens and how best it might be developed. Taken as a whole, these readings open up a number of perspectives on the role of learning in the reproduction of social life. They show how learning can be used either to reinforce or to change relative power in status or occupation, how it might reinforce or challenge an individual's sense of identity and the roles he or she chooses to play within the community. Learning is portrayed as the mechanism through which individuals and groups both adapt to their environment and change it. There are differences of view, however, as to the degree to which learning can be used intentionally to change organizations, communities or even individuals, in order to achieve predetermined goals.

Given the size of the literature which impinges upon such a broad field, it has been necessary to be highly selective. We have included chapters which fit with a view of learning as a potentially dynamic activity and one where the diversity between people and communities is developed. How and what we learn is an expression of our culture, whatever form that takes. This makes for differences not only between geographically diverse areas (for example, between countries such as those in Latin

America and those in the European Community), but also between minority communities within nations, and between different regions. We may also speak of a variety of learning cultures, by which we mean that learning takes on distinctive forms within the sub-cultures created by organizations (such as multinationals, unemployment programmes, educational institutions, voluntary organizations, and so on).

We make use of culture, therefore, as an overarching concept, signalling a concern with exploration of the social context for learning, and of relationships of power in learning. Issues of class, gender, age and ethnicity are central here in answering key questions about whose interests are served by different forms of learning, and whether new forms of learning can be developed to enable the relatively powerless to have access to effective learning, the better to contest and to change their own subordinated position.

These issues are explored in three sections, linked thematically: Part 1 deals with power, purpose and outcomes; Part 2 with adulthood and learning, and Part 3 with learners' experience and the facilitation of learning. We will now introduce each part in turn.

PART 1 POWER, PURPOSE AND OUTCOMES

There is a tendency to think of adult learners as freely 'choosing to learn'. However, learning may not be quite so voluntary as at first appears. We may be required to attend workplace training and staff development as part of our conditions of employment. If we are unemployed, financial support may be linked with participation on a training scheme, so that we experience undeniable pressure to attend. Put at its simplest, the purposes of learning can be seen as ranged along a continuum from emancipatory to oppressive, according to the degree to which they enhance or limit our life opportunities. This continuum has both a personal and a social dimension. For example, we may learn new skills, giving fresh personal opportunities, but these may still be in areas of relatively low pay or part-time work. In this case, learning may simply reaffirm a position of little power in the social division of labour, rather than transforming that position or the social division of labour more generally.

The continual development of technologies of production can, however, lead to radical changes in the workplace. This may require further training for some, but lead to unemployment for others. In this context, the promotion of learning clearly entails a struggle to give value to certain forms of knowledge, behaviour and attitudes over others. In Field's analysis of vocational education for example, he argues that the value given to this form of learning has three aims: to socialize our consent to the maintenance of the *status quo*, to contribute to employee recruitment through the development of qualifications, and to generate forms of knowledge and behaviour appropriate from the employers' perspective.

The provision of education and training is about producing some notion of 'correct' knowledge and appropriate behaviour, rewarded through assessment and qualification. The privileging of some forms of knowledge, attitudes and practices over others has been identified as central to the means by which the dominance of some interests in society over others is consented to, rather than forcibly imposed (Gramsci 1971). In different ways, this position is illustrated by Johnson (with relation to knowledge and forms of learning), Parsons (attitudes, especially concerning gender), and Field (behaviour and the risks of employer-defined learning).

Johnson's exploration of the idea of 'really useful knowledge' in working-class movements in England in the early nineteenth century has resonances for the last decade of the twentieth and beyond. It articulates the view that knowledge and power are integrally linked: power shapes knowledge and knowledge can confer power. What is valued as 'useful knowledge' varies according to our social position and the purposes we pursue. The attempt to give knowledge the appearance of a body of 'facts' to be learned is a strategy to create and recreate consent to the dominant view of a hegemonic class. The view that knowledge is independent of those who produce and sustain it, untainted by the operation of power in society, is a position which has been effectively attacked from a number of positions, philosophical, sociological and political.

Johnson's historical exploration of certain English working-class movements shows how, for those inside these movements, 'really useful knowledge' meant learning which would serve their interests as they defined them. Knowledge provided by the state in the provision of initial education was 'useless knowledge' resulting in the subjection of the working class to capitalism. This opposition to 'useless knowledge' resulted in the establishment of organizations autonomous from the state, as a strategy to create education for an alternative order, in which the working class would be free. (This position was also adopted as part of certain feminist and anti-racist strategies.) In addition to autonomy, 'really useful knowledge' was generated through informality, with learning being an integral part of the cultural politics of the movement, rather than something taking place in separate institutions. No division was drawn between education, politics and life; the use of reading-rooms and wide circulation of a radical press. Compulsory schooling by the state was seen as part of a strategy to enforce the state's view of 'useful knowledge', thus undermining working-class opposition expressed through these alternative forms of learning. Although such alternatives have not survived, the notion of 'really useful knowledge' still has a critical dimension in suggesting that what is valued as knowledge is not neutral.

A critical edge is also apparent in the feminist challenge to established curriculum design. Parsons identifies three prime areas to be tackled: attitudes, language and power. Each of these needs positive change to provide an emancipatory framework for women's learning. She demonstrates how curricula can and do conceive gender in a way which restricts the opportunities for development available to women. Issues are framed and 'resolved' in particular ways to reinforce the stereotypes of women's role in society. These attitudes are embedded in the very language we use and in what and how we learn. The various strands of feminism – liberal, radical, socialist – attempt to challenge this gender inequality in different ways, and can be used in reconstructing the curriculum so that issues of gender are at least recognized, and perhaps explored.

Behaviour has become a key focus of attention in late twentieth-century industrialized societies. Whether in the family, on the streets or in the workplace, 'good' behaviour is of critical importance in situations of rapid social chance and uncertainty. This is particularly true in relation to the economy, where technological and demographic changes are resulting in many of us having to learn new skills and patterns of work. In England, Wales and Northern Ireland, these have been enshrined in the framework of National Vocational Qualifications (NVQs), and in Scotland, Scottish Vocational Qualifications (SVQs), which specify what one has to be capable of doing in any given occupational area. We have to demonstrate that we are competent to cut someone's hair, to mend a car or to train someone, not simply that we have knowledge about these things.

As Field points out, the emphasis on behaviour in NVQs ignores the contexts in which competence is being demonstrated. These contexts do not provide learners with a framework for critical reflection on their (and our) interests as workers as a separate issue from employers' interests. An emphasis on competence as the outcome of learning reinforces a 'pedagogy of labour' in which it is assumed that our interests coincide with those of our employers, at all points.

The learning we engage in cannot, therefore, be isolated from relations of power; it is integral to those relations. This point is central to Archer and Costello's description of the role of literacy programmes in Chile during General Pinochet's regime. Extreme forms of state-led oppression included control of the mass media. Literacy activists involved in grassroots organizations soon realized that television and video played a much greater role in the lives of ordinary people than books and print generally. By working with other activists and neighbourhood groups to make videos of their own direct experience of poverty and repression they helped create a new sense of empowerment. Through creating and viewing their own videos, people realized how media images are constructed and can be used to influence behaviour and undermine opposition to those in power. By the same token, they learned how to use the technology of the media to interpret their own history in their own terms. Using Freire's phrase, they learned how to 'read' their own lives and their country's history. In the process, they also learned how to use the media to reassert their opposition to repression and to help bring to an end the rule of Pinochet.

However, it would be wrong to conclude that learning can be classified unequivocally as either emancipatory or oppressive. Particular forms may have both emancipatory and controlling aspects. For instance, Butler's research demonstrates that the skills gained in the domestic workplace can be specified in terms of competences alongside those found elsewhere in the world of employment. This is emancipatory in so far as we are able to have those skills accredited and given value within a recognized structure of qualifications (NVQs) which may result in employment; it opens up horizons which might otherwise not exist. However, it may also be oppressive in that it could result in the confirmation of women's role in the home as the basis for women entering low pay and low status jobs – that is, 'women's work' extending from the home to the workplace. This could happen either through the transfer of skills from the private to the public domain, or through the re-evaluation (devaluation) of the status of certain forms of employment into which women move. This has been termed elsewhere as the 'housewifization of labour' (Hart 1992).

Thus, there are complex issues at work in attempting to untangle the operation of power in learning in order to establish the emancipatory and oppressive dimensions to what we learn. The outcome of our evaluations depends on our purposes and is itself a reflection of the struggle between different groups – a struggle which is political in nature.

PART 2 ADULTHOOD AND LEARNING

The chapters in this part review a variety of attempts to construct a theoretical base for the learning which adults do. In various ways, it addresses the question, 'What, if anything, makes learning in adulthood categorically distinct from learning in childhood?' Squires provides an excellent introduction to this, taking us through the diversity of the curriculum, definitions of adulthood, adult forms of thought and adult development, which leads him to conclude that:

Education for adults is inherently diverse, . . . there are few if any common elements in all the different kinds of teaching and learning that exist . . . If there is a particular flavour or emphasis in the adult curriculum it is likely to lie in the greater importance of social and personal considerations in what is taught and how.

(Squires, Ch. 6: 105)

This issue of whether adult learning is different in degree rather than different in kind, has generated an extensive literature, not least because it feeds directly into considerations about whether adult education or adult learning provides a sufficient rationale for the development of an autonomous academic discipline. Knowles's re-introduction and popularization of the term 'andragogy' has generated much of the debate round the distinctiveness or otherwise of adult learning. Davenport separates out both the semantics of the term and the ebb and flow of different positions for and against. While recognizing its publicity value, he concludes that 'adult education could survive quite nicely without andragogy'. However, he does attempt to rescue the term, returning to a more literal translation of its Greek root, which would leave open the issue of methodology. Self-directed learning and facilitation may be the most appropriate approach, but that will depend more on learning style, content, goals and gender, than on age.

Notwithstanding this critique, andragogy and the debates it has stimulated have done much to raise awareness of the need for separate and enhanced provision for adult learners. This has helped move the practice of institutions of education and training closer to the needs of adult learners, and to question the priority they have accorded traditionally to their own systems. Unfortunately, Knowles has tended to overlook the constraints of these systems, and even the diversity of learners themselves and their needs. Empirical research has provided evidence that many learners resist self-direction and student-centred methods. It is perhaps ironic that Knowles's assertions are open to the charge that they are prescriptive, and run counter to the humanistic aspirations which underpin them. However, he cannot be held responsible if his terminology has been used uncritically or as a mere label or slogan within the broad field of adult education practice. Davenport provides useful clarification here, and hands back andragogy with a definition which does not beg the question of how best adults should learn. In his view, the next step ought to be a rigorous empirical testing of the assumptions of Knowles and others: 'Those assumptions which could not be verified would be discarded or reformulated instead of being accepted as gospel by true believers.'

Tennant begins the next chapter with similar concerns about the uncritical (as he sees it) application of research into the nature of adulthood to practice. He draws attention to the importance which adult educators have accorded to theories that draw general conclusions about the existence of typical or 'normal' stages in development during adulthood. He criticizes methodologies which rely on small, often unrepresentative samples and which use questionable, culturally specific measures. There are risks in the use to which this research is put, legitimating the experience of particular groups and marginalizing that of others. Tennant sees personal identity as a social construct and in a pluralist society it will be influenced by the huge varieties of interaction between individual experience and social and cultural contexts. The possibilities for learning are thus open-ended and not delimited by the lowest common denominator of life-stages and social roles.

Tennant's analysis of the methodologies of life-stages research offers a salutary warning to beware the easy borrowing of typologies and concepts for direct application to the complex practice of teaching and learning. Their value to us should be as heuristic devices, prompting questions about what we should be learning and when, not providing ready-made blanket solutions based on narrow, culturally specific tasks and roles.

Both Tennant and Kolb draw upon an implicit assumption that the relationship between learner and environment is rich, complex and unpredictable, each capable of being changed in the process of interaction with the other. Kolb's chapter is solely concerned with outlining a theory of learning which, though it is not specific to adults only, has been used most explicitly in adult learning contexts. Kolb's now well-known model of experiential learning argues for a dialectical relationship between learner and environment, in which two diametrically opposed modes of knowing provide the means through which we appropriate our experience and transform it. These divergent ways of coming to know are, according to Kolb, a supremely adaptive mechanism; they are the means by which we learn anything, whether from direct experience or from mediated forms of experience, such as reading, watching media presentations, or being trained or taught.

Kolb's theory has been applied extensively across the whole field of education and training, and used to justify an emphasis on the value of experience as the raw material for reflection, and on the importance of learning style in how people learn. This again brings us up against the danger of over-simplification through the too easy use of learner typologies, for there can only be a rough approximation between individual response and general categories of learner style. But Kolb's work has been valuable in generating further research and development into the differences between learners, and into ways in which an awareness of learning style can be used to facilitate more effective learning.

Kolb's work on experiential learning has been seminal, perhaps because, as he himself points out, he aims to produce a synthesis of existing learning theories in a 'holistic integrative perspective on learning that combines experience, perception, cognition and behavior'. He does not set out 'to pose experiential learning theory as a third alternative to behavioral and cognitive learning theories', but to draw together themes within the work of Dewey, Lewin, Freire and Piaget, in particular, emphasizing the intimate relationship between learning and the creation of knowledge.

Experiential learning is associated with the move away from perceptions of knowledge as objectively determined, neutral and culture free. Knowledge is created in a continuous process of experience, reflection and conceptualization, and it is this process which defines learning, rather than specifications of fixed outcomes which result from learning. 'Learning is an emergent process whose outcomes represent only historical record, not knowledge of the future.'

All the chapters in this part carry a strong message about the diversity of people's experience of learning and the dangers of seeing adult learners as a homogeneous group. As we examine how each person builds up their own learning cycles and approaches, we can see the need for differentiation and breaking down of stereotypes of adult learners. Every chapter, however, in different ways goes beyond the uniqueness of individual experience, to open out the social implications of the learning that adults do, both for the creation of knowledge and for the development of societies.

PART 3 LEARNERS' EXPERIENCE AND FACILITATING LEARNING

Here we turn to themes and issues focused on the micro-context of teaching and learning. The chapters analyse the interaction of learners with lecturers or trainers, the qualitative response of learners to their involvement in education and training, and the factors which influence their response. Three major sources of knowledge – practice, research, and theory – are used to identify the outcomes of learning as well as how best to promote the learning process. We have been concerned to explore the issues in these areas not as decontextualized abstractions, but through their effects for learners themselves, and in relation to current developments in the field. A concern with the micro-context of teaching and learning, therefore, does not mean that we turn aside from the policy issues of the day, or from the relationships of power which help to shape learning interactions.

The first two chapters provide a good illustration of what is at issue here. They draw on research which has been stimulated by the access movement – the growth of courses and schemes to enable entry to higher education for learners not conventionally qualified for such entry. Both Weil and Rosen base their analyses on extensive qualitative research with and for the students who have participated in this movement, whether through access courses or through mature age entry to higher education. Therefore, both make a contribution to the literature about student learning in higher education, but from a perspective significantly different from the established tradition. Their research has been into the response of students who do not feel 'at home' in higher education, whether for reasons of social class, gender, race or prior experience of a different kind.

Much research into how students learn has paid little attention to the issue of student identity and the social factors affecting learning. Perry's influential study of cognitive development in the college years, for example, drew on extensive interviews with the products of Ivy League institutions in the United States, who were largely middle class, white and, on the whole, male (Perry 1970). Cognitive psychology draws upon an experimental tradition which is more concerned to explain learning processes common to all humans rather than to illuminate the differences between them (Richardson *et al.* 1987). And while educational research has been more interested in the experience of learning, it has concentrated on the micro-world of the institution, as if it were sealed off from the influence of the wider society. Thus, we have a literature rich in the analysis of learning styles, the effects of instructional style and on surface versus deep level approaches to study (Marton *et al.* 1984). This may well reflect the fact that during the 1970s and early 1980s, when much of this research was carried out, the student intake into higher education, and the culture of learning within it, was much less subject to the pressures for increased student numbers, and to the effects of changes in government funding and policy, than it is now. It is not too far from the truth to say that this research tradition took as axiomatic the traditional goals of higher education, and the elitism of its entry procedures and attitudes to knowledge.

The access movement challenges such assumptions, and offers the possibility for studying a body of students who experience a more overt form of culture shock, and personal disjunction, during at least their early experience of conventional higher education, than those Perry might have interviewed at universities in the United States during the 1960s. Weil's analysis of this student response leads her to emphasize the personal stance of lecturers, and their ability to respond to 'the person in the student', as pivotal in helping students adjust to the demands of higher education. She shows how students enter with what may be idealized visions of higher education, and with powerful memories of earlier rejection by teachers and educational institutions generally. These students must work through much 'unfinished business' from their prior educational biographies, as well as meet the intellectual demands of first-year degree studies. Weil concludes that there is the real possibility of 'miseducation', where students are not able to reconcile the demands of the institution with their own ideals and emotional needs. She counsels against an unthinking assumption that access is achieved simply by getting more working-class students, or more women, through the entry barriers of institutions.

Rosen, exploring the experience of inner-city access students in particular, focuses on issues of race and learning. She also finds ambivalence towards higher education, and a recognition among those who have on the whole succeeded through the access movement that it has had a powerful effect on their identity and on the relationships in their lives. Part of what there is to say here is about the way in which going back into further and higher education enables people to articulate their anger at growing up with the experience of racial prejudice working against them. The difference blackness makes appears less about drawing on black culture in general than about the solidarity of those who have refused to accept a negative racial stereotype of their abilities, and who see in their own personal struggle to succeed the representation of a wider struggle for justice and rights. What learning means to these students is shaped by their perception of themselves as an embattled minority within a white-dominated culture. It may be that the most challenging aspect of their presence is that those who are not black must accept that they also have 'ethnicity', that each of us comes in one way or another from an ethnic community. It is also challenging to have to examine why it is that some people's experience is given more attention and value than others, and why some forms of knowledge have a dominant status in society.

Weil and Rosen take us inside the identity of learners who feel alienated by the learning environment of educational institutions, and who survive by drawing on a variety of personal resources and relationships. Many of the issues which the access movement has thrown into sharp relief will not be new to practitioners, but what is much more difficult is to recommend what should be done to change the culture and practices of continuing education and training generally.

One solution which has been widely promoted, is that learner or student-centred methods should be adopted whatever the context, whatever the content of the curriculum. Much of the writing on this theme operates at the level of course design, and case studies of good practice. Gremmo and Abe offer one such example, in their account of the options offered at the Centre de Recherches et d'Applications Pedagogiques en Langues, to learners aiming to improve their English. (We assume that some learners were women, albeit that the male pronoun is used throughout.)

Their argument is that we have over-learned a set pattern of role allocation and role behaviour which means that we always take for granted that decision-making, task setting and the many tasks that there are to do in a class, will be carried out by teachers only. If we open up this situation by offering learners a *choice* of learning method, including options where learners *themselves* take charge of much that has been traditionally done by teachers, then learners will start to think about how they do learn best, what *their* preferences are and the most effective plan for their circumstances. This is an approach which combines a kind of 'learner consumerism' with common sense and extensive practical experience of what works and with whom. Gremmo and Abe draw on a social psychology tradition in which role relationships and role-patterned behaviour are seen to shape what people do and, to a large extent, what they think.

Such a position could also be supported by the research which Downs and others have done, from the 1960s onwards, into the learning skill of those with few if any personal qualifications, and into the effectiveness of training in developing learning abilities. She identifies a passive approach to learning and inappropriate learning methods as powerful barriers preventing people from making the best use of further training or education in adulthood. She identifies what might almost be seen as a conspiracy of silence, between trainers and trainees, about how the training proceeds. Trainees can identify training methods which stop them learning, but do nothing to get the trainer to use them; trainers know about ways of improving learning by trainees, but see their job as teaching about a product, not helping people to learn.

Downs makes thought-provoking links between these interactional issues and the widely held notion that new forms of production require new ways of working and therefore new ways of learning – for example, workers who can continually update their knowledge and learn through their own initiatives. It may also be the case that new forms of production create many low-skilled jobs and destroy occupations without creating alternatives. The research which Downs has applied in many different employment contexts also carries practical implications for developments in formal education as well as training. The facilitation of learning is not something we should see as confined in its importance to certain sectors (such as non-vocational education) or to particular methods (for example, group discussion).

All of these chapters draw either explicitly or implicitly on a particular tradition of intellectual inquiry. Downs, for example, draws on occupational psychology and works within its acceptance of the definitions of work, and what is in the workers' interests, of those in power in the workplace. Any commitment to any paradigm or to a particular theoretical approach carries strength and weaknesses of which we can be aware even while we may not be able to resolve the problems they create. In the last three chapters in Part 3 we have contrasting positions on what is important in learning and how it might best be facilitated, each of which draws explicitly upon a particular theoretical tradition.

Carl Rogers' assertion of the importance of human relationship and of the qualities of realness, prizing, and empathic understanding are derived from a humanist tradition which gives priority to personal growth as the goal of education (indeed of experience as a whole) and human interaction as the prime stimulus for learning. The commitment to an 'inner self' reminds us that this reflects an earlier period in the history of public expectations of the formal system of education and of response to it. Some may now feel that the political pressure exerted upon teachers and educational systems everywhere makes it impossible to speak so single-mindedly 'on the side of' the growth of each individual learner. The emphasis now is more likely to be on 'what do employers need?; how can we afford retraining if output (and profits) are falling?; can we afford to provide small-group teaching *and* increase the number of places?; should we concentrate on those most likely to succeed with the least resource, rather than all who might benefit?' These are the kinds of issues which dominate current debates and make it difficult to contribute in any terms other than those provided by cost/benefit analysis. In contrast, Rogers' chapter is an account of *values* in education, and of the feelings which, in his view, need to be in play for relationships which facilitate rather than block learning. If his language and concerns now speak to us as if from another world, it is a measure of the extent to which economic values have come to dominate *all* public debate about opportunities for learning. The public policy debates of the 1980s might be judged a wasteland by those who (like Rogers) are interested in social, civic or moral values having a legitimate role to play in the goals of education and training.

Curzon's outline of behavioural objectives espouses 'instruction' and in that sense provides the diametrically opposite view to Rogers' rejection of instruction. This may also seem a language from the past. The Open University, for example, moved away from promoting behavioural objectives very early in its course production, during the 1970s. However, it has never abandoned the explicit statement of general objectives, and in other ways we can trace the influence of behaviourism in the latest practices of vocational education. The National Council For Vocational Qualifications in England and Wales, for example, has instituted a massive process of competence definition and assessment. The behavioural aspects of competence are the focus of a newly defined system of National Vocational Qualifications, to be assessed wherever possible, through demonstration on the job (see also Butler's chapter in Part 1). Primary emphasis has been given to the definition of outcomes, and to standards of performance used in the assessment of competence. The process by which these standards are to be reached has, as it were, been derestricted. What matters is that we demonstrate our competence, not how we got there. The intention behind this may have been benevolent, seeking to legitimate informal and experiential learning, particularly for those who have typically been unsuccessful in formal systems of education and training. However, one of the effects has been to downgrade the *process* of learning as an issue of importance, and to devalue the status of knowledge and its role in the development of skill.

Curzon's succinct outline of the classical view of the application of behaviourism to instruction shows that behaviourism *can* be incorporated with a curriculum oriented to knowledge and information as well as to skills. Some may argue against the way in which knowledge is packaged within a behavioural objectives approach, but that is a different issue.

The importance of knowledge is emphasized in cognitive approaches to skill, which Sloboda develops in the final chapter. Working within a definition of cognition as 'activities of knowing, of gathering, organizing, and making use of knowledge' (Gellatly 1986), he analyses skill as it manifests itself in familiar social contexts. Knowledge is a core component of skill, one which he shows as enabling other characteristics of what we would describe as skilled behaviour, such as fluency and rapidity. A cognitive approach can go along with acceptance of the determining role of social context in the definition and maintenance of skills, albeit that social factors are often undeveloped in the explanations of learning developed within the experimental tradition of psychology on which the cognitive approach draws.

The contrasting style and content of these last three chapters is indicative of the diverse traditions and sources of knowledge on which this Reader as a whole draws. Our selection of chapters reflects perceptions about who is interested in this field of research and practice, and what contributions will be found useful. In this we face all the familiar dilemmas of those who plan a curriculum for the interest and stimulus of a group of learners. We have asked ourselves what experiences you bring as you pick up this Reader, what you are looking for from your reading, and the contexts in which you might wish to use the outcomes of your learning process. As you turn now to select a particular chapter to read, we hope you will find that our assumptions on your behalf are well grounded, in a series of enjoyable and stimulating contributions.

REFERENCES

Gellatly, A. (ed.) (1986) *The Skilful Mind: An Introduction to Cognitive Psychology*, Milton Keynes: Open University Press.

Gramsci, A. (1971) *Selections from the Prison Notebooks*, London: Lawrence & Wishart.

Hart, M. U. (1992) *Working and Educating for Life: Feminist and International Perspectives on Adult Education*, London: Routledge.

Marton, F., Hounsell, D. and Entwistle, N. J. (1984) *The Experience of Learning*, Edinburgh: Scottish Academic Press.

Perry, W. G. (1970) *Forms of Intellectual and Ethical Development in the College Years: A Scheme*, New York: Holt, Rinehart & Winston.

Richardson, J. T. E., Eysenck, M. W. and Warren Piper, D. (eds) (1987) *Student Learning: Research in Education and Cognitive Psychology*, The Society for Research into Higher Education and Milton Keynes: Open University Press.

Part 1

Power, purpose and outcomes

Chapter 1

'Really useful knowledge', 1790–1850

Richard Johnson

Source: This is an edited version of a chapter in T. Lovett (ed.), *Radical Approaches to Adult Education: A Reader*, London, Routledge, 1988.

FEATURES

[. . .] Radical education [in early nineteenth-century England] was essentially an oppositional movement, gaining energies from contesting orthodoxies, in theory and practice. The first criticisms of the sorts of schooling which were provided were formed in the period up to 1820, under the shadow of a counter-revolution. The early schooling enterprises – Sunday Schools of the more conservative-Evangelical kind, the monitorial day schools, were seen as coercive and knowledge-denying. When more liberal schemes were put forward in the 1820s and 1830s – Mechanics' Institutes, the Useful Knowledge Societies, infant schools, plans for state education – they were opposed too, though more conditionally. Before the 1860s there was not enough working-class support for state education to overcome the opposition of its Tory-Anglican opponents.

Criticism was not limited to opposition. Alternatives were proposed. Education was differently defined. It was partly a matter of religion. Radical education tended to be secular and rationalist; it drew on Enlightenment ideas of an expanding human nature.[1] But there was a polarization within Christianity too. Philanthropic educators inherited a Pauline, Hebraic, Puritan-Evangelical view of human nature as finite, limited and flawed. Since social evils like crime, riot, pauperism, 'vice' and even epidemic diseases were 'moral' at root, moral and religious education was the answer. Religion was a source of order, in society and in individuals; God was a kind of policeman in the sky. Radicals by contrast, developed the legacy of natural theology (God known only through Nature), and of Christianity as a morality of co-operation among equals. The morality of 'that good man' Jesus Christ was turned against inequality and injustice. There was also a real excitement about secular knowledges, especially as solvents of dogmatic religion and as keys to understanding society and human nature.[2]

A third feature was a preoccupation with education and politics, knowledge and power. Educating yourself and others, especially in a knowledge of your 'circumstances', was a step in changing the world. Knowledge was a natural right, an unconditional good. The typical middle-class argument – that only the 'educated' should be able to vote – was angrily dismissed. [...]

Finally, radicals developed a varied, vigorous educational practice of their own. In a sense this was 'adult education'. Yet this label misleads, reading back our modern separations anachronistically. Rather child/adult differences were less stressed than they are today, or than they were in the contemporary middle-class culture of childhood. [...]

So radical education challenged the educational enterprises of 'Church Christianity' and the liberalism of the urban middle classes. It mounted alternatives in its philosophy, pedagogy and institutional arrangements. It was not merely a critical or oppositional movement, but counter-hegemonic, threatening to construct a whole alternative social order.

The success or failure of such an enterprise depended on all the relationships of force in early Victorian society, including the sheer weight of economic impositions and the control of military force. It did not depend on education alone, but on the contexts of the educational struggle.[3] [...]

TRANSFORMATIONS

So what were the modern conditions that were imposed and resisted at the time? I would not *start* with the imposition of schooling. Schooling was too marginal to daily life in this period to be the central site of change. It needs to be decentred in modern explanations too. It may be that schooling emerges as a solution to problems first posed elsewhere.

Changes at the place of waged work might be thought a better starting-point. The proletarianization of the worker was deeply formative. Like Thompson, we might think of this in terms of an initial loss: sometimes as erosion, sometimes as sudden theft of spaces for autonomy or self-activity. Marx stressed the loss or alienation of conscious sensuous human labour in the production of commodities for capital: the reduction of the worker to operative or 'hand'. Thompson sees the loss as wider, including a deeper regulation of time and public spaces for instance (Thompson 1967). Feminist historians have brought whole new features of this transition into view, features equally central to educational change.[4] Deepening proletarianization was accompanied by changes in the sex-gender arrangements of society. It sounds odd, but accurate I think, to speak of the formation of modern genders as well as classes; and so to explore the relation between the two.

We can think of gender formation, too, as deepened polarization or heightened difference, in this case between men and women in a model of heterosexual monogamy. The polarization of gender positions involved further privileging men in particular ways. Within the bourgeoisie and professional middle class, men and women were assigned to the 'separate spheres' of public life and domestic nurturance. Child–adult differences were given greater force as well. [. . .]

In public discourses about the family (and much else besides) this patriarchal arrangement was heavily preferred. It involved an intense focus on the socialization of children as a specialized and separated activity, not necessarily involving school, but always some domestic division of labour.

There were similar transitions in working-class households, but with rather different results. The changes in production often involved a similar separation of the household from the place of waged work. Yet the division of labour was less complete. The characteristic destiny of the working-class woman was the double shift (some form of earning and domestic labour). The privileging of the working-class man was as the main bread-winner. Similarly, partly for reasons of space, partly for family income, the child and adult worlds could not be so sharply segregated, though compulsory schooling itself was to bring this pattern nearer. By the 1860s one can certainly see in philanthropic commentary, the figure of the 'respectable' working man, usually a skilled worker, often a trade unionist and follower of the Liberal Party. He keeps his wife at home and he sends his children to school. He bases his industrial strategies on the family wage (and often the exclusion of women) and favours state education, compulsory, secular and free. Yet this experience was only a sectional one within the working class as a whole, not easily universalized. (Barrett and Macintosh 1980)

Any adequate detailed account of the contest of radical education and provided forms (which we still lack) would have to take account of this shifting ensemble of relationships: the combined forms of class, gender and age-rank relations. I shall argue later that the provided forms of schooling won out because they were better adapted to the new conditions, and its relationships of time, space, or power, or so it seemed, in the short run. At the same time rupturing of older patterns was so severe, and the popular legacies were culturally so rich, that alternative possibilities for learning and living could emerge and be sustained for several decades.

DILEMMAS

Radical education revolved around a complicated and layered dilemma. Radicals valued 'the march of mind' for many different reasons. As in all

periods of change there was a tension between conservation and transformation in popular responses. It was necessary actively to learn new ways
because the older common senses were not enough any more; yet customary skills and cultural inheritances seemed all the more precious because
they were threatened. Issues around literacy are a case in point. The ability
to read was especially valued because its transmission was threatened in
communities drastically affected by industrial change, handloom-weaving
districts for example. Elementary accomplishments like reading and knowing how to sign your own name did decline in some areas in the early
Industrial Revolution. Yet the desire to read and write was also very
actively stimulated by the new conditions, especially by the great surges
of popular political activity, with their extensive presses and expanding
reading publics.

There was a heightened sense too of the educational condescensions of
the rich and the powerful. The charge of popular ignorance, from Edmund
Burke's 'swinish multitude' to later liberal cajolings was deeply resented,
especially as a way of blaming oppressions on the poor themselves. As
William Cobbett put it:

> The tyrant, the unfeeling tyrant, squeezes the labourers for gain's sake;
> and the corrupt politician and literary or tub rogue find an excuse for
> him by pretending, that it is not want of food and clothing, but want
> of education, that makes the poor starving wretches thieves and beggars.
>
> (Cobbett 1967: 265–6)

Positively, radicals looked to their own education to remove superstition
and combat the ideological resources of authority. [. . .]

At the same time radicals were acutely aware of educational difficulties,
an awareness often enforced by personal experience. Sometimes these were
a poverty of resources: lack of books, teachers, time, energy, peace and
quiet. In the best radical writing about education, that most in touch, I
think, with the pressures on most working people, enlightenment
ambitions meet a powerful sense of imposed constraints, material and
cultural. Sometimes the conditions are portrayed as absolutely incompatible with any education at all. Such insights were widespread in the later
years and in movements based on the industrial North and Midlands.
[. . .]

As if this were not enough, the growth of provided education after 1830
brought further twists to the dilemma. First you were excluded from
learning by the absence of resources or household conditions. Then, once
available, the proferred knowledges turned out to be wildly inappropriate.
Far from promising liberation, this knowledge threatened subjection. At
best it was a laughable diversion – useless knowledge in fact. At worst it
added, to the long list, yet another kind of tyranny. [. . .] Cobbett, for

instance, the original de-schooler, had no doubts about the objects of the monitorial school:

> They wish to make cheap the business of *learning to read*, if that business be performed in their schools; and thus inveigle the children of poor men into those schools; and there to teach those children, along with reading, all those notions which are *calculated to make them content in a state of slavery*.[5]

[...] By the 1830s the new forms of provided education had appeared, some of them less obviously knowledge-denying than older forms. Yet a critical distance was maintained, especially from the Society for the Diffusion of Useful Knowledge and its *Penny Magazine*. There was a host of jokes on all possible permutations of 'useful knowledge':

> In conformity with the advice of Lord Brougham and the Useful Knowledge Society, the Milton fishermen, finding their occupation gone, have resolved to become capitalists forthwith.[6]

[...] So, despite the jokes, dilemmas deepened. It was *'really* useful knowledge' that was wanted; 'education-mongers' offered its opposite. [...] So how was the genuine article to be obtained? How were radicals to educate themselves, their children, their class, their brothers and sisters, within all the everyday constraints? Overwhelmingly the answer, in this period, was *we must do it ourselves*! That way, independence could be preserved, and real knowledge won. We can understand radical education best, perhaps, as the story of these attempts. [...]

FORMS

The key feature was informality. Certainly, radicals founded their own institutions. In the late 1830s and 1840s there were even schemes for a whole alternative system. The Owenite and Chartist mainstreams, however, looked askance at the more ambitious projects.

Typically, then, radical education differed from the provided kind in its actual organizational principles. Education was not separated out and labelled 'school'. It did not happen in specialized institutions. Even when Political Unions, Chartists and Owenites formed their own secular Sunday Schools, or newspaper reading rooms or Halls of Science, these were part of the cultural politics of the branch. The frequent emphasis on a meeting place of your own had less to do with specialized uses than escaping from the control of magistrate or publican (and perhaps from domestic space?) and having a physical focus for local activity. The crucial division that radicals refused, of course, was that between education and politics: hence their contestation of the 'no politics' rule in Mechanics' Institutes, and the occasional secessions to form a political forum of their own.[7]

Solutions were highly improvised, haphazard and therefore ephemeral. From one point of view – the building of a long-term alternative – this was a weakness, but it had strengths too. Education remained in a close relation to other activities, was even inserted into them. People learned in the course of their daily activities, and were encouraged to teach their children too, out of an accumulated and theorized experience. The modern distinction between education (i.e. schooling) and life (everything outside the playground walls or off campus) was certainly in the process of production in this period. Philanthropy espoused the public school as a little centre of missionary influence in an alien social world. Radicals breached this distinction, however, all the time, often quite self-consciously. As George Jacob Holyoake put it, 'Knowledge lies everywhere to hand for those who observe and think' (Holyoake 1892). It lay in nature, in the social circumstances of daily life, in the skills of labour, in conversations with friends, in the play of children, as well as in a few much-prized books.

It is often hard to separate radical initiatives from the inherited cultural resources of the people more generally. There were complex interleavings and dependencies here. It is not sensible to see the working-class family, neighbourhood or place of work as a part of radical education. Yet these were – or had been – the main educational spaces for working people. Radicals occupied them accordingly, often giving them a new twist. They taught their children to read and to think politically. They became accepted as the local 'scholar' of the neighbourhood. They led workplace discussions on 'the hardness of the times'. Similarly, when they became private school-teachers, often more out of necessity than choice, they occupied one node of educational networks indigenous to working-class communities. Radicals did not invent the proto-profession of travelling lecturer, but they certainly expanded and politicized it: hence the travelling demagogues of Chartism, the Owenite 'social missionaries', and the women lecturers who found a place in Owenism through its religious heterodoxy, critique of conventional marriage and commitment to gender equality (Taylor 1983). [. . .]

Radicals also added some inventions of their own. The simplest addition was the meeting place or reading-room, stocked with radical newspapers.[8] More ambitious and continuous radical branches organized a whole calendar of events, including lectures and classes, plus one-off special events like big public meetings or the public confrontations with the clergy sought especially by Owenites. The most important radical invention of all was the press. It was not the respectable 'Fourth Estate' that created a popular newspaper-reading public, but the law-breaking, speculative journalists of the radical press (Thompson 1963). With some exceptions – particularly the Chartist *Northern Star* – 'newspaper' is rather a misnomer. Really we are talking about argumentative, opinionated little magazines, essentially concerned with commentary and analysis, often in support of particular movements. Most were saturated with an educational content. [...]

As a form these 'newspapers' were very versatile. Some parts, like the *Poor Man's Guardian*'s expositions needed pondering over and discussing. Other parts, like Cobbett's or Feargus O'Connor's addresses, could be declaimed aloud in pub or other public place. Radical newspapers were not bought and read individually at home, but were passed from hand to hand and discussed in a pattern of multiple if not communal readership. [...]

CONTENT

Perhaps the phrase 'really useful knowledge' is the best starting point. Much more than a parody of the Society for the Diffusion of Useful Knowledge, it stressed all the key radical themes. It expressed the conviction, first, that real knowledge served practical ends – ends, that is, for the knower. [...]

'Practical', however, [...] was not an invitation to a vague pragmatism. The key discriminator was practical for what? And for whom? When 'practical' was specified more tightly all this came into view:

> All useful knowledge consists in the acquirement of *ideas concerning our conditions in life*.[9]

> A man may be amused and instructed by scientific literature but the language *which describes his wrongs* clings to his mind with an unparalleled pertinacity.[10]

> What we want to be informed about is – *how to get out of our present troubles*.[11] [emphasis added]

So 'practical' implied a particular point of view: practicality depended on your social standpoint and political purpose. One person's useful knowledge was another's useless ignorance. [...] Practical knowledge was knowledge from the point of view of 'the people' or 'the productive classes'. But this popular point of view was not just a novel descriptive angle, producing new facts, nor was it just a question of learning how to cope or have realistic expectations. The real point, the real practicality, was learning how to change your life. Really useful knowledge is 'knowledge calculated to make you free'.

So this notion of 'practical' was especially rich. When a reviewer in *The Pioneer* exhorted readers to get help from 'men of talent' in 'the highest branches of science', he met this editorial rebuke:

> No proud conceited scholar knows the way – the rugged path that we

are forced to travel; they sit them down and sigh, and make a puny wail of human nature; they fill their writings full of quaint allusions, which we can fix no meaning to; they are by far too classical for our poor knowledge-box; they preach of temperance, and build no places for our sober meetings ... but we will make them bend to suit our circumstances.[12]

I love this quotation. There is so much going on in it. There is a resistance to 'scholars' who assume knowledges which most people lack; yet there is also a sense that they have something to offer: otherwise why 'make them bend' etc. In a way, it seems the scholars are quite ignorant, and impractical to. We (the people) know more than they, especially about 'rugged paths'. Yet we also lack something ('poor knowledge-box') which they appear to possess. The solution seems to be to make 'them' (the scholars) work for 'us' (the people) – on our agenda, our circumstances, perhaps in our language too. So two important traps are avoided: being intimidated by academic pretensions, and collapsing into a self-satisfied lauding of common sense. 'Practical' does not exclude learning: a productive relationship is sought between common sense and systematic knowledges or philosophies. Practice has implications for knowledge, but knowledge has implications for practice too.

Radicalism's preferred knowledges provide examples of these general features. These knowledges had a pressing immediacy and were very much for the here and now. They were indispensable means of emancipation, directing practical actions. Their most usual expression was in practical forms, in exposing this or that instance of tyranny, or illuminating an area of daily experience. As critical theories they were capable of infinite application.

By the 1830s there were, perhaps, three main components in radical theory. For the radical mainstream, 'political knowledge' retained its pre-eminence from the days of Tom Paine. Later versions find their richest elaboration in the pages of the *Poor Man's Guardian* and in the writing of Bronterre O'Brien. Radical political theory was a blend of the belief in natural rights, the commitment to 'extreme democracy' (typically manhood suffrage with considerable ambiguity about women's rights), and a critique of the exclusive, propertied nature of the state. The state was seen as a thoroughly partisan institution, heavily loaded towards the interests of property of different kinds. From this all kinds of evils flowed: unjust laws, unfair taxes, the suppression of movements to redress grievance, the basic unfairness of the lack of popular representation. Political knowledge was, therefore, an attempt to explain everyday experiences. Why doesn't government protect us? Why does the law penalize the poor person's attempts to gain redress? Why does reform favour only the propertied?

How might we secure our democratic rights, and in doing this, change the direction of policy and law?

Radicals also developed their own economic analysis. Common justice and a sense of the importance of labour prescribed that the labourers should enjoy the full fruits of their toil; 'labour economics' or 'moral' or 'co-operative political economy' was an attempt to explain why this did not happen. Capital stole a proportion of the product in a kind of tax called profit. Lacking an analysis of exploitation in capitalist labour itself, such theories were still an attempt to make sense of the daily fact of poverty amidst the extraordinary productiveness that was all around.

Both these kinds of knowledge had, we might note, the same form. Moral economy and political knowledge incorporated criteria of political judgement – economic justice or natural rights – at their very heart. They did not pretend to neutrality. They also contained a theory, or principle of explanation. Owenite 'social science' or 'the science of society' shows a similar structure. The Owenite's central moral value was 'co-operation' or 'community'. It was this, a secularized version of Christian neighbourliness, that would characterize 'the new moral world'. Social co-operation among equals-in-circumstance was the only enduring source of social progress and happiness. The Owenites' main explanatory idea was the educative force of 'circumstances', especially of certain social institutions. Often this came down to a fairly mechanical environmentalism, posing great difficulties for a theory of change or revolution. Yet Owenism greatly extended the radical analysis. It represented capitalism as necessarily competitive, disharmonious and violent, but focused especially on the socializing weight of three institutions: the family, the Church and the school. Analysis was extended into domestic arrangements and the private sphere and, thence, to the 'formation of character' more generally. It was therefore possible to speak publicly, often for the first time, of evils silently suffered in private, especially by women. The growing division between public and private spheres was partially broken. Taboo-breaking, especially on religious and sexual issues, became an Owenite profession, not least in relation to Owenite feminist attacks on the partiality of religion in gender terms, and the exclusions operating against women within radical movements themselves.

'Really useful knowledge' meant one or other or all of these knowledges, usually with further additions. From the popular point of view, this did indeed easily transcend anything which philanthropy offered. We can see, perhaps, why the recreational fare of Mechanics' Institutes, or the very limited curricula of schooling looked so trivial and oppressive. Radicalism embraced, after all, a theory of the class nature of the state, a theory of economic exploitation, and a theory of cultural domination. It even stretched, in Owenism, to a theory of 'character' or of what we would call 'subjectivity' or 'personality' today.

So the radicals were right when they argued that their conception of knowledge was wide, comprehensive even. It was comprehensive in at least two senses: it was, or should be, universally available, but was also 'liberal' in that it was wide-ranging, critical and open. [...]

LIMITS

The shift of strategy to the demand for state education occurred in the middle decades of the nineteenth century. By the 1860s a section of the skilled organized working class had joined the Liberal agitation for a compulsory state system, while insisting on a secular curriculum, and some measure of state control. Although a proper history is needed, perhaps I have said enough about contexts to suggest how this change came about. I would give a central place to the material changes that formed the proletarian household, closed down some of the previous autonomies around the place of work (household and workshop), and forced some critical separations: home/waged labour, work/leisure, education/living, child/adult. As the need for a separate educational sphere developed, religious and philanthropic agencies supplied it in a highly regulated, but never uncontested, form. Though latterly radical education reached for more and more school-like solutions of its own, its particular strength had been its connection with pre-proletarian patterns, and, perhaps, the artisanal strata of the old working population. Schooling corresponded to the new conditions: regularized work patterns for adults and the intensification of capitalist control of labour especially. But schooling also had its own effects: especially in accentuating the child-adult distinction, favouring the more bourgeois family forms and divisions of labour including the marked gender separations, and, in its indirect effects, competing with indigenous educational resources, especially private schools and family and neighbourhood-based learning more generally.

Recognition of this *double* process is important in solving some conundrums in the social history of education, especially the difference between those who insist on 'social control' or schooling as an imposition, and those who point to working-class 'demand'. The growth of schooling was certainly not merely a matter of institutional or ideological imposition. But the idea of 'demand' (and the whole model of motivations implied) is actively misleading. Historians who argue this way, just like the modern politicians, fail to see that economic relations and changes may also coerce, transforming the very framework of choice and intentionality. What was sensible and feasible under one set of conditions, ceases to be so under new ones. The main virtue of the model of 'demand' is that it has a place for active popular agency, albeit extremely individualistically. [...] Radical education died, splintered or changed into other forms both because powerfully backed 'solutions' were offered, and the underlying social conditions became more and more adverse.

TODAY

Is radical education recoverable, as more than a memory? This is partly, I am sure, a matter of underlying conditions. It may be that radical education always depends, minimally, on widespread political excitement, and especially the expectation of major social change, and the existence of educational resources, including time free from necessary labour. This points to the need to analyse the existing situation of different social groups in our own society, to see what spaces and resources already exist. The 1970s movements are suggestive here, but may also point to quite a pessimistic conclusion. These movements have been strong precisely among those groups with the most extensive experience of formal education, especially in its more autonomous spaces in and around colleges and universities. [...]

If my analysis is right, many of the original dilemmas remain, even or especially for much wider social groups than those with a professional stake in learning. We are entering a period of deep educational reaction, or *merely* useful knowledge, to coin a phrase. In the perpetual English ping-pong between utilitarian and academic conceptions of knowledge, we are up against utility with a vengeance. [...]

Yet merely useful knowledge has plausibility, for most people, against conspicuously useless kinds. Actually, academic knowledge forms do have social uses. They seem, so far, the most appropriate forms for reproducing social elites and adding an educational justification for inequalities. They have also harboured, so far, opportunities for critical thinking, albeit divorced from popular experiences. Together these two failed forms reproduce each other. In their current deployments – academic forms for would-be climbers into a shrinking elite; training for the rest – they deepen social divisions. The continuing appeal of *really* useful knowledge is that it cuts across the division, and the personal dilemmas produced by it. Critical knowledges, which look beyond the bourgeois and patriarchal horizons, can be *both* practical and wide. [...]

Who produces the knowledges and for what reasons was a central issue for nineteenth-century radicals. Their answer was very clear: in the end it is the people's knowledges that change the world. This means that self-education, or knowledge as self-production, is the only knowledge that really matters. Others may be resources here, but in the end you cannot be taught, you can only learn. Really useful knowledge occurs only in an active mood, and must have its active centre among subordinated social groups, the equivalents of 'the people'. [...] So I doubt, in the current history, that the sites of formal education will be decisive, even in the educational struggle. I think we must look to see new forms of politics, rather, where change is not understood as a mechanical, lever-like process, but as a transformation of self and others. Until there are more contexts of this kind, which also cut across the usual social differences, I do not think that today's *really* useful knowledges will emerge in their most politically pointed, mobilizing forms. Instead, we shall continue to be stuck with today's 'quaint allusions' and an obstinate popular pragmatism which refuses all but the most conservative of its lessons.

NOTES

1 Especially through the writings of Tom Paine and, to a lesser extent, William Godwin. See especially Thomas Paine, *The Rights of Man* (London: Penguin, 1969); and Thomas Paine, *The Age of Reason*, Moncure Daniel Conway (ed.) (London, 1896).

2 This is discussed in the major histories. See especially E. P. Thompson, *The Making of the English Working Class* (London: Gollancz, 1963); H. Silver, *The Concept of Popular Education* (MacGibbon & Kee, 1965); B. Simon, *Studies in the History of Education 1780–1870* (London: Lawrence & Wishart, 1960).

3 The most detailed presentation of the research on which this chapter is based is in J. Clarke, C. Critcher and R. Johnson, *Working Class Culture, Studies in History and Theory* (London: Hutchinson, 1979).

4 See, especially, C. Hall, 'Private persons versus public someones', in Carolyn Steedman, Urwin, C. and Walkerdine, V. (eds), *Language, Gender and Childhood* (London: Routledge & Kegan Paul, 1985); E. Whitelegg, Arnot, M., Bartels, E., Beechey, V., Birke, L., Himmelwent, S., Leonard, D., Ruehl, S. and Speakman, M. A. (eds), *The Changing Experience of Women*, Part 1: 'The historical separation of home and workplace' (Oxford: Martin Robertson & Co. with The Open University, 1982). C. Hall, 'The early formation of Victorian domestic ideology', in S. Burman (ed.), *Fit Work for Women* (Croom Helm, 1979).

5 *Political Register*, 7 December 1833, quoting from *Long Island Register*, 21 November 1818.

6 *Poor Man's Guardian*, 18 May 1833.

7 Again, reactions to Mechanics' Institutes were complex and ambiguous, more ambiguous perhaps than to any other middle-class initiative. See Clarke, *et al.* op. cit (1979) p. 78.

8 E. P. Thompson (1963) op. cit., pp. 717–20. And for the later period, Dorothy Thompson, *The Chartists: Popular Politics in the Industrial Revolution* (Wildwood House, 1984), especially Ch. 2. and pp. 158–72, particularly interesting on the mix of different kinds of meeting places.

9 *Pioneer*, 31 May 1834.

10 *Poor Man's Guardian*, 25 October 1834.

11 Ibid., 14 April 1834.

12 *Pioneer*, 25 January 1834.

REFERENCES

Barrett, M. and Macintosh, M. (1980) 'The family wage', in *Capital and Class* 11, summer.

Cobbett, W. (1967) *Rural Rides*, London: Penguin.

Holyoake, G. J. (1892) *Sixty Years of an Agitator's Life*, vol. 1, London, p. 4.

Taylor, B. (1983) *Eve and the New Jerusalem: Socialism and Feminism in the Nineteenth Century*, London: Virago.

Thompson, E. P. (1963) *The Making of the English Working Class*, London: Gollancz.

——— (1967) 'Time, work discipline and industrial capitalism', *Past and Present*, no. 38, 56–97.

Chapter 2

Feminist challenges to curriculum design

Susan F. Parsons

Source: This is an edited version of an article which appeared in *Studies in the Education of Adults*, vol. 22, no. 1, pp. 49–58.

Over the past decades with the growth of feminist writings in so many areas of enquiry, the emergence of this new consciousness is affecting the underlying philosophy and the practical tasks of curriculum design. For the most part, the impact of feminism has been one of challenge, and this chapter is an attempt to give a broad overview of some of the issues which arise at the points of intersection. [. . .]

The challenges of feminism have generally been of two kinds. One kind of challenge is critical, since its major concern is with questioning the present order of things, asking for more clear justification of existing practices, and suggesting that there are social, psychological, moral and philosophical reasons for considering serious alternatives. Obviously at this level of challenge, feminists are most threatening and learn to shield themselves against the accusations of being 'militant', 'aggressive', or 'destructive'. The second kind of challenge is constructive, and in this area feminists are concerned to develop new practices, to think more open-mindedly and laterally about methods and resources, and to create new areas of enquiry which may redraw the map of traditional academic disciplines altogether. We need to examine both of these kinds of challenge to understand and assess the potential impact of feminist thinking.

THE CRITICAL CHALLENGE

In their critique of education, feminists are concerned primarily and broadly with demonstrating the potent interaction of personal and social factors which combine to form the context of gender identity and relationships in which we live. This prevailing ideology regarding gender is deeply embedded in our society and is also engrained in existing educational structures, making its authority both more elusive and more powerful. Feminists have been concerned to expose the development of this ideology by a close examination of different historical periods, of social structures and mores, of philosophical traditions – all of which form the background against which contemporary views can be more clearly seen. This ideology takes both explicit and implicit forms in various academic disciplines, in matters of educational method and technique, and in the description of the social and personal needs to which education responds. Several examples of the critique will have to suffice to give the general picture.

One area of criticism has to do with attitudes to gender. These are reflected in the various stereotypes which are the most obvious signs of ideological pressure exerted upon one's self-understanding. In the early days of recent feminism, these were questioned, and the roots of such opinions traced back through previous educational philosophers whose ideas have had such impact upon our own. From Aristotle's claim that women should not spend too much of their energy on rational activity, particularly when pregnant, to Rousseau's argument for the gentle training of girls in femininity, the notions of what boys and girls are to be educated 'in' or 'for' have been closely allied with assumptions regarding their most true natures as male and female. Questioning these attitudes has resulted in equal requirements of home economics and woodworking classes for boys and girls at school, and has more recently affected the growth of 'returning to education' programmes especially useful to young mothers. However, the impact has yet to be felt fully and effectively in other subjects like physical education, at the level of careers advice, and in higher education where statistics reveal only small changes in the ratio of women to men in many disciplines. The challenge of feminism at this point is to consider how the design of a curriculum reinforces attitudes towards gender which may be experienced as oppressive, and which may have limiting effects on the future possibilities of people's lives.

A second area of criticism has to do with language. It has been recognized for some time that language reflects and reinforces the ideology of gender and thus constitutes a significant factor in its persuasiveness. Feminists have pointed to the exclusiveness of language, whereby women are effectively excluded from any obvious participation in discourse by being rendered invisible. This occurs both particularly through the use of masculine pronouns, and more generally through the use of the male as the standard from which the female is the derivative (steward/stewardess, and so on). Special effort is thus required to recognize the presence of the female at all in many discourses, and her invisibility in language renders her an ineffective participant in dialogue. There is thus pressure for inclusiveness in language which acknowledges the presence of two genders and allows both to join in the communications network. In addition, there is a growing awareness that such exclusivity in language expresses the bias of most academic disciplines towards the male, a bias which threatens the credibility of some subjects, or at the very least causes some disciplines to be imprecise or inaccurate. Textbooks which are written with such language become a problem, and make it difficult for students to frame their own thoughts in other ways. It is the challenge of feminism at this point to realize that curriculum design can either be 'part of the problem or part of the solution', and that closer attention to language becomes a necessary component of positive change.

The third area of criticism has to do with analysis of the social milieu in which education is set and to which it is responsive. Here it is obvious to feminists that the pattern of gender relations is set very deeply into the total social structure, and that the whole framework of interrelating pieces has provided a persistent and effective social ordering of power and authority. This recognition can tend to reinforce a conservative view of education, whereby it continually fits new members for participation in the existing society, and is thus basically dedicated to preservation of the *status quo*. The career structure and lines of authority within educational institutions can be seen as a microcosm of this pattern, so that teachers model for students the kind of thought and behaviour which will one day be required of them. However, this could also be a liberating recognition, if it encourages the creative use of educational materials and methods to open up new possibilities. The breakthrough of women into the medical sciences during the late nineteenth century provides an example of the way in which curriculum design reflected and strengthened existing institutional interests, and the kind of power struggle which was necessary before any significant changes could be made. The close links between institutional power and the status of academic disciplines makes a sobering realization for those who are interested in the process of redesigning today. [...]

These three features of curriculum – attitudes, language, and power – form a circle of inter-linked forces, and it is the initial challenge of feminism that we should recognize our participation in this process. Personal attitudes are not just my *own* feelings about things which I hold privately, but are expressions in language of the structures of interactions to which I belong and which determine the power relations between myself and others. The first fundamental aim of feminism is thus to nurture critical consciousness continuously.

Let me give an example of this kind of critique at work in the design of a philosophy syllabus, which used to be part of the BA in Humanities course at Nottingham (formerly Trent) Polytechnic. At each step in planning this programme, issues concerning attitudes, language, and power were relevant. It is certainly true that initial convictions about the nature of the philosophic enterprise itself affected this in important ways. I consider philosophy to be a way of pursuing both knowledge and understanding, and it demands clear and careful ways of thinking for this to be achieved. Therefore, philosophy is a discipline in which the connection between process and content is inextricable. To teach is to be engaged oneself in the material under discussion, and to demonstrate through one's style and approach the nature of the fundamental philosophic quest. This Socratic model guides my own thinking, and it has been the result of applying such a model in practice that critical consciousness has emerged.

I planned the syllabus to begin with *Images of Man*. This study was to involve exploration of descriptions of human nature offered by a wide range of thinkers, from which could be seen a variety of configurations of the world, of society, and of moral values. The second level of study would involve an examination of *Science and Belief* from the seventeenth century to the present day. This study of the history of ideas allowed a more broad consideration of topics, and demonstrated some of the underlying methodological problems which philosophers uncover and contend with. The third level was then to examine in greater depth several of the *Perennial Problems of Philosophy* – namely (i) the nature of the 'self' or the 'personal', (ii) arguments for and against the existence of God, and (iii) the nature of the ethical dimension and various intractable moral problems. This design seemed a fairly straightforward one, from the more popular and approachable material in the first year, to the more difficult and abstract in the final year. Since students were studying this subject along with two others for the liberal arts degree, there could be many interconnections made between disciplines. Cross-disciplinary thinking was therefore encouraged, and this is something to which adults as mature students on the course were particularly attracted. Likewise, this kind of study encouraged both the use of one's own experience as the raw material of reflection, as well as the development of greater self-awareness in examining one's most basic assumptions and prejudices. It proved therefore to be a popular course with adults, and one in which they were actually better equipped in many ways than younger students to handle the subject's demands.

What happened in the course of teaching the syllabus was an increasing awareness of the critical challenges of feminism. Having glibly labelled the first year unit *Images of MAN*, and having found appropriate textbooks, I was struck by the preponderance of women in the classroom who had come to learn. This caused me to look more closely at the content of the material being used – a range of thinkers from Plato to B. F. Skinner – and to discover there the expression of certain attitudes to gender. In more or less explicit form, these attitudes seemed to be generally less favourable towards women than towards men, and to raise certain expectations of social place and moral behaviour. To question these attitudes was, then, to discover the problem that language presents. On the one hand, there is the widespread belief that discussions about 'man' are actually inclusive discussions; that when we hear 'man', we should not hear an exclusively gendered term, but rather an inclusive word meaning 'human'. Women are thereby effectively rendered invisible, and more importantly, the actual assumptions which are made about her gendered identity can pass by almost unnoticed. On the other hand, therefore, it was only when this pretence of inclusivity was questioned that the real material regarding women's nature and identity could be exposed and discussed directly by students. When this happened, an empowering exercise was taking place, which challenged both the root assumptions of the discipline of philosophy and its conservationist political role.

A similar process occurred in the second year. The history of modern science is, at one level, the documentation of the dualism that 'man is to culture as woman is to nature'. To trace this attitude to gender in the writings of scientists, to expose the framework of language in which such views became embedded, and to realize the authority which such beliefs still carry was an exercise in feminist challenge. By the way, it was a sobering exercise to conduct also with B.Sc. students – the majority of whom are men and the majority of whom will not have such encouragement to critical thinking in the course of their higher education. Since the content at this second level was basically concerned with a continuing dialogue, it was appropriate that students also engage in the dialectical process of question and answer regarding basic presuppositions about the universe and our place within it.

Third-year students were then able to investigate more deeply the implications which such challenges might have for some of the weighty philosophic problems. In all three of the problems selected, it became obvious that attitudes to gender, the limitations of language, and the reinforcement of existing power relations all contributed to shaping these issues in a particular way. Descriptions of the self as a detached thinking and observing being housed within a body reveal a particular construction of the personal, whose relevance to women's experience was problematic. Arguments for the existence of a divine being whose nature is defined by contrast with known and lived reality reinforce the controlling and masterful image of a male deity. Finally, the nature of the moral life as self-discipline according to rational principles is called into question by many women's experience of moral decision-making. In wrestling with these issues, the pressures of ideology can become intense and its atmosphere suffocating.

THE CONSTRUCTIVE CHALLENGE

How to break into this circle is the next stage of the feminist challenge. The other side of their critique is the hope for realizing new possibilities that will be more fulfilling of human potential than present ones. The constructive task of these challenges is to bring about positive changes in attitudes, language, and power relations. This too lies at the heart of the feminist enterprise as it affects educational curriculum design, and it is in this area that feminists of different types are divided in the objectives they seek.

The objectives of liberal feminism are determined by their search for equality of treatment, of opportunity, and of status between men and women. This approach is considered by many to be the most easily accommodated by the present educational system, partly because the ideology of liberalism generally seems so widely accepted. It has become fairly basic to the political and economic rhetoric of Western countries that individual freedom is highly desirable, and that status and authority should not be determined by reference to biological features such as race or gender. That commitment to this ideology does not run very deep is one of the more painful discoveries of feminists, who have in recent years become pessimistic about this approach making any substantial change. Indications that girls actually do better in all subjects at school in single-sex classes, that professions lose social prestige and status in proportion to the number of women that enter their ranks, that the social structuring of the family enforces a privacy on women's lives that does not happen to men – all of these combine to present a picture of deeper problems which liberal alterations do not modify. It is important that such liberal consciousness be kept active however, since in so many curricular decisions this is the first point at which levels of awareness are challenged. Ground which has already been covered by these arguments can then hopefully be of use in considering multicultural issues as well.

The objectives of radical feminists have differed from those of their liberal sisters, since radicals are much more keenly aware of the distinctive determinations of the female consciousness. Because women are understood to be unique and to have quite special contributions to make in all areas of life and work, educational objectives must be centred on the nurturing and development of women in their own right. This means providing different kinds of opportunities which will express the insights and talents of women particularly. Thus, there is a demand for 'women only' classes in which women will not be overpowered by the voices and ideas of men; there is a concern for the development of women's writing as the expression of special kinds of experiences; there is an interest in discovering those unique insights which women will bring to bear on traditional disciplines; there is a hope that the area of Women's Studies will become a new discipline in its own right. The question which hangs over this approach is its effectiveness in long-term social change. It would seem that many educational institutions are happy to let the steam out of the pressure cooker for a while by allowing groups of women to 'do their own thing' in fairly innocuous activities. The minor irritation caused by their irruptions of enthusiasm can be easily contained, and, once exhausted, are believed to be of no further concern. In all of these constructive suggestions however, radical feminists have been striving for curricular change that will allow the emergence of women as women into the public world. Their uniqueness is to be fostered and encouraged by any redesigning that takes place.

The approach of socialist feminists differs yet again from these two because its major interest is in education for social change. These feminists are not content with the objective of equality since it does not address the underlying structural aspects of gender that are such powerful determinants of educational philosophy and practice. Likewise they are not happy with separatism in the curriculum, since this reinforces dual status and creates the illusion of power that is nowhere else affirmed. Socialists will emphasize that we are human first, and women second, so their constructive suggestions are centred on the need for change which benefits all. This means closer consideration of the ways in which each subject area has been affected by particular assumptions regarding gender, assumptions which are overlooked to the detriment of students whose minds are not as opened as they might be. Nearly every discipline has had its underlying presuppositions examined, not just for curiosity's sake, but because this can reveal most clearly how that discipline constructs reality and where its strengths and weaknesses may lie. In the process of this examination in which so many common threads can be found, educationists can legitimately argue that the working map of the disciplines needs now to be substantially redrawn. How this is to happen becomes the constructive interest of these feminists. Some of the concerns which cross 'traditional' boundaries are now of greater interest – for example, the nature of mothering and fathering, the meaning of human praxis, the emergence of sexual and gender consciousness, the linguistic construction of reality, the ideological nature of morality, the growth of 'green' philosophy, and so on. Each of these constitutes an area of academic interest which challenges the narrowness and bias of disciplines. In so doing, the socialist feminist aim is to discover and to take advantage of the possibilities for change that are contained within every existing order.

The three types of feminist approach can be illustrated in the handling of a philosophy syllabus, and in fact represent to some extent the stages of my own thinking as I tried to come to terms with this. For liberals, the challenges of feminism can most easily be accommodated by the inclusion of materials about women, and by women writers, in order to give equal time to these concerns. One session spent discussing Plato's view of man's nature could then be balanced by one session discussing his interpretation of the nature of woman. One session discussing Kohlberg's theory of moral development based on a sample of men could be balanced by a session on Gilligan's *In A Different Voice* using material from women (Gilligan 1982). In this obvious attention to balance, it would be hoped that both women and men could pick and choose, from among the theories offered, those which seemed most appropriate to their own experience. Equal time given to *Images of Man* and *Images of Woman*, equal attention to the material on examinations and in essay titles, equal numbers of male and female authors, equal volumes of books ordered for the library and appearing on bibliographies – in general, equal shares in the discipline: all of these contribute to the atmosphere of openness in which free choices can be more reasonably made. The liberal hope is that in the process of such investigation, greater self-awareness will be fostered for the individual. Growth in self-knowledge rates high on the liberal educational agenda. It is based on faith in the fundamental rationality of human beings, as those who can rise above natural or habitual determinations to become self-determining. This process requires greater detachment and objectivity which the balanced curriculum can provide.

What is discovered in the process, however, is something which more closely approximates the radical feminist critique. At some point it becomes painfully obvious that theories of woman's nature are not on a par with those of man's, since the presuppositions which guide the investigation of humanness are biased in favour of those qualities which the man most closely embodies. If Aristotle's description of humanness, for example, begins with the notion of the perfection of the male from which every other creature is a degradation, one wonders what the freedom of women to choose or to reject this theory can actually mean. If this is reinforced by a social structure in which women's role and value is directly linked to such an understanding of her nature, in which she ought to be what she is, we have a closed system in which education can only fit people for survival. To notice this same circularity of approach, found in proofs of God's existence, in discussions of the nature of selfhood, and so on, is the crucial ideological challenge of radical feminism. At this level of awareness, it is difficult to avoid the conclusion that the entire philosophical enterprise has been a male projection of its own gendered bodily experience. If this is the case, then the simple addition of samples from women's experience will prove facile. What is needed is the experience of a wholly different approach, from a wholly different set of basic presuppositions, using a wholly different gendered bodily experience, and with a wholly different perspective on the world. This suggests the need for a separate syllabus in which such an alternative can be fully explored and its implications considered. Educationally, this represents an objective that is concerned with giving space for the construction of a new worldview from a group which is normally invisible and powerless. Its ultimate aim is the creation of a serious and viable alternative to the *status quo* by those committed to its realization.

Problems with this approach emerge in relation both to the consistency of its fundamental principles and to the universality of its ultimate educational aim. If, for example, the dualistic division of the world is problematic in 'male philosophy', then its remedy is surely not another dualism.

Likewise, if a new version of rationality, or of the moral life, is being discovered and proposed, it is of more than local interest to a select few. The socialist feminist approach is concerned to make possible a new way of structuring gender relations, and it is the function of education to help this to occur. One of the best methods for the accomplishment of this objective has been found in the discovery of experiential teaching techniques. Devising exercises for people to engage in, developing critical situations for them to enact, provides a lived experience of the problem under discussion. This exercise can encourage the realization of the limitations which restrict our existing relationships with others, making us acutely aware of the baggage of assumptions and expectations which burden our interactions. This can also open windows, helping us to find the openings in this confined and confused space. How we recreate these situations to achieve more satisfactory and fulfilling solutions for all concerned is the creative project of this approach. This is not individualistic education, since the stress is on the communal nature of the human person, and its purpose is ultimately the discovery of more just ways of interacting with others, both at the personal and the social level. It is getting down to the guts of the matter by involving both heart and head, and in that sense is profoundly true to the original Socratic understanding of philosophy.

In terms of developing a philosophy syllabus, each of these feminist viewpoints has something to offer, and I would not wish to diminish their distinctive contributions, nor to suggest that one challenge should take priority. [. . .] This is further complicated by the many structural considerations that affect the possibilities for curricular change. There are problems with acquiring new resources in institutions which are facing crippling financial cutbacks. There are difficulties in staffing due both to shortage of people and to the inadequacy of appropriate training in the relevant areas. There is the usual tendency of institutions to reinforce only what has been tried and tested before, and the hold of traditional disciplines in their separate kingdoms is very powerful. There is thus the inevitable power struggle for recognition of the things which have heretofore been invisible or understood to be dangerous. These matters must be taken seriously by those who attempt any realistic change, but providing the creative impulses of these feminist challenges can be kept alive, there is real scope here for positive development in curriculum design. [. . .]

REFERENCE

Gilligan, C. (1982) *In A Different Voice*, Cambridge, Mass.: Harvard University Press.

Chapter 3

Competency and the pedagogy of labour

John Field

Source: This is an edited version of an article which appeared in *Studies in the Education of Adults*, vol. 23, no. 1, pp. 41–52.

Like all educational practice, vocational education can be seen as possessing a treble function. Evidently it is an agency of socialization, (re)producing a labour force with appropriate skills, knowledge and attitudes; it is patently also an agency of selection, offering qualifications which distribute the population between different roles. And vocational education shares with the rest of the educational system the function of generating new knowledge and skills, and even new frameworks of meaning, which enable the institutions of human activity to change and survive; in this third sense, it is future-oriented and even emancipatory. What is notable about recent reforms is that many situate work itself – the process of human labour – at the centre of the learning transaction, at a time when work is losing its centrality in the values and aspirations of Western culture.

In Britain, for example, the national system of vocational qualifications is being organized under the leadership of the National Council of Vocational Qualifications (NCVQ). Established in the wake of a 1986 Review of Vocational Qualifications (undertaken by the Department of Education and Science and the then Manpower Services Commission), the NCVQ is charged with bringing all vocational qualifications within a national framework, whose standards are described in terms of 'competence', and divided by levels (Level 1 reflecting elementary skills, Level 5 incorporating professional and graduate qualifications). Competences for different sectors will be defined by employer-led Lead Industry Bodies for each major sector (Ashworth and Saxton 1990). [. . .]

Why is the role of qualifications within the labour market now changing on such a wide scale? It seems to me that in two of the three functional areas of education, the legitimacy of the existing vocational qualification system has broken down. It no longer commands credibility as a means of sorting and distributing the population; and it is now impossible to create a consensus about the desirable future towards which vocational educational inputs will lead us. Competency-based vocational education has been widely canvassed in Britain and Australia as a secure basis for a system of vocational qualifications that is accurate, efficient and 'relevant to industry's needs'. Most British discussions of competency-based education have been content to accept these claims, and added to them the view that it will also help secure greater equality of opportunity; much of the literature is concerned with exploring the best technical means for achieving a competency-based system that meets such goals. This chapter is an attempt to situate the competency movement within a wider context: it seeks to establish that the competency movement is the latest refinement in what might be called 'the pedagogy of labour' – that is, the sponsoring of structured and planned learning from the activity of work, and for work. What is new about these moves is that they attempt to develop a 'pedagogy of labour' that can be applied comprehensively – cutting across different occupations and industrial sectors, and across what have previously been considered distinct age ranges and different and separate levels and domains of skill and knowledge.

These developments appear to mark a new stage in government-dominated attempts to match the functions of socialization and qualification with what is perceived as rapid changes within the workplace and in the organization of work. The main thrust here, then, is to explore relations between the competency movement and changes in the labour market. The labour market does not, though, operate in a vacuum; the implications of the competency movement cannot be understood without also exploring changes in the wider framework of societal values that have accompanied the shift towards post-industrial status; competency-based qualifications are seen as promoting not only supposedly desirable economic goals but also the subordination of labour in a society where the unquestioned status of the work ethic has been weakened (especially perhaps amongst the young, young men above all), and where the goals of production themselves are now under challenge. Finally, all policy-driven educational innovation constitutes an intervention within the institutions which provide educational services; the NVQ framework is being used, as are other assessment-driven curricular innovations, to overcome teacher-led resistance to change. In turn, though, the professional education lobby (and in this case especially the Further Education Unit) has, if often implicitly, been critical of industry's alleged unwillingness to move from a perspective of training as mainly a substitute for employment (Gleeson 1989) or a short-term reaction to a more 'pro-active' approach which rests upon steady investment in the development of human capital. The forces behind the competency movement, then, are diverse, and they stand in a sometimes complex and even potentially conflictual relationship.

VOCATIONAL EDUCATION AND THE BRITISH STATE

Vocational training in Britain in modern times has traditionally belonged to what has been effectively constituted by employers and their lobby as the 'private' domain. Despite persistent expressions of belief that poor training and education were handicapping economic performance, public intervention in training was rare and limited in scope. Only in crisis was the state to step directly into the labour market as a training provider: obviously during the two world wars, and even then its scope was limited to training wartime workers – often women – for essential industries, best seen simply as a temporary extension of its peacetime role in training civilian employees in the arsenals and dockyards; the state also trained disabled ex-servicemen and women prior to their discharge. This temporary role was not entirely abandoned in peacetime, but its civilian scope was always redefined in terms of the 'public' domain, effectively as an arm of the welfare services. More sustained provision was a matter for the local state, where it long remained as a disregarded and low-status activity. Its scope did not, though, embrace the policy and practice of training within business and the professions, which were regulated by employers and the examining bodies, with little outside interference – even trade unions had little or no interest in training policy (Lowe 1986, Field 1988).

Locally provided technical training supported the two broad types of training which were deemed sufficient to provide specialized labour power to carry Britain through the industrial revolution, then the Fordist period of mass manufacture: apprenticeship and 'sitting by Nelly'. Apprenticeship of the young to the more experienced provided a cadre of skilled workers who could carry out integrated and complex tasks, often on highly differentiated jobs such as shipwrighting, where every product was different. The problem with this labour process was the considerable power it afforded to the skilled worker. Fordist regulation – so-called, of course, from the application of 'scientific management' in the motor industry – appeared to offer a means of simultaneously reducing labour costs through higher productivity; and the creation of a consumer market through wage improvements (Braverman 1974, Barratt Brown 1984, Gorz 1989). I certainly accept that Fordism's impetus towards popular consumerism has profoundly affected adult education as a whole, but the focus here is on the implications for training policy and systems.

The chief purpose of Fordist mass production was to raise productivity by breaking the grip of the skilled worker over the labour process, repackaging the latter into small, repeatable, visible and therefore measurable and controllable steps. Each step could be carried out, time after time, by the worker and machine, in the way parodied by Chaplin's *Modern Times*; new workers learned by observation and practice. Fordism also required specialized strata of professional managers, sales staff, technicians and development scientists. Simultaneous with the growth of Fordism was the expansion of the Welfare State, with a very rapid growth of employment in local government, the health service and education; in these three areas too, new quasi-professional groups – including a small but growing number of technical college teachers – emerged with a strong administrative hierarchy and a public service ethic.

The consequence was the emergence of differentiated forms of vocational educational qualification, with differential access. Training for the Fordist production worker, such as was needed, took place on the line and was so empty of any wider content than repetition that there was serious policy concern over the utter absence of any wider awakening of the young mind – to civic virtues, to culture, to discoveries in technology and science which would produce the new, white-hot future. By contrast, highly specialized occupational training emerged for the other two groups within the labour market: scientific production, personnel management and human relations for the Fordist managers, and a series of separate functional tracks for the Welfare State professions. Alongside these, the range of technician-level courses also expanded steadily. Qualifications proliferated, most of them conferred by awarding bodies that were in turn either governed or regulated or advised by industrial or professional bodies, each jealous of its autonomy and each seeking to limit the role of other parties to the process.

It is not too difficult to see how this situation broke down. It is not simply that Thatcherism destroyed the cosy corporatism of the awarding and regulatory bodies; nor merely that industry and profession-based proliferation led to confusion. Fordism or Taylorism was, if you like, a second industrial revolution. Even in the 1950s, the use of scientific work management systems derived from Taylor met with resistance from workers; as a predominant mode of organizing labour its decline became unmistakable, in retrospect, in the 1970s. At about the same time, the steady expansion of Welfare State employment started to falter, then to stagnate. Given the extent of change – epitomized in such expressions as 'post-industrial society', and even in Germany, 'the end of the work-society' – it may be important simply to establish the main lines of continuity. A number of characteristics of Western capitalism have persisted, first and most obviously the fact that capitalist organization of the economy still predominates, and that the creation of surplus value – profit – remains its driving force. Second, like the Fordish industries, most economic activities continue to be conducted by very large organizations; indeed, this is now true not only of privately owned concerns but since the 1950s and 1960s it has also been true in local government, education and the public health system. Third, 'post-industrial society' has not abolished the working class; neither has it undermined the existence of a distinctive working-class culture, although it has wrought significant changes in it (Alheit 1989).

Broad patterns of economic change have been so widely observed that little further elaboration is required. So far as the organization of work is concerned, the main discontinuities would appear to be:

- the tertiarization of the economy: many more people now work in retail, financial services and administrative organizations than in manufacturing;
- the feminization of the labour force: as personal service and home-based activities are commercialized, so women come to form a more strategic and numerous part of the labour market;
- increasing core-periphery divisions: there are growing numbers of self-employed, part-time and contract workers, and growing attention to the 'personnel' and identity aspects of the core of full-time employees;
- globalization produces 'flighty capital': transnational ownership requires managers to show greater sensitivity to unit labour costs, and export work to low wage economies, using high wage economies only when they offer greater added value;
- greater returns on 'flexibility' and adaptability of labour: adoption of new techniques within existing plant, rather than opening new plant elsewhere.

There also appears to be a persistent, if paradoxical, coexistence of a permanent 'surplus' of labour with selective skill shortages (which are predicted to grow through the 1990s, for technological and demographic reasons).

Such changes have been observed as keenly, and anxiously, by the professional education lobby as by government. With the decline of youth unemployment programmes, there has been a strong lobby, both from within the public education service and from central government agencies such as the Training Agency, to persuade employers more systematically to train and update those who are in work. This attempt to create a constituency for training, though, requires at least lip service to the idea of a consensus about the kind of training required (Oakey 1990: 38). To take one example among many:

> Economic, social and demographic changes are leading to a generally recognised need to reform our structures of education and training. The need to develop a better educated, more flexible workforce, with education and training continuing throughout life, is increasingly under-stood, and has been given prominence in a range of Government policy proposals
>
> (UDACE 1989: 4)

Yet notions such as 'flexibility', far from being consensual, are highly contested, for example by trade unions. And the 'tacit utopia' of this lobby, with its assumption that the desirable future is one of higher productivity and faster growth, is also very much open to challenge. Perhaps the most significant change of the period since the early 1960s, in the long term, is the emergence of what are sometimes called 'post-materialistic values'; certainly it is difficult to identify any period in the past when there was substantial support for political and social movements which challenged the very idea that progress equals economic growth. Yet that is precisely the challenge of Green movements today.

Finally, the new system appears to be firmly in the grip of business interests. In practice it is hard to say whether this is more formal than real, and it may be better to say that the NCVQ framework has been designed to exclude education interests; thus education providers are not even represented on the Lead Industry Body for Training and Development. The most plausible explanation is that the NVQ system is not just about the labour market; like the Training and Enterprise Councils, it is a state-driven creature, in large part designed to effect and secure change in the public education and training system. The system itself, with a large work-force protected by the values of teacher professionalism, is notoriously impervious to outside attempts at change and restructuring. However, in the past ten years a number of reform efforts have emerged which have sought to use the assessment process to drive changes in teacher behaviour. Examples are GCSE, the national curriculum, and now NVQ.

THE LOW-TRAINERS AND NO-TRAINERS: A PROBLEM FOR POLICY

These developments are familiar enough; and it would be odd if, taken together, they did not produce pressures on the system of vocational qualifying education. But competency-based qualifications are only in part an attempt to cope with the desire for flexible workers. They are also an attempt to manage the risks created by the unpredictability of employers' investments in human resource development (HRD), at a time when we appear to be witnessing a growing diversification of the labour market in rapid and often complex ways. Of most concern to the new training lobby are those sectors of the labour market where conditions actively work against involvement in the vocational education system.

First, there are very large sectors where employers and workers perceive themselves as having few or no training needs. This would include those industries where employers' immediate needs are for speed, obedience and low unit labour costs, and workers' needs are for short-term cash pay-offs: thus in the fast food and retail sectors, which remain labour-intensive despite computerization at the check-out and in warehousing and administration, outlets are often intrinsically close to the consumer and are as a result being systematically subjected to hi-tech Fordism; at the lower end of the market (for example, burger bars) there is often not even any perceived need to train in interpersonal skills; even at the higher end there is often no pressure from employers for retail staff to know much about the products they sell; literacy, youth and low unit labour costs have solved most of employers' perceived problems, while in companies which do offer training in-house, much of what is offered is company-specific.

Second, there are sectors where employers perceive their training needs as highly specialized and as having little connection, or being in competition, with other employment sectors. Some of these are high wages areas where there is great interest in recruiting the highly skilled but little or none in offering continuing qualifying training which might be used by workers to change employer. The entire software industry is a case in point. It may offer continuing training, but it rarely carries a qualification. Workers themselves, though, will often commit personal investments to gain advanced qualifications but on the basis of incomplete information, with the consequence that there are recurrent 'cobweb cycles of over- and underproduction of specific qualifications in various educational and labour markets' (Timmermann 1983).

Third, there are low wage sectors where qualifications offer an entry threshold but otherwise carry little currency. In these sectors, workers' qualifications are gained despite the employer, often at public sector institutions while at the pre-entry stage, and carry little external currency. Nursery nursing is an obvious instance.

Such low-training sectors have multiplied in recent years. Training investments may simply look irrational, both to employers and, often, workers. Their significance is in generating pressures, at a time of general withdrawal from corporate structures and overall regulation, for a state-led and national (potentially supra-national) system of vocational qualifications. Hence the use of Training Agency contracts with employers and providers of vocational education to create an artificial 'command market' for qualifications accredited by the NCVQ. The question remains whether the next stage – competition for scarce labour leading on to the offer of training as part of the overall recruitment and benefits package – is anything more than a pipe-dream.

TOWARDS A CRITIQUE

Most of the critical comment on NVQ has focused on technical problems. For example, how do you ensure accuracy and comparability of performance specifications? How do you consistently interpret words like 'satisfactory' (vs 'unsatisfactory')? What about potential for future performance? What size are the units of competence? It is as though the NCVQ approach was entirely new and squeaky clean. It has, though, a history, in attempts to apply behaviourist psychology to a range of fields of human learning. The advantages of behaviourist psychology in education are that it stresses outcomes of learning, their predictability and their measurability. It has equally been criticized, both in Britain and the United States.

Behaviourism has been attacked by adult educators on philosophical and conceptual grounds, but they have not been widely noticed for what appear to be sectarian reasons. Jack Mezirow (1978) accused behaviourist adult educators in 1978 of 'indoctrination to engineer consent' and of addressing 'the wrong reality to begin with'. Three years later he returned to the theme:

> There is nothing wrong with this rather mechanistic approach to education as long as it is confined to task-oriented learning common to the 'technical' domain of learning . . . It is here such familiar concepts as education for behavior change, behavioral objectives, needs assessment, competency-based education, task analysis, skill training, accountability and criteria-referenced evaluation are appropriate and powerful.
>
> (Mezirow 1981)

Mezirow did not see behaviourism as appropriate for his other two 'domains' – social interaction, and above all the most adult of learning transactions, 'perspective transformation'. Similarly Jarvis has attacked behaviourist approaches for at best confusing the processes of learning with the outcomes and at worst ignoring processes altogether (Jarvis 1987).

This is a critique from the viewpoint of liberal adult education, which may be weakened in its impact by its particularism. Like many adult educators, Mezirow and Jarvis ignore the fact that humanistic and liberal philosophies are shared by much of the teaching profession in schools and other mainstream post–16 institutions, from youth work to universities. And in a sense this is also inevitably a practical problem for NVQ's advocates: unless they are to bypass the mainstream public system they have either to persuade educationists that NVQs are entirely compatible with humanistic philosophies or that humanistic philosophies should be amended or abandoned – neither of them a simple or conflict-free task.

Many educationists now doubt the value of any generic theory of learning. Rather they stress the virtues of pluralism, taking the view that learning outcomes appear to be context-specific and can vary enormously from one child to another, from one set of circumstances to another. [. . .] In a mass schooling system, where large numbers of young people (and adults, increasingly) are in the classroom because someone has said they must be, teaching is inimical to mere rule-following. Routinization of the kind which NCVQ envisages may avoid the problem by bypassing teachers, operating through in-house mentoring systems of various kinds, which NCVQ clearly intend should be routinized and managed from above by performance monitoring and so on. However, it has yet to be shown that a routinized learning process can work.

Workers in other fields have also drawn attention to behaviourism's lack of attention to contexts; for example, Lindsay Prior in a survey of evaluation research in mental hospitals points out that:

> in many respects, behaviourism is only another form of reification in which human 'problems' are projected onto the isolated, decontextualised human frame and detached from the meaningful contexts in which they occur. Thus, people become bodies who behave, and their problems are seen to rest in their behaviour rather than in their social condition. Their behaviour is subsequently sorted into constructive and unconstructive, useful and useless, dependent and productive categories.
>
> (Prior 1989: 145)

Prior suggests that inappropriate attempts to promote assessment practices based on a behaviourist psychology have been so widespread because behavioural changes are easy to record and quantify, enabling managers to believe that they can account for what it is that they do. They cannot because of the unpredictability of social contexts and learning.

The specific context which most closely affects NVQs is the labour market. It has yet to be seen whether NVQs will substantially change the present somewhat tenuous relationship between vocational qualification and actual occupation, where the possession of credentials is only one of the variables involved in gaining and advancing in a particular job, and one whose importance varies in different conditions (Dale and Pires 1984). NVQs will in principle lead to more intelligibility and transparency of the qualifications system, and thus may make for greater 'match' between certification and occupation; as against this existing hierarchies of control at work are to be utilized, in order to assess competencies gained directly at work, rather than challenged. Accordingly it is difficult to see how competency can greatly affect equality of opportunity either way. Further, NVQ contributes to subordination precisely by its reinforcement of the divisions between different aspects of the work process: its five-tier structure of course makes explicit the hierarchies of the workplace, and the known difficulties of applying a competency-led framework to the fourth and fifth levels makes clear what it is that is being excluded from the lower levels: any development of the kinds of the qualities needed to take decisions and manage enterprises, even within the impoverished and limited frameworks of relative powerlessness in which most managers are given the illusion that they rule. Mezirow implicitly accepts this when he accepts the 'relevance and power' of mechanistic behaviourism so long as it is confined to the 'technical domain'. Why is perspective transformation not as legitimate in the technical as in any other domain? Why assume that perspective transformation and technical learning cannot substantially overlap? They are only separate when the purpose of technical learning is circumscribed by the need for labour to be subordinate to the demand of the enterprise.

Competency based assessment, in its present form, threatens to become the new Fordism of the education system. The proliferation of competency specifications and the increasing precision with which competences are stated parallels the 'parcellization' of the work-force and labour process. As competences are differentiated more finely, so it becomes more and more possible to narrow the scope of initiative and field of responsibility of each individual in her work; the coherence and goals of the organization accordingly become less rather than more intelligible (Gorz 1989). As well as inviting bureaucratization, this process is likely to foster alienation from work rather than revive the work ethic.

A wider critique, then, would start from the assumption that what is at stake is not simply the competence and allocation of labour power at the macro-level, but also its continued subordination, and indeed the meaning and value of work itself. If the goal is to produce human beings who are creative and flexible in their handling of work, as of their other human activities, a more holistic approach is needed. Atomized and mechanistic approaches are more likely to foster the learning of strategies of manipulation and resistance: Australian researchers report on 'the apparent extent to which students would forget material once they had finished a particular competency' (Candy and Harris 1990: 55). Indeed: this is rational and learned behaviour; it is in a way a higher-level competence. The competency movement, then, is a deeply contradictory one. In its conventional forms, it seeks to impose uniformity of standards of performance and its measurement, in order to strengthen employer control over labour, and support strategies to 'add value' through the more efficient distribution of the work-force. Yet in order to work towards these ends, it also has to allow for flexibility in the face of constant technical and organizational change, as well as the movement of labour and its skills between different employers. The example of movement across national boundaries makes the point: it requires standardization and flexibility.

These are common problems in education, and taken with education's inherently future-oriented nature they raise a number of questions of legitimacy. With the erosion of industrial society and the growth of what are sometimes described as 'post-materialistic' values, it is no longer possible to construct a consensus around the desirable future to which vocational education inputs will lead. Not only are there no shared work-based utopias; on the contrary, increasingly the future is perceived and represented as full of threats. Education, which has for so long taken the desirability of technical-scientific progress as a given, is faced with questions which can only find provisional and often disturbing answers; and to many of which any given answer will be inherently contestable (Oelkers

1990). Will a more productive economy simply produce a more polluted society? Will faster growth lead to war over energy supplies? Is greater affluence in the West possible without poverty and envy in the South and East? And what of work – is it now an avoidable evil, or a scarce social good which should be more equitably shared among the population? Since it is largely the act of production which creates so many of our difficulties (from low pay to pollution), there is no likelihood of any qualification system being able to secure legitimacy for more than a short period of time if it is subordinated to the goal of greater production. This being so, there is no intrinsic reason to abandon the goal of a wider transforming and humanistic general education as part of the matrix in which changing vocational qualifications are provided and gained.

REFERENCES

Alheit, P. (1989) 'Krise er arbeitsgesellschaft – ende der arbeiterkultur?', in D. Mazur and M. Buessenschuett (eds), *Bildung in der Arbeitsgesellschaft*, Universitaet Bremen.

Ashworth, P. D. and Saxton, J. (1990) 'On "competence" ', *Journal of Further and Higher Education* XIV, pp. 3–25.

Braverman, H. (1974) *Labor and Monopoly Capital*, New York: Review Press.

Brown, M. Barratt (1984) *Models in Political Economy: A Guide to the Arguments*, Harmondsworth: Penguin.

Candy, P. and Harris, R. (1990) 'Implementing competency-based vocational education: a view from within', *Journal of Further and Higher Education* XIV, pp. 38–58.

Dale, R. and Pires, E. (1984) 'Linking people and jobs: the indeterminate place of education credentials', in P. Broadfoot (ed.), *Selection, Certification and Control: Social Issues in Educational Assessment*, Lewes: Falmer Press.

Field, J. (1988) 'Unemployment, training and manpower policy in inter-war Britain', *British Journal of Education and Work* II, pp. 39–49.

Gleeson, D. (1989) *The Paradox of Training: Making Progress out of Crisis*, Milton Keynes: Open University Press.

Gorz, A. (1989) *Critique of Economic Reason*, London: Verso.

Jarvis, P. (1987) 'Adult learning in the context of teaching', *Adult Education* 60, pp. 261–6.

Lowe, R. (1986) *Adjusting to Democracy: The Role of the Ministry of Labour in British Politics, 1916–1939*, Oxford: Clarendon.

Mezirow, J. (1978) 'Perspective transformation', *Adult Education* [USA] XXVIII.

—— (1981) 'A critical theory of adult learning and education', *Adult Education* [USA] XXXII.

Oakley, D. (1990) 'Adult education, work and leisure: a critical analysis', *Studies in the Education of Adults* 22, pp. 31–48.

Oelkers, J. (1990) 'Utopie und wirklichkeit', *Zeitschrift für Padagogik* XXXVI, pp. 1–13.

Prior, L. (1989) 'Evaluation research and quality assurance', in J. Gubrium and D. Silverman (eds), *The Politics of Field Research: Sociology Beyond Enlightenment*, Beverly Hills: Sage.

Timmerman, D. (1983) 'Financing mechanisms: their impact on post-compulsory education', in H. Levin and H. Schutze (eds), *Financing Recurrent Education*, Beverly Hills: Sage.

Unit for the Development of Adult Continuing Education (UDACE) (1989) *Understanding Competence*, Leicester: NIACE.

Chapter 4

Chile, Santiago
Breaking the culture of silence

David Archer and Patrick Costello

Source: This is an edited version of a chapter in D. Archer and P. Costello, *Literacy and Power: The Latin American Background*, London, Earthscan, 1990.

History is ours for it is made by the people.
Salvador Allende, Chilean President, 11 September 1973, while the National Palace was being bombed by Chilean air force bombers.

In the culture of silence the masses are 'mute', that is, they are prohibited from creatively taking part in the transformation of their society . . .
(Paulo Freire)[1]

In 1973, the Chilean military, under the leadership of General Augusto Pinochet, seized power from the first democratically elected Marxist government in the world: the Socialist Popular Unity government of Salvador Allende. The generals declared a state of siege, dissolving Congress, destroying the electoral register and suspending the Constitution. Sympathizers of Allende were killed, tortured, imprisoned or exiled. Between 1973 and 1977 an estimated 30,000 people were killed, 2,500 disappeared and tens of thousands passed through the prisons and concentration camps. The silencing of a people took other forms beyond immediate brutality. Popular organizations – political parties, unions, student bodies and neighbourhood committees – were either banned or their leaders replaced by military personnel. Newspapers were closed, with many journalists arrested or blacklisted.

Control of the mass media was critical to suppressing the voices of dissent. For example, in 1973 there were four Chilean television channels: a national network and three university channels. Under the socialist government, there was a large element of social influence over their output mediated through various bodies including a national television council on which government and workers' representatives sat with the university rectors. The military *junta* moved quickly, eliminating workers and parliamentary representatives from the council and appointing new rectors for the universities, all of them military men. The Directorate of National

Television was replaced by a Director-General appointed directly by the government. All powers of the university television corporations were vested in the new rectors. In summary, all social administration of Chilean television was lost and replaced by direct military control.

A climate of fear combined with a rigid control of information to create a society where the working classes had been effectively silenced. This allowed the state to implement a strict monetarist economic strategy without popular resistance. [...] The results were a consumer boom in the late 1970s and recession from 1981 onwards. [...] Unemployment, 5 per cent in 1973, had risen to 25 per cent by 1982. The official figures hid the full extent of poverty. Government schemes such as the minimum employment scheme (PEM), provided wages significantly below the minimum wage in order to take people off the unemployment lists. In 1980, 4.5 per cent of the population were on PEM receiving a wage that was a quarter of the legal minimum.

A NEW MOVEMENT

Women have been the most dynamic sector of the population since 1973.

(Herman Mondaca)[2]

Before the coup, few women were involved in the popular organizations. The systematic destruction of these, coupled with unemployment and poverty, forced women into a more active role. An example comes from the experience of a group of fourteen women in Lo Hermida, a *barrio*[3] of Santiago, Chile's capital, that houses 60,000 people. As in all the popular *barrios*, standards of housing and services are basic. One woman we met had recently constructed an extension to her house out of mud and wire meshing found on a tip.

During the period of Popular Unity, there was money and work ... we had what we needed in the house. Our husbands were working ... we'd go hungry ... but it was hunger of one day, not like now, when we pass several days without eating.[4]

Unemployment challenged traditional family roles. With the loss of work opportunities for men in the formal economy, new ways of making an income were required and it was women who were forced to develop these alternatives. Despairing husbands were left to look after the children while women abandoned what they saw as the protected space of the home to search for ways of feeding their families. For many women, this involved overcoming both the fear of a largely unknown and inhospitable world as well as the resistance of husbands ashamed of their wives leaving the home. [...]

The first step for the women of Lo Hermida was setting up a canteen for children. Food was supplied by Catholic aid agencies and the Church provided a location for the cooking. The canteen fed the children but did nothing for the adults. A meeting was held to see what the alternatives were. [. . .] The women decided to set up a laundry as a source of income. A site was found and the Church supplied the necessary materials. From there they had to decide on norms of working, find clients through house visits and by using local radio as publicity, do accounts and set up an organized structure to supervise and direct the work itself. The whole process was a learning one. Work was shared and profits divided equally.

What started as a way of surviving economic hardship became a means to understanding why that hardship came about. In the years immediately following the *coup d'état*, the Church was the only institution allowed to function with some degree of independence. It operated as an umbrella, the only shelter available for the work of semi-clandestine organizations. Through individual clients as well as through Church organizations that the laundry worked for, the women in the laundry came across many people who had been involved in Popular Unity and others who had suffered from violence.

We saw that our problems are not individual but collective and that we had to unite to deal with them.

First working with groups of the unemployed, then groups of relatives of the 'disappeared',[5] they began to involve themselves in the wider struggle against the regime. In 1978, they organized a hunger strike for the detained and a candle-lit march on which people were arrested by the army and tear gas was used to 'restore order'.

Far from frightening us, it did the opposite . . . we continued in a more dedicated way.

Literacy

In 1984, the Cultural Action Workshop (TAC), an independent non-governmental organization, started working with the laundry workers. They wanted to help them recover the history of their experiences, in the form of a book to be written by the women. To help the research, the team distributed written summaries of previous meetings. They were surprised to discover that over a third of them had serious reading difficulties – this in a country with official literacy rates of 91 per cent.[6] [. . .]

TAC decided to set up literacy classes – along Freirian lines[7] – in Lo Hermida, as a strategic task to overcome the obstacles that put a brake on participation in popular organizations. They began with nine people, mostly members of popular organizations, using improvised materials and

MIEDO

Figure 4.1 Miedo ('fear') – an image from the TAC primer Learning Together

teaching in the church. At the end of the year, certificates were given at a party to the two women from the laundry who had participated. The following year the TAC developed a primer with the people who had learnt to read and write in the first workshop. The themes were chosen to reflect the reality of the population, and the codifications were drawn by a local artist. Themes included tea (sugared tea is a major part of the diet), the taking of land for housing, fear (see Figure 4.1), unemployment, games and hospital.

TAC's work has contributed to participation in *barrio* organizations. It has also given a boost to the expression of local culture. Alongside the literacy work, short story competitions have been held on specific themes including literacy itself and life in Lo Hermida. Some of these have been published. In addition, they have now set up a team of local teachers to multiply the work and set up groups in different parts of Lo Hermida. The team has four groups operating in the different sectors of the *barrio*. One of the most active members is Rosita, who learnt to read and write with the laundry and who is now teaching others to lose their fear of ignorance. The teaching team has written a guide in order to be able to extend the experience beyond Lo Hermida to other *barrios* of Santiago and other urban populations in Chile.

Literacy's relevance

When the 'soaps' are on TV, no one will turn up to classes.

(Rosita)

For all its successes, TAC's use of literacy work to recover culture and strengthen organization faces the serious problem of lack of motivation to learn by many of the people they are trying to reach. Literacy is no longer the exclusive means of access to the outside world and the importance of the written word is on the decline:

It is not a part of the culture to read papers, magazines and books. It seems to be only part of school.

(Raoul, literacy teacher, Lo Hermida)

The written word doesn't play a big role in urban daily life because other forms of communication have displaced it. In *barrios* like Lo Hermida, television is everywhere. While only half the homes have a sink for washing dishes, four in every five households own a television. Average television viewing in Santiago is 28 hours a week.[8] It is at first a shock to see, even in the poorest homes, a television usually in the dominant position in the house, providing a constant stream of censored news, soap operas[9] and game shows interspersed with a mountain of publicity (up to 40 minutes an hour) for consumer goods and foodstuffs that are far beyond the budgets of any of Lo Hermida's viewers.

In the 1960s, a strong critique of the mass media developed in Latin America which assumed that the institutions were part of the ideological apparatus of domination and instruments of US imperialism . . . it was easy to put TV and the school together as instruments of domination. So much of the effort of popular education was reactive, trying to develop an alternative to TV. We think this is a defensive position and it ideologically condemns TV, and so doesn't use its possibilities.

(Valerio Fuenzalida, director of CENECA)

Popular education groups perceive television as a threat. For many, it presents a world view at odds with any critical perception of reality, and one which promotes passivity in the face of hardship. News programmes present demonstrations as the work of terrorists threatening the peaceful order of the Chilean state. Soap heroines don't achieve their goals by organizing workshops. The woman of the popular *barrio* is notable by her complete absence from the screen. Yet the screen has a profound emotional influence on these women, 'to the point that women who only own a black and white TV describe some programmes in colours'.[10] The position taken by popular educators, of rejecting outright a medium which is so influential on the people they are teaching, is bound to marginalize their role. If education is to start from people's reality, this is an example of reality being ignored.

A NEW LITERACY

[. . .] Television demonstrates the power of visual images as a form of communication. Literacy teaching recognizes this on one level: the codification of the literacy primer is a visual image. The dialogue generated by the decoding of the image is associated with the word. For Freire, reading the word is ultimately about reading the world. The codification, then, is a recognition of the need for the visual image as a representation of that world. What theories of literacy have not recognized is that visual images have their own language, and that 'visual literacy' is assuming a greater significance in a country like Chile where 90 per cent of homes have a television and where video is set to become a mass medium. [. . .]

At first, the idea that visual images can be read or written seems absurd. After all, everyone can watch (or 'read') television so the concept of the visual illiterate seems untenable. But this is also true of alphabetic reading:

> Of course, illiterates can read . . . can recognize the shapes and colours of words on buses so that they don't get lost . . . this means that an illiterate can 'read' because she can recognize the key words in her daily life . . . but illiteracy limits the ability to analyse and create new words, new experiences.
>
> (Raoul)

Reading is not a technique, but a way of analysing experience critically in order to be able to participate in a wider society. If the word offers less access to communication than the image then visual literacy attains greater importance. To 'write differently', then, is to produce visual images using film and video. This makes it necessary for us to learn to 're-read differently' – to analyse those images in an active, interpretative manner rather than passively accepting their intended content. [. . .]

The Incas were traditionally thought to have run an empire without writing. There were no manuscripts found by the *conquistadors* and the empire was thought to have been run on the basis of accounts which were kept by means of the special arrangement of knots on coloured pieces of rope. However, these knots, as encoded information, were a form of writing with their own language and grammatical rules. Computer analysis of the designs on Inca ceramic materials suggests that these images conceal further remains of a written Inca history. Information is encoded on the basis of the spatial arrangement of shapes and colours. To restrict the concept of writing to linear, alphabetic writing is to fail to understand different ways of thinking, some of which are becoming relevant again as images become the dominant way in which our thoughts are structured.

It is conceivable that what we now think of as writing is merely a short historical interlude in the modes of representation and communication of human thought.

As yet, there are no literacy groups in Chile that have taken on board the idea of a new literacy. However, in the work of other groups elements of what might make up a teaching programme for the new literacy are highly developed.

Literacy materials

In 1982–3, there was no video work in Chile. We did an investigation and found that young people had very clear images of the government and the opposition . . . they identified the regime as authoritarian/dictatorial, but in relation to images . . . colourful and happy, while audiovisually, the opposition were perceived as morose, serious and in black and white.

(Herman Mondaca, PROCESO)

PROCESO made their first video documentary in 1982 with minimal technology: a borrowed camera and a tape recorder. The aim was 'to rescue the memory' of the inhabitants of marginal *barrios*, a memory that had been systematically silenced by the regime's censorship of all media. They had showings in the *barrios* and among the students of Santiago: 'Our support came from the new social movements emerging at that time . . . women's groups, groups of the unemployed' (Herman Mondaca).

The next video was a 30-minute piece on human rights involving the testimony of different people and some discussion. 'With the second video, we saw that we were doing something different . . . we removed the narrator or commentator . . . we wanted to give a voice to the participants' (Herman Mondaca). The video was effectively a codification: it encoded the contradictions and complexities of the reality of the people who watched it – and it generated dialogue:

We showed it in Lo Hermida . . . 350 people came to see it and it generated a big discussion . . . two human rights committees were set up afterwards, overcoming traditional political divisions among the people. The video didn't say 'organize!'. It just showed the reality . . . people saw it and spontaneously reacted.

(Herman Mondaca)

In 1983 the opposition movement became more vociferous in its demands. Popular organizations such as the women's movement were operating more openly though still subject to police repression. PROCESO decided to use the opportunity to make more videos which went deeper into specific themes: women, the young, human rights. They decided that the popular sectors of society should be the source of all information and commentary in the videos, which were also to be used to make a contribution to popular education among those sectors. The videos were distributed through other organizations, students, women's groups and the Church. [...] PROCESO set up a distribution and feedback department so that the viewers could have a voice, giving their criticisms, responses and ideas for new videos. [...]

Reading

After the coup, many university departments were transformed. Study of media and communications was heavily attacked because of its association with left-wing politics. [...] As a response, in 1977 a group of academics set up a research body (CENECA) to continue monitoring and evaluating the media, independently of the university system. Their work involved studying the transformations in communication and culture since the coup: monitoring censorship as well as analysing new laws and their impact.

> We investigated how people saw TV and we found it confirmed that people don't watch TV passively ... People see their TV from the perspective of their material conditions, and their educational, social and political position ... there was an active reading and we had to strengthen that in order to make it more so.
>
> (Valerio Fuenzalida)

To complement the research side of their work they set up a number of programmes of 'social and cultural animation', designed to spread the experience and insights of the research. One active reception course was organized with sixty women from the urban women's movement (MOMUPO) and unions of domestic employees. It aimed to 'stimulate creativity, critical understanding of reality and validate solidarity and social participation'. [...] The course used the different types of programme – soaps, news, games shows – in order to develop the active reading of television.

The way in which any television is watched and the effects that it has are dependent on a complex of social factors. For example, soap operas are usually considered a form of escapism, a way of living in fantasy what is impossible in reality. A study of the viewing habits of women residents of popular *barrios* revealed a more complex reason. The women preferred the Chilean soaps to Mexican or US imports, in spite of the greater opulence and potential for escapism in the latter. This suggested that the identification of the women with soap heroines was rooted in something more than a desire to forget their own problems. The conflicts on which the dramatic structure of soaps are based are ones which are not far removed from their own lives: abandoned children, incestuous fathers, single parents, barriers to love and so on. While the material way of life of soap heroines creates a distance from the viewers, these conflicts form the basis for a strong emotional identification with the heroine. It is this rather than the type of dress the heroine is wearing that spontaneously generates topics of conversation amongst the urban women on the subject of their favourite soaps.

For CENECA, this is the basis for active reading/reception. In a class of women, a discussion of reasons for liking soaps can lead to a consideration of why certain heroines are admired, and to think about why family conflicts are presented in soaps whereas economic ones are not. Ultimately, the women are in a position to think about the kind of conflicts that they would use if they were writing a soap themselves. [. . .] Women began to read the contents of their favourite programmes more critically. [. . .] Even the television of Pinochet's Chile can be a codification of life in urban popular *barrios* if read in a critical, active manner.

Writing

> Official TV arrives at our communities and we are simple adornments of the propaganda of the mayor or state functionary who opens a public toilet; foreign TV arrives or sometimes alternative TV and it only shows the misery or the poverty. But we want neither, we want to show the beauty as well, the beauty of our lives.
>
> (Video workshop of the urban women's movement)

At a meeting in 1985, members of PROCESO and the women's movement MOMUPO decided to make a documentary. The difference from previous work was that the women themselves were to make it. It would be about their view of the history of popular women's organizations during the dictatorship.

> We were familiarized with the machines and the basic techniques. It took us a long time to learn these things: sound, lighting, editing and ways of presenting things to the camera. We had to learn the language of video and television.
>
> (Coty Silva, MOMUPO)

PROCESO's only role was in teaching the techniques and doing the camera work itself. Each of the women involved was an activist in a different *barrio* of Santiago. Every meeting was recorded over the following months by the PROCESCO workers as the women discussed the nature of women's organizations developing out of specific conflicts. The women took on the role of investigative reporters of the realities in their own areas. Over a year, more than 50 hours of recording were made. Four years later, the edited video (*Gestación*) is still the most popular one shown by women's groups in Santiago and all over the country. It deals with themes such as the personal changes experienced by women leaving the home to participate in organizations, the relations between men and women and the role of women in society.

> By making videos, we could use our own words, our own language, our own way of seeing.
>
> (Marina Valdes, *Gestación*)

Two more videos have been made since *Gestación* under the direction of the workshop. One is on subsistence and the way in which women have survived the recession, the other is on the recuperation of culture and dignity through the process of organization. In both productions PROCESO assisted with the camera work, but the women were involved in direction at all stages from planning to final edit.

Opportunities to 'write' the moving image are still very limited in Latin America. Among groups involved in this work, there is a debate about the role of the professional in facilitating the writing process. On the one hand, PROCESO sees the camera work as a neutral technique that helps the direction, rather like the lines on a piece of paper, guiding the newly literate.

> By professionalization, I don't mean following the formal, classical language of television. But you can't have a single fixed camera view for five minutes, or people won't watch.
>
> (Herman Mondaca)

There is a danger that anything which fails to match the professional standards of television will be seen as the work of amateurs and rejected by its potential audience. PROCESO make their videos on the principle that certain technical and artistic criteria must be used to prevent such a rejection.

There are other groups who believe it impossible to distinguish any aspect of the production – or 'writing' – of video as professional or as a technique. In this view it is essential that the people themselves write their history, regardless of aesthetic criteria. This may well mean the withdrawal of any professional advice. If the product appears amateur or unclear, that is secondary to the authenticity of its origins. [. . .]

Camera techniques are seen as part of the hidden agenda of modern television. Chilean television has made huge technical advances since 1973. Presentation and production are slick and use of modern post-production techniques is widespread. Hand-held camera is never used on the screens. Instead the camera is 'hidden', giving an artificial appearance of objectivity, as people are not made aware of the process of filming while watching the product. Cameras in the hands of the people could break these norms, thereby helping to expose, for example, the hidden selectivity of news coverage. Learning to 'write' in this way might reinforce people's ability to 'read'.

In the language of literacy, this debate questions to what extent videos written by non-professionals need to have their grammar and spelling corrected in order to be read seriously.

BREAKING THE CULTURE OF SILENCE

A new impact

As the economic recession worsened in the mid-1980s, popular resistance to the dictatorship grew bolder. Large-scale demonstrations spilled over into riots in 1983 and 1986. Pinochet himself was the object of an assassination attempt as the new social movements felt their strength. [...]

Visual literacy played an important part in breaking the culture of silence. First, it promoted the growth of organizations. Video showings like that in Lo Hermida (which spawned two human rights groups) were repeated all over Chile. Video groups like PROCESO became more skilful in using the medium for organizational ends. One technique was to show a documentary in a public area and video the viewing as well as interviews with viewers and discussions among them afterwards. This new video, of the viewers, would be shown the following month to the same people. Seeing themselves on the screen had a dramatic effect:

> The people feel that they are appropriating the TV . . . and seeing TV
> again . . . losing their helplessness. Specialist courses are not necessary
> . . . just seeing the TV inserted in their own reality can produce the
> 'click'.

> (Herman Mondaca)

Video can be responsible for a very rapid conscientization. The mechanics of producing images become clear. Television loses its monopoly as the mouthpiece of truth when moving images are democratized. One viewer responded after seeing himself on the screen for the first time 'now I've been on television . . . they're not going to lie to me any more'.

Once people realize the way in which the world is presented to them, they are much more likely to try and change it themselves, recognizing that it is their world as much as the world of the presenters. Changing it is suddenly within their reach.

More recently PROCESO have set up a mobile video service for fifty-five women's groups in and around Santiago. Using a giant screen, they show videos such as *Gestación* to groups of women in the popular *barrios*, sometimes in closed spaces such as chapels, but often publicly, in streets where anyone can join in, watch and participate in the discussions afterwards. [...]

As the popular movement gathered strength, video was also important for providing information about events censored by the official media. Some video groups, rather than concentrating on the literacy side of the work, were producing an alternative news magazine. By distributing through unions, political parties, women's groups, cultural associations and of course the Church, these acted as a form of information for the literate. Since 1984 TELEANALISIS (now called Nueva Imagen) have produced a video every month, following the protests and demonstrations, national strikes, Church activities, as well as the international news excluded from Chilean TV. [. . .]

The state was not slow in recognizing the significance of video. At first, any videos of public protests had to be shot from parked vans or the top of buildings. There were no laws but rather an inevitable police response and the workers couldn't afford to lose their equipment.

> We wanted to show our images and we didn't want it to be clandestine . . . so we started going out into the streets, wearing medical service cards or boy scout cards as identity on our shirts.
>
> (Herman Mondaca)

Police saw the badges and, reading them from afar, took them as a seal of official approval, a perfect example of the ascendancy of the visual image over the written word. This provided some immunity until the state realized the scale and increasing importance of alternative video. Scare tactics were used. People were followed, received telephone threats, had their houses observed. Newspaper articles were published in which video groups were accused of being subversives, with titles such as 'Video: Principal Ideological Arm of the Chilean Left'.

> In September 1987 one of us, Mario Nuñez, was kidnapped with four civilians. They were beaten in the face and testicles and questioned about their activities. They searched his house and mine and took some 'evidence' . . . photorolls and tapes including some of my four-year-old kid. At dawn, the prisoners were released on a road outside Santiago. On the same day, we won a prize in Brazil for one of our documentaries.
>
> (Herman Mondaca)

Scare tactics were ineffective and the army could do little more because by this stage PROCESO was networked with over 150 organizations. The national movement was too strong. For example, the Catholic Church had video equipment in almost every parish. Repressing video had become an impossible task.

Visions of democracy

[...] The 1980 Constitution instituted by the military government set elections for 1989. In 1988, Pinochet announced that there would be a Yes/No plebiscite in November to decide whether he should carry on as leader. Effectively this was a tactic, an attempt to avoid full elections. However, legal requirements offered the opposition access to national media. For the first time since the coup, the opposition ('No') campaigners were given daily 15-minute spots on national television. Groups like TELEANALISIS and PROCESO suddenly had an opportunity to use the networks themselves. [...] The polls initially showed a big proportion of indecisive voters. Many of these were people who were frightened of voting 'no' to Pinochet. The government campaign concentrated on showing images of pre-1973 as chaotic, playing on people's fears of disorder. The 'No' campaign was directed at this fear.

> The TV spots used the language of advertising to produce the conviction that the 'No' was a just position, a happy position, and one of non-violence ... it created a feeling that to vote 'Yes' was non-ethical, an option for aggression and the violation of human rights.
>
> (Valerio Fuenzalida)

One image was of the police beating an undefended person lying on the ground. Full speed was followed by slow motion of the same sequence. Each blow was circled and amplified with sound effects. The text wasn't saying that those in power must be punished but rather that this must never happen again:

> This man is a Chilean [the demonstrator]. So is this man [the policeman]. This man wants peace. So does this man. This man is fighting for what he believes. So is this man. Let them both have what they want. Vote NO!

This was one of very few images dealing directly with violence. The aim was to overcome past associations of the opposition with morose black-and-white images. The symbol of the campaign was the rainbow. [...] In spite of being broadcast late at night, the No spots attracted record audiences and are recognized as the major factor in the success of the campaign. As the momentum increased the campaign took to the streets. To wear a T-shirt with the image of the rainbow was a sign of a loss of fear. Video was involved here too. PROCESO filmed discussions in villages on the plebiscite and used the mobile video unit to show them.

In the ballot, Pinochet was beaten and the showdown was set for the elections the following year. An alliance of all parties opposed to Pinochet was organized under Patricio Aylwin, a Christian Democrat. [...] Faced with inevitable defeat in the elections, Pinochet made a number of last-minute moves to ensure that complete power would not be left in the hands of the new government. One of the bills rushed through Congress involved the privatization of television. Aware of the power of the medium, he sought to ensure that big business – which would remain sympathetic to him – gained control and would retain it even in the aftermath of a lost election.

The future

[...] The new government in Chile presents the same dilemma for the popular movements and for education groups as did the Borja government in Ecuador. Is it worth using the limited democratic space offered by the government to try and open that space further? Or is it better to stay in opposition to avoid the assimilation of any protests? [...]

The new government's policy is to democratize the television, creating legal mechanisms so that the national channel is autonomous of government and responsive to the regional needs of different branches of its network, restoring the universities' independent control over their franchises and setting up a new 'pluralist and representative' national television council to regulate and supervise broadcasting.

With television genuinely responsive to its audience, the literacy of that audience becomes vital for the success of the democratization. 'Active receivers' will be able to articulate the demands that make it their television. As writing develops, the opportunities will exist for different organizations to express themselves through the networks. [...]

Time will tell what the effect of campaigns based on making and watching television programmes will be: whether they create new forms of participation and organization, or whether, with the military in the wings and the economic situation in the popular *barrios* unchanged, they will merely form part of the social palliative for the de-read democracy which has swept the continent.

NOTES

1 Paulo Freire, *Cultural Action for Freedom* (London: Penguin, 1972).
2 Director of video group PROCESO in interview with authors, August 1989.
3 Urban neighbourhood borough.
4 *Lavando la Esperanza*, written by members of the laundry workshop with Taller de Acción Cultural (TAC) (Santiago 1985). Other quotations in this subsection are taken from the same publication.
5 The 'disappeared' are a surprisingly large group. It is so common in the Southern Cone (Chile, Argentina, Uruguay, Paraguay) that it has become a verb: I was disappeared, You were disappeared, She is disappeared, etc. Few reappear.

6 National Report 1986, quoted in, *Situatión Educativa de America Latina y El Caribe* (Santiago: UNESCO/OREALC, 1988).

7 Freire's work challenged the idea that knowledge, whether of mathematical tables or the history of a revolution, can be taught as though it consists of packages to be fed to students who, by memorizing the information, magically acquire the attribute of being educated. For Freire this view of knowledge is responsible for transforming education into a business transaction

> For Freire it is not enough to change the content of an education for it to be revolutionary, it is necessary to change the very structure of teaching. Popular education requires that the knowledge it produces is one developed *between* teacher and students, in relation to a lived reality.
>
> A text or literacy primer based on the Nicaraguan revolution could not simply be a description of the new reality which students memorized. Nor could the process of learning to read be reduced to the rote learning of the alphabet. The aim of the crusade was not to dictate the aims of the revolution or to transfer the techniques of literacy. Rather, through a 'problem-posing' text, the idea was to promote creative participation in the revolution via creative use of the written word. In adult literacy, mastering oral and written language constitutes one dimension of the process of being expressive. Another dimension involves enabling people to 'read' their reality and 'write' their own history.
>
> (Archer and Carletto 1990: 24)

The method developed from this is one where the words and associated images used in literacy primers reflect key aspects of the lives and current experiences of the learner. The words used are said to be 'generative' in that they generate both dialogue and new words, by rearranging the syllables. The images used are seen as 'codifications' of reality, which stimulate learners to reflect critically on the meaning of their lives and of the shared history of their country. They 'de-code' these images and thus learn not only to read words, but to 'read' their own history. (Eds.)

8 Research into television in low-income areas from Fuenzalida, Valerio, *Estudios sobre la Televisión Chilena* (Santiago: CPU, 2nd edn, 1986).

9 The soap opera or *telenovela* in Latin America is slightly different from its European or North American counterpart. It rarely runs longer than twenty episodes and finds its dramatic origins in the melodrama of the radio-soaps, and before them the musical sagas of the continent.

10 Fuenzalida, Valerio, and Maria Elena Hermósilla, *Visiónes y Ambiciónes del Televidente* (Santiago: CENECA, 1989).

Chapter 5

Unpaid work in the home and accreditation

Linda Butler

The aim of this chapter is to discuss the argument that since many millions of individuals in the home engage in unpaid work that is the same as, or similar to, work undertaken elsewhere for pay, then those individuals' potential to achieve credit on the basis of their current competence towards vocational awards is the same as it is for their counterparts in, or experienced in, paid work.

The opportunity to explore this argument has arisen because vocational qualifications are being reformed by the Employment Department, Industry Lead Bodies, the National Council for Vocational Qualifications (NCVQ) and the awarding bodies (the RSA, BTEC, CGLI, etc.) to become competence-based.

Competence-based awards are:

- assessed on the candidate's performance of the units or elements of an award, as opposed to what he/she can write about them;
- assessable irrespective of the *mode* (for example, formal course; 'sitting by Nellie'), *duration* (for example, five-year apprenticeship; five weeks' study), or *location* (for example, college; own back yard) in which the competence was gained.

It is therefore no longer necessary to undertake a taught course to gain, for example, the competence required for a new vocational qualification in management. Candidates can instead *demonstrate* their competence by actual performance, whether planned or naturally occurring in the workplace.

Can this same approach to assessment and accreditation, for the same vocational qualifications, be applied to unpaid work in the home? To explore this argument, it is necessary first to consider whether activities carried out unpaid in the home constitute work. There is after all a long-standing and deeply held societal perception of unpaid work in the home as a vocation, something like a calling, and therefore so different and separate from the paid work world as to have no relevance to it. Home work is done for love, not money, for family approval rather than for external awards, and for private satisfaction rather than paid work advancement. This perception, however, confuses the activity with the motivation behind it. Contemporary understanding of the nature of work generally eschews definitions of work which are dependent on exogenous factors such as whether it is paid, and look instead to the nature of the activity itself. Thus, in functional analysis, which is the dominant contemporary analytical tool applied to capturing the functions which people carry out in jobs and occupations, work is defined as purposeful activity with critical outcomes.[1] Whether or not an individual is paid is irrelevant to defining what he/she is doing as work.

The functional analysis definition is important, since the Department of Employment adopted functional analysis to derive, in the late 1980s and early 1990s, and in conjunction with industry, the new occupational standards which themselves constitute the foundation of the reformed vocational qualification system. The definition of work as purposeful activity with critical outcomes no doubt gave strength to the NCVQ's decision to publish their statement in 1991 that 'previous practice has perhaps tended to fall into the trap of equating 'work' exclusively with conventional paid employment.[2]

The theoretical basis for regarding unpaid work as work is supported by reference to many contemporary writings on the changing nature of work, which follow a general theme of a working career evolving as an individual portfolio of paid work, fee work, free work, home work and study work (see, for example, Handy 1991).

If unpaid work is work, how much of it is undertaken? It is certainly the case that both free work, that is community and voluntary work, and home work, are very widely practised. As an example of community work, 1.4 million women and men provide care in the home for more than 20 hours per week for a sick, disabled or elderly person. As for volunteering, if prompted to adopt a broad definition of volunteering, about one in two people are said to have considered themselves as undertaking some form of voluntary activity in the last year.[3]

In the case of home work, the weekly hours spent in 1989 were 25.9 hours for male full-time employees and 42.2 for female full-time employees; for part-time female employees, 58.6 hours per week (no figures given for males); and for housewives (assumed to be female, no figures given for males), the hours per week were 65.3 (The Henley Centre for Forecasting quoted in Central Statistical Office 1991). These data, in conjunction with common observation, suggest that unpaid work in the home is undertaken by more persons, and for much more time, than is community or voluntary work.

We need now to consider whether this great volume of unpaid working activity contains activities which are the same as, or similar to, working activities carried out for pay. In respect of the nature of the activities carried out in community and voluntary work, it has long been claimed that almost any job done for pay is done by someone as a volunteer, and any single community or voluntary organization is likely to offer experience in several – and sometimes dozens – of different jobs. Drawing parallels between paid work and community or voluntary work is therefore relatively easy.

The range and level of the activities carried out in unpaid work in the home has been much less clear. Such work, commonly called housework, is subject to two contradictory preconceptions. On the one hand, it is most readily understood by women and men as a limited set of functions such as cooking, cleaning, washing and ironing, which are common to all housewives, whether male or female, and which are stereotypically perceived to be low-skilled. On the other hand, there is a long-standing body of research and educational practice which attempts to differentiate and upgrade the functions of housework, often by pointing to the apparent relationship between the management of the home and business management. This body of work, which refers almost exclusively to women's rather than women and men's unpaid work in the home, is regularly subject to the criticism that it reflects the functions only of middle-class white women.[4, 5, 6]

A national project to clarify and define the competence acquired in unpaid work in the home was undertaken in 1991 for The Employment Department Group.[7] The project explored the hypothesis that unpaid workers in the home develop competence and are competent in ways which can be classified and related to the competence which is required in paid employment. This relationship was explored using functional analysis, and the project deployed the same recognized process used to derive occupational standards in all industrial or commercial sectors. The project also deployed the normal fieldwork procedures – namely, the initial mapping of the domain, the conduct of a series of workshops with expert participants, supporting individual interviewing, and an expert review of the completed draft standards.

The design of the recruitment and workshop procedures did, however, take special account of the possible alienation of the occupational group from their competence, because of a stereotypic understanding of such competence as low-level and limited. Workshop participants might be so competence-blind that the project would fail to elicit an accurate and comprehensive account of unpaid work. The steps taken to mitigate this problem included recruiter briefing, time-log sheets and briefing exercises in the workshops.

The use of time-log sheets played quite an important part in putting participants in better touch with the amount and variety of their unpaid work. All participants were asked before they attended their allocated workshop to complete two time-log sheets, one to cover a typical and one an untypical unpaid working day. These time-logs were then used as personal *aide-mémoires* during the course of the workshop. Participants' attention was drawn to them at specific points in the day – for example, at the beginning of the workshop day in order to help generate an overview of the extent of unpaid work in the home.

Almost all workshop participants completed their time-log sheets and said they were easy to do. The project advised counting as work anything which they could pay someone else to do for them. Participants appeared to have almost no problem with counting what they were doing as real work, although they were often surprised at how much they did. Participants were asked to decide for themselves what they wanted to include. Some women, for example, had meal breaks which they did not count in; many others, whose meal breaks were spent supervising children, counted their meal breaks, too, as work.

However, it was apparent that while participants were easily able to record the length of their unpaid working day, they recorded only brief and stereotypic details of their working activities. It was only after the initial workshop exercises that participants said they had omitted to record important information about their days – for example, work on more abstract functions such as planning projects. Those women selected for the expert review workshop were asked to repeat the time-log exercise, and on this occasion the sheets were much more fully completed.

The workshops provided the project with its main source of information. They were conducted using a variety of exercises designed to elicit information. A typical workshop consisted of:

1 a brief introduction outlining the aims of the project and introducing the facilitators;
2 an ice-breaker exercise (usually not needed);
3 feedback from the time-logs recorded by the respondents;
4 a presentation on how new standards-based qualifications concentrate on the demonstration of competence, and relating this to the respondents' own experiences;
5 a brainstorming exercise to produce information on broad functional areas (usually in groups of five or six, led by a facilitator), producing information on key roles, units, and element structure;
6 a further exercise concentrating on a unit and elements, producing information on range and standards (sometimes in small groups of two or three, with or without facilitators);
7 filling in of the repsondent questionnaire;
8 feedback on the day from the respondents and the facilitators.

Typically, participants had an opportunity at the beginning of the day to provide lists of the activities which they undertook. These were compiled against a number of headings, with the aim of providing an initial view of the main activities which occur. To gather information in more depth, we focused on a particular activity, and probed what happened during that activity, the alternative ways of doing the activity and who else was involved, and we asked questions about the skills and knowledge required to do it.

We also asked why an activity was undertaken, since purpose is important to determining outcome. The timing of this question was important. If asked too early on in a discussion, the response was usually puzzlement; asked later on, it produced reflection and reasons. We then asked further questions about what other activities achieved the same purpose. This was an important iterative process in establishing the domain of unpaid work in the home.

The final workshop was used to review a refined version of the functional analysis. In this workshop, the facilitators explained the draft analysis, which was followed by focused, intense debate as to its structure and content. This workshop proved particularly successful, and led to some very valuable changes in the analysis. It was also interesting to find that although the participants were being asked to deal with the language and structure of functional analysis for the first time in this review workshop, they coped with the translation of their activities into functions very well.

The functional analysis was based on a sample of nearly 200 women, a large one for a functional analysis. The sample frame was as advised by MORI, the national market research group, to be broadly representative of British social class, age, urbanity and ethnicity patterns. The units and elements structure of the analysis are shown as Figure 5.1 and two sample units are shown in detail as Figures 5.2a and 5.2b. The complete functional analysis is unpublished at the time of writing.

A number of points should be considered in reading the analysis. First, the project brief specified the development of a functional framework of key roles, units and elements, but not performance criteria. The purpose of performance criteria is to enable assessment to the described standards. Since the project was intended to test the transferability of unpaid work competence, rather than its assessment as a vocational qualification in its own right, the development of performance criteria was considered irrelevant. However, the description of each element does include range statements, which delineate the variables affecting the performance of each element. The range includes descriptions of methods, materials, people, places, etc., which could be encountered in the activity, and descriptions of the standards which are generally applied by those performing the element. These standards are not described with the precision normally associated with performance criteria, but they do provide some idea of the standards which are self-imposed or accepted by those undertaking unpaid work. Indeed, it was significant to discover, counter to the dominant stereotype of unpaid work, that common standards do apply to

Key Purpose: To establish and maintain a home which sustains and develops its members

Key Role	Unit	Elements
Key Role A Develop and manage systems to meet routine and non-routine needs	*Unit A1 Develop and establish systems for the operation of the home*	Element A1.1 Plan systems to meet routine needs Element A1.2 Set standards for the functioning of the home Element A1.3 Manage systems for the functioning of the home
	Unit A2 Plan change and manage unforeseen circumstances	Element A2.1 Plan projects and events to meet non-routine needs Element A2.2 Manage unforeseen circumstances
Key Role B Optimize the acquisition and use of material and financial resources	*Unit B1 Secure, plan and monitor financial resources against budgets*	Element B1.1 Identify sources of income and credit Element B1.2 Obtain, secure and exploit income and credit Element B1.3 Plan budgets and allocate expenditure Element B1.4 Monitor cash flow to modify income and expenditure levels
	Unit B2 Negotiate and agree the purchase of goods and services	Element B2.1 Determine specifications for goods and services Element B2.2 Negotiate terms for the cost and delivery for goods and services Element B2.3 Order and monitor the delivery of goods and services Element B2.4 Arrange and check payments for goods and services
	Unit B3 Optimize the use of goods and services	Element B3.1 Conserve and recycle resources for further use Element B3.2 Provide goods and services for gifts or substitution Element B3.3 Establish networks for the sharing and exchange of goods and services
Key Role C Obtain, record and provide information to others	*Unit C1 Obtain and store information for analysis and decision-making*	Element C1.1 Determine and specify information requirements Element C1.2 Identify and locate sources of information which meet information requirements Element C1.3 Obtain information from organizations and individuals Element C1.4 Record and store information for further use
	Unit C2 Provide information to organizations and individuals	Element C2.1 Provide information to meet the needs of organizations and individuals Element C2.2 Exchange information within peronal networks Element C2.3 Provide recommendations to assist decision-making
Key Role D Support and care for adults	*Unit D1 Support and care for independent adults*	Element D1.1 Provide emotional support and care for adults Element D1.2 Provide advice and guidance to adults on personal matters Element D1.3 Support adults in their careers, hobbies and pastimes
	Unit D2 Develop oneself and others	Element D2.1 Develop one's skills, knowledge and personality Element D2.2 Develop other adults' skills, knowledge, personality, and physique Element D2.3 Develop teams' skills, knowledge, and physique
	Unit D3 Supervise, support and care for dependent adults	Element D3.1 Maintain and develop support mechanisms for the dependent adult Element D3.2 Provide social support to the dependent adult Element D3.3 Provide emotional support and care for the dependent adult Element D3.4 Mediate between dependent adults and organizations

Key Role E Care for and supervise children

Unit E1 Protect children from danger
- Element E1.1 Provide a safe home environment for children
- Element E1.2 Monitor children's relationships with other children and adults
- Element E1.3 Instruct children in safe and unsafe practices
- Element E1.4 Organize the supervision of children by other adults

Unit E2 Teach and aid the development of children
- Element E2.1 Provide a disciplined environment for children's development
- Element E2.2 Teach cognitive, behavioural and manual skills
- Element E2.3 Provide guidance on the acquisition of knowledge and understanding
- Element E2.4 Provide development opportunities for children
- Element E2.5 Provide support for children in their development activities

Unit E3 Exchange information with children
- Element E3.1 Provide information and guidance to children
- Element E3.2 Obtain information from children

Unit E4 Provide children with social situations
- Element E4.1 Support children in their social activities
- Element E4.2 Provide opportunities for children to socialize with other children

Unit E5 Supervise, support and care for children
- Element E5.1 Provide emotional support and care for children
- Element E5.2 Mediate between children and organizations

Key Role F Maintain the health and safety of household members

Unit F1 Maintain the health and fitness of adults and children
- Element F1.1 Monitor and encourage the health and fitness of adults and children
- Element F1.2 Direct adults and children on dietary intake
- Element F1.3 Promote physical fitness in adults and children

Unit F2 Supervise treatment processes for adults and children
- Element F2.1 Care for and monitor adults and children during illness
- Element F2.2 Obtain and evaluate advice from specialists and others
- Element F2.3 Administer medications and theory to adults and children
- Element F2.4 Evaluate and maintain/modify the treatment process

Unit F3 Maintain health and safety in the home
- Element F3.1 Detect, secure, and isolate health hazards
- Element F3.2 Detect, secure, and isolate safety hazards
- Element F3.3 Secure the home and contents from intrusion and damage
- Element F3.4 Establish standards of hygiene and cleanliness
- Element F3.5 Clean and wash areas of domestic use
- Element F3.6 Dispose of food waste and clean preparation areas and dishes

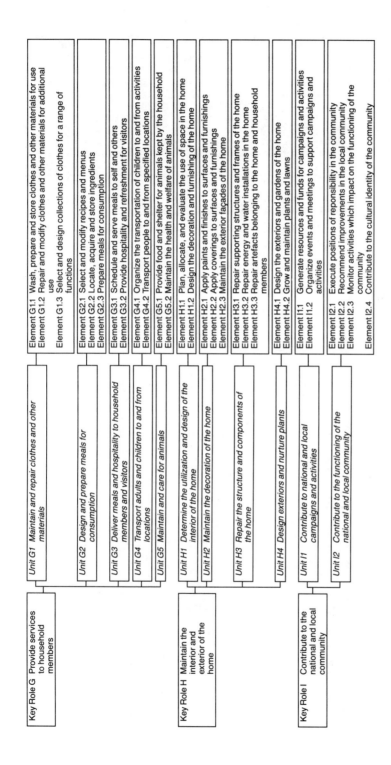

Figure 5.1 Competencies in unpaid work in the home: functional analysis overview

---

Element B1.1   Identity sources of income and credit

Sources of income: employment: of partner, self, and other family members; interest from savings: stocks, shares, unit trusts, PEPs, building society accounts, deposit accounts; marketing promotions: brand coupons, special offer packaging; competitions: free-entry competitions, market promotions; state benefits, allowances and grants: housing benefits, income support, family support, child allowance, death benefit, disability allowance, pensions, special one-off payments etc; sale of goods and services.
Sources of credit: institutions: banks, building societies, finance houses; promotions: interest free offers, low-finance offers; scheduling of payments: credit cards, bills, etc.

Standards: sources of income are correctly identified; a range of income sources are identified if possible.

Element B1.2   Obtain, secure and exploit income and credit

Obtain income by: negotiation with partner, and other family members; selling goods and services; establishing and demanding state entitlements.
Income secured by checking: till receipts, change, bills, fees, commissions; security of: purse/wallet, cheque books, credit cards, pass books, certificates.
Exploit by utilizing: interest-free credit, delayed payment offers; interest rate levels and movements, tax advantages, size of investment discounts, etc.

Standards: the effort, time and cost of acquiring income is balanced with the revenue due from that income; income is secured safely; income is invested with reputable organization; investment balances risk against return.

Element B1.3   Plan budgets and allocate expenditure

Types of budget: investment and cost centres.
Budgets headings: food, clothes, and routine expenditure; car: purchase, petrol, repairs; holiday; house repairs, decoration, extension, purchase; children: pocket money, education expenses (uniforms, sports kit, books, and tuition fees).
Size of budget: from minimal daily expenses to house purchase values.

Standards: resources effectively balanced between budget headings; expenditure is accurately forecast; information on costs is accurate; records of important expenditure are maintained.

Element B1.4   Monitor cash flow to modify income and expenditure levels

Monitor balances of: cash in hand, bank accounts, building society accounts, stocks and share holdings, unit trusts, PEPs, endowments and annuities maturations.
Factors to monitor: price of goods and services, interest rates, stocks and share values, currency exchange rates, general economic performance, specific employment-related company performance; expenditure of the household.

Standards: income and expenditure are effectively balanced over varying lengths of time; money is switched between budgets to cover contingencies for over and underspending (virement); factors affecting cash flow are monitored carefully to determine expenditure schedules.

Figure 5.2a Competencies in unpaid work in the home: Key Role B, Unit B1

Element F3.1   Defect, secure, and isolate health hazards

Health hazards: toxic substances: detergents, disinfectants, caustic soda, cleaning agents, lead, asbestos, animal waste products; drugs: medicaments, tablets, alcohol; food: dirty storage areas, decaying food, past sell-by-date items, mixing incompatible foodstuffs; hygiene: dirty toilet, sink, washing areas; general health dangers: damp, fumes, lack of ventilation, pest infestations, temperature inappropriate.
Detect by: inspecting, monitor manufacturer's instructions; research: BSI, consumer magazines/articles, government health warnings.
Secure and isolate: remove, place in locked or inaccessible cupboard/drawers, dispose of safely, modify.

Standards: materials are only used for the purpose stated by the manufacturer; inappropriate use is detected immediately, and help summoned immediately if required; hazards are kept out of the reach of children; cleaning routines are maintained to self-determined standards.

Element F3.2   Detect, secure, and isolate safety hazards

Safety hazards: heat: fire, matches, cooker, hot liquids, cold liquids, acids, heaters, cigarettes; electrical appliances: trailing leads, overloading of supply, fusing, water contact, misconnection; obstacles: loose staircarpet, fittings, shelves, stepladders; sharp objects: knives, glass.
Detect by: inspecting, monitor manufacturer's instructions; research: BSI, consumer magazines/articles, government health warnings.
Secure and isolate: remove, place in locked or inaccessible cupboard/drawers, dispose of safely, douse, modify.

Standards: materials and equipment are only used for the purpose stated by the manufacturer; inappropriate use is detected immmediately, and help summoned immediately if required; hazards are kept out of the reach of children; cleaning routines are maintained to self-determined standards.

Element F3.3   Secure the home and contents from intrusion and damage

Home: structure: house, flat, maisonnette, bedsitter, room, mobile home; permanent or temporary; main residence, additional residence; property: owned/rented by self, other.
Contents: people: residents, visitors; goods: money, valuables, appliances, car, bikes.
Intrusion by: criminals: burglars, arsonists, rapists etc; unauthorized visitors: canvassers, salespersons, promoters of causes; unwelcome visitors.
Secure by: doorlocks, chains, window bolts/locks, alarms; questioning routines, pre-notification of visit, identity cards, references; monitoring: neighbourhood watch, notification to neighbours and police of absence, watching for strangers, unusual activity/noise.

Standards: locks and other devices are used when doors/windows not in use; intrusion and damage is notified to police immediately before other action taken; violent intruders only confronted when no other option is available; level of defence is appropriate to nature of perceived threat; unauthorized or unwelcome visitors dealt with politely but assertively; persistent nuisance is notified to police; visitors are scrutinized as to their purpose and identity, and are not allowed in if there are any doubts, or a proper appointment is made and their identity is checked; unusual activity in the locale is monitored and police informed if there is a perceived problem.

Figure 5.2b Competencies in unpaid work in the home: Key Role F, Unit F3

Source: A. Leigh and L. Butler, *Competences of Unpaid Workers in the Home*, the final report of the project 'Unpaid Work in the Home: A Functional Analysis', funded by the Employment Department group through TEED, 1991.

individuals' home work. What were often initially perceived by the sample to be personal standards were used by most as the accepted way to achieve a function. Any variation in performance was due to the different circumstances impacting on the individual. She/he might pay someone to clean the house for example, but the cleaning would be supervised to commonly found standards.

Second, activities were only included in the analysis where they were purposeful, with critical outcomes, and where they also had an economic exchange value. Economic exchange value is implicit in paid work; in the case of unpaid work, it was made explicit in order to differentiate between work activities carried out in the home and all those other activities which are part of private life. Thus, only activities which could be paid for by the homemaker, if she decided to do so and had the resources to do so, or which she could sell to others, were included. Examples include childminding, the treatment of sick people, and the storage and supply of information. Hobbies or leisure activities did not feature in the analysis, since individuals cannot pay another person to have a hobby or leisure activity for them. Where individuals sell the skills and products of a hobby or leisure activity, such as dresses or hand-knits, then they sell a service or product, which means that they must enter the market. Such activities can then be included in the analysis.

Third, the activities listed in the analysis are what most unpaid women workers in the home do; the criterion was that most unpaid workers do most of this at some time. Therefore there are no particularly esoteric activities, such as building one's own home or a car.

As already described, the functional analysis was conducted with a sample of women, and the question, therefore, arises as to whether it also applies to men. The project was designed to focus primarily on women in unpaid work in the home, since it was known that women do more unpaid work in the home than men. It is often contended that even where unpaid home work is shared, there is a strong, continuing division of domestic labour between women and men. The project sought to test the relevance of the functional analysis to men by reviewing the analysis in a men's workshop. However, attempts to recruit such a workshop were unsuccessful. Local advice to the project was that men in the localities, even when carrying out unpaid home work as their main work activity, were subject to social norms which were unlikely to allow self-perceptions such as home manager or househusband.

The functional analysis shows an extensive range of activity in unpaid home work. The key roles indicate that unpaid work in the home includes a wide range of financial control activity; the resources which come into and go out of the home are carefully monitored and controlled. The home is also the site of the establishment of management systems and supporting information systems which lead to the ordering and effective running of the home. The care and supervision of adults and children takes up significant effort, and in some cases, where people are supervising severely disabled adults for example, the functional levels are extremely demanding. Health and safety in the home has a wider range and greater criticality than many paid work settings. Cleaning is only one aspect of home systems for maintaining health and safety standards. Services to supply and maintain clothing, meals, hospitality, transportation and animal care are all offered in the household. Home maintenance is defined in the functional analysis as the aesthetic and operational design of the working spaces of the home, as well as maintaining and fixing things in it.

Unpaid work in the home involves the use of many pieces of equipment, dealing with a huge variety of people and organizations, and the level of responsibility which is placed on the individual can be very high. Unpaid work is ordered by self-discipline and the setting of standards of performance. There is team-working and the supervision of others, as well as the autonomy to be proactive in a wide range of activities outside the home in community and volunteering work.

The depth of competence, that is how much skill and knowledge was used in the achievement of the function – varied between functions and between people fulfilling the same function, as it does in paid work. Individuals tended to acquire skill or learn knowledge when they needed to, rather than upskilling themselves without a directly applicable end point. None the less, the range of skills and knowledge was significant, across the manual, cognitive and management/supervisory range.

The determination of the level of competence acquired in unpaid work was somewhat problematic, but the NVCQ guidelines on the determination of level offered an approximate guide. Levels I/II are supervised or routine unsupervised functions, while Level III involves the supervision of others. Levels IV and above require the use of bodies of knowledge and are professional awards. Using these guidelines, and examining the analysis function by function, it is possible to determine which level is appropriate to the specific function.

There are many functions in unpaid home work which involve the supervision of others, which would suggest they should be located at Level III. Some functions, for example those related to finance, go beyond the occupational standards for junior management or even middle management (Levels IV and V respectively). Some other functions are relatively simple to fulfil in a routine context, and therefore seem to relate to Level II. However, if complexity is taken into account, the requirements on the individual, and thus the level of the competence, may increase substantially.

Instead of labelling the whole of unpaid home work at a particular level, it should be seen as a domain in which the full range of levels can be discerned. The level will vary from function to function, from individual to individual, at different points in time, just as it does in paid occupations. There should be no assumption that the levels of competence are low. Generally, the expectations that unpaid workers have of themselves may be higher than those placed on them by employment, and it is quite possible, particularly for women, that those entering or in paid employment from unpaid work, actually step down a level or two.

We can now consider how unpaid home work competence relates to the competence required in paid work. It is clear that unpaid work overlaps considerably with paid work, and is not just a pale shadow. The unpaid worker in many ways already performs the required underpinning functions of paid work: autonomy, self-management, proactivity, teamworking, setting one's own standards, working to standard, and taking responsibility for self-development.

Transfer from unpaid home to paid work competence in some respects is not problematic, and indeed is already practised, as information from the project's participants showed. Participants who had been in the past or who were currently in paid work in nursing, policing, cleaning, care (children and adults), customer service and management related their unpaid work competence to these areas of paid employment. One woman, for example, said:

> I do the same for the old people as I do for my own kids – food, drink, toilet, bathing, bed, company and emotional support. In the home I work in now, talking's more important than cleaning. They really rely on you, sometimes you're the only person they've got in the world.

This transfer should not be seen as particularly remarkable, since the home is a small organization fulfilling an economic need. As an economic entity, the home demands the type of functions which other economically active organizations do. By this argument, there appears no reason why the unpaid worker should not be able to transfer a wide range, and differing levels, of some or all of his/her competence to a new, paying organization. Of course, this would require some retraining, as it does for a paid worker moving from one job, or orgnaization, or even section, to another.

Turning to how unpaid home activities relate to specific occupations and jobs undertaken for pay, early studies in the USA have shown a strong relationship between unpaid home work and paid work in managment, supervision, office and business administration, and occupations emphasizing interpersonal skills, such as teaching and counselling. Some of these relationships were endorsed in the UK research and practice referred to earlier[4, 5], and by the views of the project participants, who also identified, without prompting, other possible paid jobs or occupations which related to one or more of the functional analysis Key Roles. Examples included library/advice worker, counsellor, telephonist, painter/decorator, interior designer, personnel officer, gardener, entertainer, trader, animal welfare worker, buildings caretaker.

Professional careers advice sought by the functional analysis project endorsed these relationships and identified others, such as retailing, travel and leisure and crafts trades. From these occupational and job relationships, it was possible to begin to identify the relevant vocational qualifications where credit for current competence might be sought.

We can now consider whether unpaid workers' potential to achieve credit towards vocational qualifications on the basis of their current competence is the same as it is for their counterparts in, or those experienced in, paid work. Since unpaid home workers acquire competence, and work to standards which are clearly related to paid occupations and jobs which have associated vocational qualifications, then such workers must, logically, have the potential to achieve credit towards such qualifications. At this point, it is clear that the more pertinent question is not whether they have the same potential but whether they have the same opportunity. Will, for example, an unpaid worker seeking credit towards a management qualification on the basis of his/her unpaid work competence be able to do so as readily as someone who is a paid manager? The answer to the question is no. There are no examples of any such credit being offered to an unpaid worker for his/her home-based competence, in contrast to the well-established procedures for accrediting paid managers.

However, at lower NVQ levels, the transfer of competence from the unpaid to the paid workplace has begun to be explored. Projects with two Training and Enterprise Councils (TECs) are beginning to introduce credit for competence acquired in unpaid work towards NVQ levels II and III qualifications in Business Administration. At level II, it appears likely that at least half the award may be accredited from this source. Examples of relevant competence include making and receiving business telephone calls, drafting routine business communications, handling mail, maintaining business relationships, making and receiving payments, and arranging travel and meetings. Students acquire their evidence by treating the home as a workplace like any other. Opportunities to demonstrate competence – for example, by drafting a business letter – are logged, and the letters copied and produced as evidence for the assessor, who may or may not also wish to check competence by questioning or an additional skills test. By this means, it appears possible to enable students to complete their programme in about half the normal time.

It must be stressed, however, that this practice is currently very unusual. The attitudes and expectations of both unpaid workers themselves and education and training systems and employers contribute to this situation. As described earlier in this chapter, the sample of women taking part in the functional analysis were alienated from their unpaid work competence, being able to describe fully or accurately neither the nature nor the amount of the unpaid work they did. Thus, for example, participants were surprised to discover that nine out of ten of them worked more than 40 hours per week in unpaid work, and five out of ten for more than 61 hours per week. They also, at least initially, described their unpaid work in the most crudely stereotypic terms: washing, cleaning and ironing, and so on. Women in this frame of mind, whether seeking paid work, education or training, cannot attempt to claim credit or other reward for competence which they do not even know they possess. In addition, while after the functional analysis workshops participants were very positive about their unpaid work competence, they still expressed strong doubts about its acceptability in the paid work world. As one women put it, 'Employers – men – won't accept these qualifications if they know housewives can get them'.

Even if women and men could accept their unpaid work competence themselves, could their education and training providers and employers do so? There are pressing incentives. Current government targets for updating the skills of employees in companies are as follows:

- by 1992, all employees should be taking part in company-driven training or developmental activities;
- by 1995, at least half the employed work-force should be aiming for updated or new qualifications within the National Vocational Qualification framework and should have individual action plans to which their employers, as well as they themselves, are committed;
- by 2000, a minimum of half the employed work-force should be qualified to Level III of the National Vocational Qualification or its academic equivalent (A-level).[8]

Such ambitious targets are much more likely to be achieved if the unpaid work competence of employees is taken into account: as we have discussed, unpaid workers in the home are regularly working to Level III and often above. Moreover, women over 25 years old, who are currently the least formally well-qualified sector of the paid work-force, are also the group projected to be most likely to compensate for a severe shortage of young people entering the paid work-force as the decade progresses. The impact of this shortfall is forecast also to affect the numbers of places taken up in education and training institutions, who therefore also have an incentive to develop a new market for their products among adults. Accelerated training towards qualifications suggests itself as particularly attractive to women who often re-enter the paid work market in their mid- or late 30s.

In the face of such incentives, and despite the endorsement of the awarding bodies and the NCVQ, it is still the case that credit for competence acquired in unpaid work is barely understood or practised. To explain why this is so, we need to take into account the impact of a male-dominated economic culture which has consistently excluded women from paid work except where there is an overriding benefit in allowing them into such employment. At the start of this chapter, we pointed to the presentation of unpaid work in the home as a vocation or calling, and therefore as something quite different from paid work. In this way, it is possible to maintain that home-acquired vocational competence is at the margins of relevance to paid work, and this in turn justifies treating women coming into paid employment as inexperienced or low-skilled. Recognizing the reality of women's unpaid work competence directly challenges this position, with consequent substantial disbenefits to current systems such as pay and promotion structures based only on paid work experience.

Wittingly or unwittingly, the key components of the reformed vocational and educational training system continue to reject the status of unpaid work competence as equal to the same competence acquired in paid work. Employment Department Group budgets for research and development in this area are minuscule, although unpaid workers in the home are the largest single occupational group. Lead Bodies, who define occupational standards, have no guidance or direction from government to consider the competence acquired in unpaid work in the drafting of their standards. Indeed, Lead Bodies themselves may specifically exclude it. The Management Lead Body, the Management Charter Initiative (MCI), in contradiction of the NCVQ's endorsement of unpaid work, currently rule that evidence from voluntary work is only acceptable as supplementary rather than primary evidence towards NVQs carrying its endorsement.[9] Functional analysis is merely a methodological tool; it reflects the experience and values of those consulted in the process of the development of standards, and those who are consulted are almost without exception only in paid employment. The awarding bodies, in conjunction with the Lead Bodies, have developed levels of awards which reflect existing hierarchies and stereotypes in paid employment. Thus, for example, the complex and sophisticated roles of the paid care assistant – usually female – working perhaps with the dying or the severely handicapped, are graded at NVQ Level II, the same level as tyre-fitters.

Education and training providers are in many ways the servants of this system rather than its masters. Nevertheless, they can add to the problem by adopting a remedial or deficit model in their treatment of unpaid worker clients and students. Thus, for example, women returners – that is, those entering or re-entering paid work from unpaid work – may be offered a variety of special treatments to remedy what seem to be perceived as deficiencies of experience and competence. These include access courses, sometimes a year long, preceding entry to vocational courses entered direct by young people with little or no paid or unpaid work experience; special course content, such as introductions to paid work skills, which while they may sometimes acknowledge relevant unpaid work competence do not go so far as to accredit it; and special teaching arrangements, especially women-only recruitment and women-only staffing, apparently aimed at reducing the stress and building the confidence of students seen to be returning to the unfamiliar world of work but in effect ghettoizing such students outside the mainstream of institutional provision.

All these practices clearly show up current and widespread vocational education and training and employment ambivalence towards the worth and transferability of competence acquired in unpaid work. At the moment, such recognition is at the margins of practice, and acceptable only as far as it relates to lower-level awards in female-dominated occupations. Recognizing such competence is economically dangerous and yet economically potentially valuable, and socially just, yet widely and deeply challenging to existing power structures. What has to be faced is that so far, the established system has merely held up a mirror to itself and declared that to be the true image. The extent of future change is likely to depend less on the justice of the case than on economic, demographic and political imperatives.

NOTES

1 Critical outcomes are those outcomes which are important to the achievement of the function. Thus, for example, in Business Administration, an outcome that desk drawers are kept tidy is relatively unimportant compared with being competent to record and relay information. What is important is subjective; it is most usually defined by reference to the consensus of opinion within the occupational area under review.
2 *Assessing Competence in Unpaid Work*, NVQ notes (London: NCVQ, 1991).
3 Information from The Volunteer Centre UK. A distinction between community and voluntary work was not drawn in arriving at this figure.
4 R. B. Ekstrom, A. M. Harris and M. E. Lockheed, *How to get college credit for what you have learned as a homemaker and volunteer* (Princeton, USA: Educational Testing Service, 1977). This manual, first published 25 years ago, is addressed directly to potential students interested in claiming college credit at first degree level and below for their learning from volunteering and home work. Students identify their own skills from an extensive taxonomy, and use them to negotiate a credit claim towards a relevant vocational award.
5 K. Howard *Managerial Skills: Yes they can be developed in the home* (Linlithgow, Scotland: Howard Affiliates Ltd, 1986). Howard's study was the first in the UK to research the managerial skills in home-making. It was undertaken in 1985 for the Equal Opportunities Commission (EOC). The job descriptions of a sample of housewives and a sample of middle and senior managers were drawn up and their skills exhaustively analysed. From these data, Howard dervied a list of similarities and differences and concluded that 'there is a great overlap in the skills used . . . when there are differences, they are in skill areas where organizations normally provide specialised training'.
6 Women Returner access courses such as NOW (New Opportunities for Women), WOW (Wider Opportunities for Women), and Women into Management often try to encourage women to recognize the skills they have from their

unpaid work experience in order to relate that experience in their CV to the requirements of paid employment.
7 This project was undertaken by the author, in conjunction with Dr Alan Leigh, for the Training, Enterprise and Education Directorate (TEED) of The Employment Department Group. Dr Leigh's contribution to this chapter is gratefully acknowledged.
8 From a speech given by the Secretary of State for Employment, 1989.
9 Verbal information from the MCI to the author, February 1992.

REFERENCES

Central Statistical Office (1991) *Social Trends*, London: HMSO.
Handy, C. (1991) *The Age of Unreason*, London: Business Books.

Part 2

Adulthood and learning

Chapter 6

Education for adults

Geoffrey Squires

Source: This is an edited version of a chapter in G. Squires, *The Curriculum Beyond School*, London, Hodder & Stoughton, 1987.

INTRODUCTION

There is no single point, in a modern industrialized society, at which a person suddenly and unambiguously becomes an adult. In the United Kingdom it is a process which is often thought to begin at the age of 16 with the termination of compulsory pupil status, and to be complete by the age of 21, with the attainment of full adult rights, roles, and responsibilities. In between, there are many important markers, such as the right to vote, drink, or marry without one's parents' consent; and of course the social and psychological processes of maturation may vary greatly from one individual to another. In educational terms, the definition of 'adult' tends to come later rather than earlier, primarily because there is already distinct provision for 16- to 19-year-olds and for some 18- to 21-year-olds in higher education. Adult education therefore is often thought to begin where these end, and is sometimes referred to as 'post-initial' for that reason. Some institutions even use the age 25 to distinguish between ordinary and 'mature' students; whereas others are more concerned with the number of years spent outside the educational system. By contrast, some regulations specify only post-compulsory (16) and post-secondary (18) status. It is clear that definitions of 'adult' in adult education, are not and cannot be clear.

This is true also of the 'education' in adult education. It is much more difficult to specify or classify the range of provision and activity in this sector of education than in any other: indeed, it is hard to call it a sector at all. Some forms of adult study and learning go beyond not only formal education, but beyond formality, and become virtually indistinguishable from the everyday learning that characterizes, and indeed makes possible, our lives. Nevertheless, it is useful to think of education for adults under four broad headings:

1 Educational institutions which exist primarily to teach adults, such as local authority adult education services, university extra-mural departments, the Open University, adult education residential colleges, and the Workers' Educational Association (WEA);
2 Educational institutions which teach adults along with younger students, such as polytechnics, colleges of higher and further education, and universities;
3 Non-educational institutions or organizations which teach adults as a secondary function or by-product of their main activity, such as companies, armed and civil services, churches, trade unions, voluntary associations, and clubs;
4 Non-institutionalized, independent adult learning, carried out by individuals using whatever resources are to hand: friends, shopkeepers, the mass media, bookshops, libraries, museums, and so forth.

The scope of 'education' in adult education is thus very wide and rather ill-defined, particularly in the cases of 3 and 4. However, the problems of scope and definition are not due only to the elusiveness of the terms 'adult' and 'education'. Adult education as a phrase, has had a particular meaning in the United Kingdom for many decades, connoting courses of a non-vocational, liberal, or recreational nature which do not lead to any paper award. The reasons for this restrictive connotation are complex and cannot be gone into here, but one consequence of the restriction has been the almost theological distinctions that are made by those in the field between adult education (in its older, restricted sense), adult education (in its newer, inclusive sense), the education of adults (all-encompassing), continuing education (typically but not always vocational-professional), lifelong education, recurrent education, and *education permanente*.[1] To many of those who work in adult education, these labels are important, because they signify particular emphases in a field which has always been normatively strong even though structurally and financially weak, as much a movement as a service. Consequently, one finds the labels of departments, agencies, and institutions continually changing, somewhat to the bewilderment of those outside the faith.

The headings that are used in Figure 6.1 are either institutional, or are commonly used in writing or talking about education beyond school. The model therefore matches the reality reasonably well, and indicates the range and specificity of most post-school education. Models, however, are more useful if they not only describe but help one to analyse, and it is in this sense that the model is more problematic. The three key dimensions of general education – knowledge, culture, and ability – can still be used. Academic education is clearly conceptualized in terms of bodies of knowledge, disciplines, or interdisciplinary fields. The criteria used in planning and assessing courses are primarily epistemological criteria, to do with

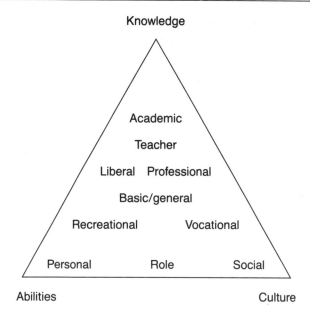

Figure 6.1 The curriculum beyond school

reasoning, evidence, argument, verification, logic, and so on. At the other points of the triangle, the planning of social education courses of whatever kind is clearly carried out with prime reference to society, or in Lawton's terms, culture; and courses in personal development with reference to concepts such as ability, capacity and potential, growth or development.

It would be a nonsense, however, to suggest that the curricular reality is uni-dimensional or two-dimensional; that academic courses exist in a social vacuum, or do not involve abilities and potential; or that there is no knowledge content or development of skills in social education. This model is presented in two-dimensional form in order to emphasize the characteristic specificity of post-compulsory education in both purpose and scope, as compared with the schools; but there are always three dimensions involved, and the reality of the curriculum beyond school lies [. . .] in a tension which is impossible to represent graphically. Likewise, the headings in the model should not be seen as discrete or isolated; they are, rather, identifiable points in a complex field of force. [. . .]

Whereas the older meaning of adult education confined it to two or three of the headings in Figure 6.1 (liberal, recreational, basic) the newer meaning – any form of education or training that adults engage in – excludes nothing in the diagram. Some adult education is academic or professional, and there is continuing in-service education for teachers. In recent years, there has been a growth of interest in continuing vocational education and training. Some forms of adult education have always been concerned with roles, social change and awareness, and personal development. Much local authority adult education is recreational, and the work of the WEA and university extra-mural departments is intended to be of a liberal nature. Basic education for adults is now an established service in the United Kingdom, and of course much more important in developing countries. If the old conception of adult education was rather restricting, the new, all-inclusive sense is liberating in its scope. But it has an important consequence in curriculum terms. Where one could in the past associate adult education with certain of the headings in Figure 6.1, and where one can still associate 16–19 provision and higher education with other headings, one cannot now associate the education of adults with anything in particular: in curriculum terms, it has become coextensive with education itself. Thus, attempts to define adult education in terms of the curriculum – that is, in terms of what is taught – seem doomed to failure. Does this mean that adult education is simply education for people who happen to be adults? Obviously there are forms of adult education – for example, role education of some kinds – which are peculiar to adults. But is the rest any different in curriculum terms from what is taught to younger people? Is it essentially the same content, inflected towards older, voluntary, and probably part-time students? If so, adult education cannot be defined in terms of unique purpose or content. The counter-argument, that adult education, although increasingly catholic and eclectic, does have a unique identity and underlying unity, has been made in three ways: in terms of its students (as adults); in terms of its orientation (towards groups as well as individuals); and in terms of its mode of operation (not only formal, but non-formal and informal). These three kinds of arguments will now be examined.

ADULTS AND ADULTHOOD

There is nothing inherent in the concept of education which links it to childhood and adolescence. Nevertheless, the fact that most education is still so linked has led some adult educators to define the nature of their enterprise in terms of the atypical nature of their students – namely, the fact that they are adults. This leads to a view of adult education which is student-centred not in the simple sense of using methods which allow the student a good deal of control over curricula and teaching, but in the profound sense that the whole activity of education turns on the student, rather than on, say, organized knowledge, or formal certification.

This implies some idea of what an adult is. Much of the early work on adult learning stressed age and ageing as the primary characteristic of adulthood, and for this reason tended to see adults' educational potential

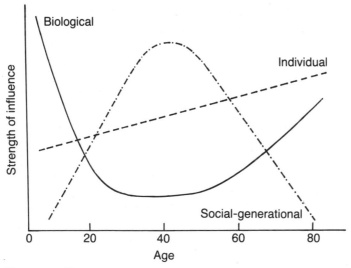

Figure 6.2 The conceptualization of adulthood

Source: Adapted from P. B. Baltes *et al*. 'Life-span developmental psychology', *Annual Review of Psychology*, London, Academic Press, 1980.

very much in terms of decrement and decline.[2] In recent years, however, the emphasis has shifted away from age as a determinant of adulthood, to age as an aspect of adulthood, and this allows other kinds of factors to be admitted. One useful model has been suggested by Baltes *et al.* (1980), who argue that there are three main kinds of influence on adulthood: biological ageing; social experience as a member of a particular generation or group; and individual life-events. Moreover, Baltes suggests that the influence of these three factors varies along the life-span (see Figure 6.2). Biological factors are very important in childhood and old age, but recede into the background during most of adult life, except in the case of serious illness. Generational factors, weak at first in the confines of the family, become more and more important as the adult reaches maturity and becomes engaged in society through work, leisure, and other social involvements. Thereafter, the influence of this factor may decline gradually, and then perhaps sharply in old age, when many people withdraw or disengage from society. It is much more difficult to assess the importance of individual life-events in adulthood (events such as getting a job, marriage, having children, becoming unemployed, getting divorced, deaths in the family), but Baltes suggests that the cumulative effect of these is to make individuals more different from one another as time goes by, and hence he argues that their importance increases with age.

It should be stressed that what is being said here is an interpretation of a model which the author himself presents as tentative. However, Baltes's approach seems to provide a useful framework for thinking about what adulthood is. This is a prerequisite for any theories of adult education which refer primarily to the nature of the student. The model also suggests that, with the exception of old age, the most important aspects of adulthood are social-generational and individual-experiential, rather than biological (though that is not to discount interactions between all three factors). If adult education turns primarily on the nature of its students, therefore, one would expect a strong emphasis on individual and collective experiences, on roles, significant life-events, self-concepts, and relations with others. Such an emphasis does indeed appear in the four ways of thinking about adult students that are described briefly below: in terms of adult learning, adult thinking, adulthood and adult development.

The first of these is concerned primarily with teaching and learning, but has important implications for the curriculum. The word 'pedagogy' refers, strictly speaking, not to teaching but to the teaching of children. Although Knowles (1978) did not invent the word 'andragogy' (the teaching of adults), he has given it wider currency than any other writer on adult education in the English-speaking world. While Knowles does not suggest that there is a clear cut distinction between children and adults as learners, he does argue that teaching based on andragogical assumptions is appropriate to people in their late teens and beyond. The simple antithesis between pedagogy and andragogy has caught the imagination of many who work in adult education, perhaps because it offers a means of defending a rather embattled professional identity. It is worth pointing out, however, that Knowles is somewhat ambiguous about identifying andragogy solely with adult education; in some cases he presents it as a more enlightened approach to teaching younger age-groups as well.

A rather different approach from that of Knowles is that of Riegel, who is concerned not so much with how adults learn as how they think, although clearly 'learning' and 'thinking' overlap. Riegel's starting-point is Piaget's theory of mental operations which distinguishes between four stages/levels of development: sensory motor intelligence; pre-operational intelligence; concrete operations; and formal operations. Riegel goes on to add a fifth stage/level: that of dialectical operations. He argues both that this is the highest mode of operation, and that it is characteristic of adults, whereas formal operational intelligence is of use mainly in the more arid aspects of formal education:

> it has never been shown convincingly that the highest level of operation (i.e. formal operational intelligence) characterizes the thinking of mature adults. Only under the most exceptional circumstances of logical argumentations and scholastic disputes would a person engage in such a form of thinking . . . Piaget's theory describes thought in its alienation from its creative, dialectical basis. It represents a prototype reflecting

the goals of our higher educational system that, in turn are reflecting the nonartistic and noncreative aspects in the intellectual history of Western man.

(Riegel 1979: 49–50)

Adult thinking, by contrast, embraces contradictions not as a failure, or a sign of incomplete development, but as a characteristic feature of the mature consciousness.

The mature person achieves a new apprehension of contradictions. Contradictions are no longer regarded as deficiencies that have to be eliminated by rational thinking at all costs but in a confirmative manner as the basic source for all activities. In particular, they form the basis for any innovative and creative work. Adulthood and maturity represent the period in life during which individuals knowingly reappraise the role of formal, that is non-contradictory thought, and during which they may succeed again (as the young children have unknowingly succeeded in their primitive dialectics) in accepting contradictions in their thoughts and actions (scientific dialectics).

(Riegel 1979: 130)

Riegel is an interesting, if eclectic and sometimes polemical writer. His theory involves two critiques: first, of the disjunction between theory and practice, as exemplified for him in formal operations and to some extent academic education; and, second, of the idea of human development as an evolutionary, gradualist affair. In support of his first critique, he cites Hegel; in support of the second, Kuhn, among others; in the first case, he stresses the importance of dialectical thought; and in the second the importance of crises. Dialectical psychology, according to Riegel, is committed to the study of action and change. Where the influence of Dewey can be discerned in Knowles's approach, in Riegel's case it is Hegel and Marx, and the more general European (rather than American) critique of alienation or alienated thought. This is a complex critique, and here one can do no more than hint at some of the main problems with Riegel's approach.

The first point has to do with what is meant by 'dialectical operations'. Some writers interpret this very much in theory/practice terms: 'In the process of dialectical thinking, abstract thought, i.e. ideas and concepts, are reunited with concrete reality and experience' (Nottingham Andragogy Group 1983: 6). The problem with this is that it implies that 'concrete reality and experience' are in some way independent of or free from abstraction: an example of a more general tendency in some writing on the theory/practice issue to treat terms like 'experience', 'concrete', 'action', 'context', and 'use' as if they were obvious and unproblematic. The counter-argument is that even these apparently practical matters are shot through with theory and abstraction; that there are no facts without concepts; that practice embodies ideas, whether one realizes it or not; that there is nothing which is not interpretation. Indeed the whole effort of phenomenology to 'discover' the structures which constitute what we call the world, or real life, or everyday existence, has shown how difficult it is to find anything which might be called direct or primordial experience. It is one thing to say that dialectical operations are concerned with contradictions in thought, but it does not necessarily follow that such contradictions arise only out of a separation and reunion of 'abstract thought' and 'concrete reality'.

A second problem lies in Riegel's assertion that dialectical operations are somehow higher or more advanced than other kinds of thinking. If this is not simply to be a *parti pris* inherited from Hegel and Marx, one has to ask why or how they are higher? Part of the answer seems to be that they are less 'alienated', but this raises the question: alienated from what? The unstated assumption is that there is a 'natural' mode of thought or state of existence from which we have either grown away or been forced away, and that it is the job of the dialectic to return us to our natural home. But one may ask whether this is not a kind of romantic nostalgia for a primordial existence in which nature and community were somehow organic; in the end, a suppressed desire for an order pre-dating modern consciousness.

Third, Riegel asserts that dialectical operations are not simply a higher, but a later stage in thinking, associated typically (though not necessarily) with adulthood. This view can be criticized on the basis of a contingency model. It may well be that adult thinking in certain circumstances is concerned (often fruitfully) with contradictions, or at least with problems that are other than obviously 'logical' or 'systematic'. But in other circumstances it may not; and a contingent model of mental operations would suggest that adults can often deploy a range or repertoire of approaches or modes of thinking, and vary them as appropriate. Indeed, some of the research on cognitive styles suggests as much: that people are not always locked on to a particular style, but can to some extent choose how to think or approach problems (Kogan 1976, Messick *et al.* 1978, Squires 1981). There is a need for some empirical work on this aspect of adults' cognitive styles.

If the 'difference' of adults lies not so much in how they learn or think, perhaps it lies in the state or status of being an adult, in the adulthood of adults? After all, even in everyday conversation we do not use the word 'adult', or its associated terms, lightly. We tell people to 'grow up', 'act their age', not to be 'childish' or 'immature'. Even humorous phrases like 'for children of all ages' tell us something about our expectations of adults and adulthood, expectations which are moral and social as well as psychological. In sociological terms, this is most likely to be expressed in terms of role; adults have many congruent and incongruent roles which involve expected patterns of behaviour, and when these patterns are transgressed or absent, the conception of adult is itself modified. Such roles may be quite closely related to age, in that we expect young adults, middle-aged adults, and older adults to do or not do certain things. Age-roles cross-cut with social and gender roles, and in any case seem to have become more fluid in recent decades; [...] Adult students bring their roles with them into the classroom – how could they not? – and although what they study there may not be a direct extension of those roles (indeed, it may be an escape), role is a significant element in any adult teaching situation: not only the roles of the students, but the role of the teacher or trainer in relation to those roles.

The argument that the adulthood of adults constitutes an important and even defining aspect of adult education can also be stated in more philosophical terms. [...]

It is clear that in recent decades there has grown up a school of thought about adults and adult education which is quite different from the traditional philosophical approach (Lawson 1975). This school of thought comes under the broad heading of life-span developmental psychology, and it stresses not so much the state of adulthood as the process of adult development. Its main sources and influence have been in the United States, though it has had some impact in the United Kingdom as well. Cross (1982) provides a useful overview of the field, but one of the most detailed expositions of the various facets of the notion of development – cognitive, moral, ego, and so on – is to be found in the book edited by Chickering *et al.* (1981), who argue that it provides a new rationale not simply for adult education but higher education.

At their simplest, models of adult development draw attention to the fact that adult life is not some kind of plateau, but full of ups and downs and changes: changes in jobs, changes in family circumstances and personal relationships, role changes, changes in attitudes and beliefs, and to some extent physical changes. Such models dispute the fairly widespread assumption that adults, having attained maturity, simply settle down into a predictable routine, and cease to learn or develop in any way, until biological ageing obtrudes and forces them into decline. At this level, the writing on adult development is a very useful corrective to the simplistic, even unthinking attitudes towards adult life, and in particular middle age, which have for long permeated our educational thinking.

Beyond this, things become more problematic. Cross draws an important distinction between thinking about life-phases and life-stages. Life-phases refer to the chronologically identified periods in the life-span which are age-related (though within wide margins) and which Shakespeare, to mention only an early example, described in his Seven Ages of Man speech. Conventionally, it is common for people to distinguish between early adulthood (Young Turks, and so on), the prime of life, middle age, retirement, and old age.

It is also fairly widely recognized that the age of transition from one phase to another may vary considerably from one individual to another ('You're as young as you feel . . .') and also as between groups: women and men, different social classes, different cultures. In some country districts, a man of 30 may still be called a lad by older men, whereas in a modern city environment, that would be unthinkable. Developmental psychologists attempt to describe each of these phases in terms of its characteristic conditions and tasks: for example, finding a job, choosing a partner, rearing children, coping with ageing relatives, or fighting ill-health. While many of these headings are apt and recognizable, they may also seem a little simplistic and linear, failing to take account of both the unique trajectory of individual lives, and the deeper kinds of changes that take place.

It is the attempt to model those deeper changes, however, that is most problematic. In Cross's terms, this is the writing about life-stages, rather than life-phases, and the basic idea here is that adult life is a matter not only of change, but of development, or regression: of more or less, better or worse, with the emphasis usually on the potential for the positive. Some of the writing in this vein has been about specific facets of development: Perry's (1970) work on cognitive development, and Kohlberg's (1973) theories of moral development are obvious examples. Some of it is about development in a more general sense, what one might call the development of the person or the self, and here the work of Erickson (1968) and Loevinger (1976) is widely referred to. It is worth noting that the latter, more general models of development owe a good deal to earlier work in psychotherapy (Jung, for example) and indeed to philosophies and theologies which have explored the notion of individual or spiritual growth.

There is not room here to discuss life-stage theories properly. They can be criticized for abstracting individuals from their social and economic context, of being individualistic in a pejorative sense: there is little sense in much of the writing of the social constraints under which most people live, or little evidence for concern with the development of the community or society. They appear naïvely optimistic about the horror of old age as described by, say, Proust or Yeats, and seem remote from the more ironic or pessimistic strands in European culture. The chief problem, however, is that they attempt to identify a path of development which is not based on any coherent or consensual view of human existence. It was one thing for Buddhists or Christians to map out a spiritual path (however tortuous) in the days when those religions supplied the general world-view in their particular cultures. In a modern, pluralistic, and in some ways more sceptical culture, that task is infinitely more difficult. This kind of objection applies not only to the general writing about human development of someone like Erickson; it can be raised in connection with Perry's more limited work on cognitive and ethical development. Perry, broadly speaking, maps out a progression from initial dualism, through relativism, to commitment within relativism, and the implication is that the last is better than the first. It is by no means self-evident, however, that relativism is an advance on dualism (what if the world *is* a battle between good and evil?) or that commitment is in all cases preferable to detachment (a view that Buddhists would at least want to question).

Life-phase, and even more, life-stage theories of adult development thus appear to raise some serious problems, of both a descriptive and normative kind. On the other hand, they stimulate some very interesting questions about the nature of personal and social education for adults. These headings are never entirely absent from any curriculum at any stage, but adult development theories give them a particular prominence. They point to an aspect of education where perhaps it begins to turn into something else; they blur the conventionally sharp distinction between knowledge and self-knowledge.[3]

The four conceptions of adult students described briefly here – in terms of adult learning, adult thinking, adulthood, and adult development – all have possible implications for the curriculum. Of the four, it is the third (adulthood) which seems most compatible with traditional liberal and academic forms of education; the other three in various ways seem to point towards more personal and social concerns. But the assumption in all cases is that the education is still largely of the individual and for the individual: an orientation which is not shared by some who teach adults.

INDIVIDUALS AND GROUPS

It is one of the paradoxes of compulsory education that although its aims are individualistic, its means are collective. Examinations test individual achievement, not the achievement of a group. Norm-referenced examinations in particular set one child in competition with another. The stated aims of the schools are often expressed in terms of 'individual development' or 'personal development', yet most work in schools is done in groups, in classes ranging from under ten in a sixth form to more than thirty in some lower forms. [. . .]

On the other hand, teaching has become slightly less collectivized. [. . .] There has been increased use of small group work (three or four students working together on a project or topic) and of independent study using prepared materials. The quantum jump in educational technology represented by the micro-chip will probably mean that independent study, long heralded as the way forward in teaching, will in fact increase in importance; though one must be sceptical as to how quickly or widely any new methods will be adopted at any level if they impinge on traditional teaching patterns and roles.

In higher education, individual ends are also pursued by collective means, though here the pattern is rather different from the schools. Teaching alternates between extreme collectivity (mass lectures) and extreme individuality (library-based studies or tutorials), though a middle ground of small group/seminar work has become much firmer in recent years. Scientists have always worked in small groups in their laboratories. But the aims or ends of higher education are still typically stated in individual terms: the development of this person's intellectual capacities, that person's competency to do a job, or the other person's general maturity. Indeed, one can argue that in the United Kingdom particularly, the emphasis on treating students as individuals is especially strong (Squires 1980). This can mean various things: an awareness of individual differences, implied by individualized teaching and favourable staff–student ratios; a concern for the student as a person, embodied in tutoring/counselling/pastoral/ support provision; or an attempt to develop the student's autonomy, as evidenced in the apparently *laissez-faire* attitude to work, and regulations, and the aversion to 'spoon-feeding'. British academics on the whole pride themselves on not only the quality of research and teaching in their institutions, but on the quality of care, and look askance at the disorganized impersonality of continental universities and the organized impersonality of the larger American ones. No doubt the care is often deficient, and doors which are always supposed to be open, are not, or if they are, the lecturer is not there. But 'treating students as individuals' is part of the formal rhetoric and the informal vernacular of British higher education.
[...]

It has been necessary to look briefly at the themes of individuality and collectivity in some of the other parts of the education system to put such notions into a proper perspective in adult education. For in adult education – or, rather, in certain forms of it – there is a distinct and different tradition of concern not only for the individual student, but for students as or in a group. This manifests itself in various ways. There is the tradition of adults coming together as a group, deciding what they want to learn, and finding someone who can teach them. This may range from an existing group which invites a visiting speaker, to a study group which hires a tutor to do a whole course. There is the tradition of negotiation between tutor and group as to what shall be covered or accomplished in a particular class – a kind of consensual specification of objectives. There is also a tradition of groups of adults coming together and teaching themselves, combining and exchanging whatever expertise they already have. There is the tradition that even the amateur learner or person who thinks he knows nothing has something to contribute to the group's learning. There is the emphasis in some forms of adult education on group projects (a collective production such as a survey or book) or on group action (actually doing something about housing/local amenities/co-operative production/political conditions).

In all these cases, the typical individualism of educational purposes is modified by a concern with people as or in a group (De Sanctis 1984). Of course, things are not necessarily as democratic or collective as they seem. The will of the group may be the will of a few activists; tutors may provide what they want to provide rather than what is needed; negotiation may be a ritual rather than a reality. The action or development that arises out of the group work may be pre-planned or short-lived. What is important here, however, is the ideology of collectivity in adult education, and its contrast with what prevails in the rest of the system.

This ideology is expressed in, and takes, several forms. The mildest of these is suggested by the word 'association'. Associations are groups of adults freely coming together to pursue a common interest or purpose. Many of those interests and purposes will not be specifically 'educational', though systematic learning always goes in a non-formal or informal way. Some associations are explicitly educational: for example, the WEA. Some will aim to influence people and institutions outside themselves. Many will have a mixture of aims and motivations, including providing a meeting-place for people, giving them a pleasant time, improving or reforming society, educating members, monitoring situations of interest to them, and so forth. One becomes a member of an association deliberately: simply living in a particular place or doing a particular job is not enough (there are, of course, professional associations which compel membership). Conversely, one can deliberately and freely leave at any point. The adult educator tends to see himself, in theory anyway, in a service role vis-à-vis the association; as someone who acts as a resource for the members.

Adult education may also be sometimes oriented towards 'the community' (Fletcher and Thompson 1980, Brookfield 1983). [...] As Michael Newman (1983) points out, 'community' can mean many different things: the working class; the quiescent poor; the disadvantaged; the 'whole community'; the 'acceptable community'; and society. Nevertheless, there is a common thread running through most 'community education' and 'community development', and that is its concern for people in groups, rather than simply as individuals. In Third World countries, this often means the village or rural community; in industrialized countries, it tends to be the poorer areas of urban communities. Communities unlike associations, are not something that one deliberately joins or leaves. One is a member, like it or not. Of course, the term 'community' may also suggest a strong interaction between people living or working together, which may not exist. Thus it is possible to say, somewhat paradoxically, that there is 'very little sense of community in this community'. Adult educators tend to believe in the 'community' in the first sense, and see themselves in a catalytic role *vis-à-vis* its members, as a facilitator, *animateur*, or person who enables the community to articulate its consciousness and raise it (Freire 1983).

Whereas the term 'community' suggests people living together or working together, the word 'movement' suggests people progressing in a particular direction. Adult education has in the past been linked with various movements. The political purposes of much adult education latent in the word 'association', implicit in the term 'community', become explicit in the word 'movement'. Education is seen as a resource for action: action engaged in by groups. One is reminded of the slogan of one such movement (the Irish Land League): agitate, educate, organize; which might well stand for all of them. Movements, by their very nature, require not only formal adherence but real commitment. Whereas associations can and do tolerate 'sleeping' members, movements cannot. There will be great importance attached to role models (charismatic leaders) past and present. While the term 'movement' nowadays tends to connote political purposes, it should be remembered that in the past many such movements were primarily religious, and only saw themselves incidentally as social or political. The role of the adult educator in the movement is neither a service nor a catalytic one, but as a committed functionary, contributing his particular expertise and know-how to the common cause.

There is another, and very different, form of collectivity in adult education. That is where people have to be trained or educated in groups because they operate or function as a group. To train them individually would miss much of the point of the exercise, which is to improve communication, co-ordination and teamwork within the group. There are obvious examples of this in sports and military training. A football team has to be trained as a team, though individual skill training has its place as well. And in the armed services, training exercises may involve a whole ship's company or battalion or squadron. Individuals are expected to have acquired their skills before the whole thing is 'put together'. Group training or education is also found in professional, commercial, and industrial contexts. Much of the non-formal or informal continuing education of, say, a primary health care, or social work, team will be concerned with how that group operates as a group: with questions of liaison, control, interaction, and feedback. Staff meetings in educational institutions are also partly taken up with such matters: and sometimes a residential weekend is devoted to analysing how and where the institution or department is going. Continuing education for managers may also involve group sessions: anything from a routine meeting in which such issues are discussed, to more specific day- or weekend-schools. And there has been some use of group training approaches with production workers. Through all these examples runs the realization that work is typically not carried on in an isolated, individualistic way, but involves communication and co-ordination with others.

The collectivist aims or methods of adult education come under fire from various directions, and for various reasons. Professional educators sometimes regard the activities of associations and community groups as amateurish. The professional historian or archaeologist may have mixed feelings about the quality of work of the local history society, or the amateur archaeological association. The professional social worker or counsellor will often be wary about the use of voluntary workers in these fields. True, the traditions and ethos of adult education in the United Kingdom make most adult educators view such activities in a favourable light, as something to be welcomed and built on and perhaps refined. But there is often a vague question mark hanging in the air about the 'standards' of adult education work.

Educators may also worry about the activities of associations, community groups and movements in respect of indoctrination. The local country-dancing club or bee-keeper's association is unlikely to be a source of concern in this respect. But what about the local housing action committee, or ratepayer's association? What about political parties, religious or 'cult' groups, feminist groups, animal rights groups, environmental pressure groups? How far do these educate or indoctrinate their members? How far does the ultimate aim of doing or changing something lead people to subordinate analysis to commitment, individual doubts to collective will? Indoctrination tends to be associated with certain types of educational content (religious, political, social) and with doctrines which challenge rather than reinforce existing norms. (Thus we tend to accuse the Young Socialists of indoctrination, rather than the Boy Scouts.) But it is more accurate to see it as a process, applicable to any kind of content, which lacks or rejects certain of the characteristics which are associated with the word 'education': the making explicit of assumptions and values, the exposure to conflicting ideas and arguments, the tolerance of doubt and indecision, the encouragement of rationality rather than belief, and the limiting of pressure on the student to conform.

A good deal of education probably fails to satisfy these conditions, and in any case they are open to criticism themselves. Do they not encourage a kind of amoral detachment? Do they not imply an overemphasis on cognition at the expense of affect? Do they not 'teach' that thought is separate from action? Do they not foster a pseudo-neutrality? There is room here only to register these points rather than discuss them in detail. [. . .]

THE FORMAL, NON-FORMAL, AND INFORMAL

Adult education has been, and has had to be, much concerned with the failures of compulsory education: failures both in the sense of the students who are dubbed, and dub themselves, failures; and in the more abstract sense of the shortcomings or defects of the school system. A good deal of adult education is, and always has been, compensatory rather than continuing: it does not build on what went before: rather, it starts the job anew. And sometimes it has to demolish some bad construction work before it can begin again.

The reasons why students or educational systems fail are complex, and have been the object of a great deal of research into both student characteristics (ability, motivation, social background, learning styles, and so on) and system characteristics (among them, teacher-training, teaching methods, curricula, institutions, assessment, and guidance). Failure itself has been conceptualized in terms such as under-achievement, wastage, and also the more elusive measures of attitudes to education. Adults, and the educators of adults, may attribute 'failure' in varying degrees to the student himself or to the system. Adults themselves often seem to internalize 'failure' and attribute it at least partly to themselves, whereas 'irrelevance' they will typically attribute to the system. It is one thing to be bored, but another to be 'no good'. Adult educators tend to blame the system, partly because they have a generally optimistic attitude towards 'potential', and partly because they can cite many instances where a second chance has reversed the initial verdict. Of course, these students are only the ones who come back to education; and most 'failures' do not.

There is another way in which adult educators have to be concerned, not so much with the failures as with the limitations of formal schooling, and that is where organized school education, as a system, fails to engage the commitment or meet the needs of whole communities. This is most dramatically the case in some developing countries, where the schools cater for only a small proportion of the population, or may provide something which does not seem to meet the general needs. The school system in such cases provides a narrow, steep, and rather academic ladder to urban desk jobs or elite occupations in the modern sector of the economy. It seems to do little for agriculture, for the 'petty trader', or for the health, welfare, and development of the local community. Education – formal education – seemingly does not reach the great majority of the population, or if it does, is perceived as a selective mechanism, not as a source of knowledge and skills. This kind of 'failure' is less dramatic and less obvious in industrialized countries, but in these, too, questions can be raised. What does the formal education system do for the unskilled factory worker? For the unemployed? For the self-employed? For the neighbourhood? For people's problems with health or money or work or housing or personal relations?

Both the individual failures among students and the more generalized failure of the education system have led many educators who are concerned with adults to look for alternative ways of engaging adults in education: ways which would not simply repeat the 'mistakes' of schooling. Over time, these alternatives – and they are numerous and various – have come to be known generically as 'non-formal' education. It must be stated right away that 'non-formal' is not a precise term, although definitions of it exist.[4] It is relative to 'formal', and there are many ways in which education can be considered formalized: uniforms, regulations, designated buildings, professional labels, teaching methods, time-frames, knowledge categories, syllabuses, authority structures, examinations, qualifications, styles of talk and interaction, standardized environments (desks, classrooms, black-boards), and even smells. When one goes back into a school building as an adult after a long absence, there is a sudden rush of recognition, a hundred sensory cues which constitute 'school'. It is these, rather than what one learned, which come back suddenly; and it is these, and the memory of these, which in many people's minds constitute the experience of education.

Non-formal education can vary and do away with any or many of these characteristics. The teacher may not be a 'proper' teacher; she may be called a facilitator, or group leader, or resource person, or *animateur* – anything but a teacher. Or there may be no one specifically in charge at all. There may be no textbooks, no red ink on written work, no set syllabus, no examination. The class, if it is called that at all, may be held in someone's front room, or a library, or, in the country with a warmer climate, under a tree. There may not even be a *group* of students, but rather a network of mutually assisting individuals or a one-to-one helper–learner relationship. There may be no 'teaching' but rather 'discussion' and 'talk' and 'interaction'. One may not know who the 'teacher' is for a while. Chalk may be deliberately banished. Indeed, the whole thing may be so unlike school that people may not even realize that education is going on. Non-formal education is found not only in social and recreational education for adults: many of the methods and procedures used in continuing professional and vocational education are strikingly non-formal as well (Houle 1980). Some novel and interesting techniques, such as 'audit', have been developed in addition to the use of more conventional means such as journals, conferences, short seminars, and distance study packages. [. . .] The growth of non-formal education has opened up a wide range of questions about what is normal or necessary in formal education.

These questions have been sharpened by the rapid growth in some countries of what a recent Carnegie Commission report has called 'Corporate Classrooms'; namely, organized education outside the formal education system, in corporations, professional bodies, government departments both central and local, and all sorts and sizes of business and industry (Eurich 1985). When these activities are added to the non-vocational, non-formal activities of voluntary organizations, and the educational and educative potential of distance learning, using radio, television, computers, or learning packages, it may be that, whereas formal education for adults is still the most visible form of education, it is no longer the *normal* form. This may come as something of a shock to those who work in the formal system. If it does, it is a reflection on the monopoly that formal education has at the compulsory and consecutive stages, that education or learning outside the system should be considered marginal or abnormal. [. . .]

Non-formality or informality in learning can, however, be seen in a different and more individual light. (The distinction between non-formal and informal is being treated here as a matter of degree.) Some years ago, the Canadian researcher Tough (1971) put a very simple question to a number of adults: have you spent at least seven hours over the last few months trying to learn, understand, or master something to the point where you could teach another person a bit about it? Many of Tough's adults at first said they hadn't, but on reflection and with prompting, began to realize that they had. These 'learning projects', as Tough dubbed them, were interesting in several ways. First, they were quite numerous. Second, they were relatively evenly distributed across social and educational categories, more so than formal education achievement and participation. Third, they often involved little or no contact with formal education provision. And last, they varied enormously, from fairly 'intellectual' activities, through essentially interpersonal ones, to practical skills and tasks. Learning projects can involve anything from learning how to cope with a baby, to planning a foreign holiday, to mastering a new piece of equipment at work, to installing double glazing. [. . .] The originality of Tough's work lay not so much in directing attention to informal learning, but in finding a way of showing that it is not purely random and inconsequential: that it is significant, according to certain criteria of time, mass, and outcome. [. . .]

The emphasis on non-formal and informal learning may affect the formal curriculum through the accreditation of experiential learning. It has always been recognized that people learn a great deal from their experience, whether at work, or in the family or community, or in some of the specialized roles they play. What is relatively new, however, is the suggestion that they should get formal recognition of and credit for this. This credit is not for the experience, but for what has been learned from it, where it corresponds to something that might have been learned as part of the formal curriculum. The main work on the accreditation of experiential learning has been done in the United States under the auspices of what is now the Council for Adult and Experiential Learning (CAEL). Some interest has been shown in it in the United Kingdom, particularly by CNAA. Getting people to describe or demonstrate what they have lear experientially, and assessing that learning in educational terms, is a complex and fairly time-consuming business, and there is no room here to discuss the conceptual or practical problems. The point to be made here is that over the longer term the accreditation of non-formal or informal learning could affect the formal curriculum not simply by giving students exemptions or advanced standing on some courses, but in terms of how one conceives of organized knowledge, and in particular the relationship between theory and practice.

IMPLICATIONS

The analysis in this chapter suggests that in the education of adults the process of curriculum disintegration which begins with the break-up of the compact model of general education reaches its logical, specific conclusion. The curriculum in adult education is more diverse in terms of aims, content, and form than anything that precedes it. The answer to the question: what is taught to adults? is everything. Nothing in Figure 6.1 can be excluded. What is more, the form and context of teaching are more varied than they are in school, 16–19 education, or higher education. The scope of the adult curriculum is so wide that it tests the limits of education itself, by turning into politics, therapy, entertainment, or work. The form of adult education at its most informal is indistinguishable from everyday experiential learning. [...]

One is forced to the conclusion that education for adults *is* inherently diverse, and that there are few if any common elements in all the different kinds of teaching and learning that exist. [...] If there is a particular flavour or emphasis in the adult curriculum it is likely to lie in the greater importance of social and personal considerations in what is taught and how.

This is partly a matter of the form of the curriculum. Continuing education for adults may sometimes take a full-time, consecutive form, as when mature students embark on full-time degree courses, or graduates do intensive one-year conversion courses, but in the main continuing education takes an intermittent form, alternating with the other activities of adult existence – work, family life, leisure interests, community responsibilities. The natural form for adult education to take is therefore modular, not necessarily in relatively long, assessed modules, but typically in short bursts of a day, weekend, or few weeks, or on a part-time basis over a period of months. This kind of format interleaves adult education with everything else that is going on in the adult's life, and thus makes it more likely that what is being studied will be located in the adult's social and personal context. Adults are not usually professional students, with the degree of role closure which that allows.

But the emphasis on the social and personal also derives from the thinking about content and process reviewed in this chapter. What was said by Knowles about adult learning, by Riegel about adult thinking, and by others about adult development all point towards a greater embeddedness of 'knowledge' in existence and experience. The non-formal and informal modes of learning imply much weaker boundaries between education and everything else. The orientation of some adult education towards groups rather than individuals points to the relating of knowledge to 'context' or 'society' or 'action'. It has been argued in this chapter that of all the areas of post-school education, adult education is the least susceptible to generalization; indeed, it can hardly be called a sector at all. But there may be a kind of underlying tendency in different sectors of education which does not necessarily manifest itself in structural unity. Thus in the 16–19 phase (perhaps even 14–19) a kind of 'vocational drift' may affect whatever structures or policies are put in place, a tendency on the part of many students to judge curricula in terms of employment. In higher education, the phrase 'academic drift' has been widely used to describe the tendency for institutions and curricula to gravitate towards an academic norm or ideal type. If there is any such tendency in adult education, it is likely to be some form of existential drift, a vague but nevertheless powerful pull towards, for want of a better word, life.

NOTES

1 The older restricted definition was a consequence of the way in which some key, early reports on adult education in the United Kingdom interpreted its scope, and of the terms of reference given to the 'responsible bodies' and later the local authority services. A detailed account is given by Kelly (1970), who distinguishes between adult education (restricted sense) and the education of adults (broad sense), a distinction pursued by Lowe (1970). [...] The newer labels are to some extent associated with particular agencies which helped to popularize them: recurrent education with OECD, lifelong education with UNESCO, *education permanente* with the Council of Europe. It will become clear in this chapter that I tend towards an all-inclusive definition (any educational or training activity engaged in by adults) which subdivides into a number of much more specific fields such as adult basic education, continuing professional development, higher education for adults, and so on. The distinction between adult and continuing seems to me to be merely a re-translation of the non-vocational/vocational one, with all the problems that implies.
2 For useful overviews of the research on adult learning see Knox (1977), Cross (1982), and Allman (1983). The generally more positive view now taken of adults' learning capacities is due to several factors: a realization that earlier studies were confounding ageing and generational effects; a rethinking of the measures used, which had led both to the distinction between fluid and crystallized intelligence and to a search for capabilities which may be characteristic

of adults rather than children (complex decision-making, self-awareness); the recognition that test conditions may not be a good guide to normal behaviour; and a growing belief that positive interventions may improve adults' physical and mental performance at least over the short term. There is now a fairly good consensus that most adults can learn what they could have learned as young people, with the exception of fast, complex skills, and before old age takes a marked physical toll.

3 Mezirow (1983) has written interestingly on what he calls 'perspective transformation', drawing on Habermas's (1974) concept of emancipatory knowledge: both phrases suggest to me a blurring of the conventional distinction between what one knows and what one is. That distinction is buttressed by the firmly impersonal conventions of much of education – in particular, academic and technical education; but it is worth noting that knowledge may mean a great deal to academics and technicians in a personal sense. One of the most difficult things for most academics to deal with is not disagreement, but indifference: to confront the student to whom it means nothing. That indicates that knowledge is meaningful for the academic in two senses: the internal logic or coherence of the field or discipline, and the existential significance of the knowledge.

4 The distinctions between informal, non-formal and formal education are usually traced back to the work of Coombs *et al.* (1973) on education in the Third World, but since then the terms have become common currency in industrialized countries as well; see Fordham (1979), for example. Broadly speaking, formal education refers to education conducted by the mainline educational system, both compulsory and post-compulsory; non-formal education is education carried out by institutions or agencies whose primary purpose is not education; and informal education refers to the systematic and cumulative aspects of everyday experiential learning. [. . .]

REFERENCES

Allman, P. (1983) 'The nature and process of adult development' in M. Tight (ed.) *Adult Learning and Education*, London: Croom Helm.

Baltes, P. B. *et al.* (1980) 'Life-span developmental psychology', *Annual Review of Psychology*, London: Academic Press.

Brookfield, S. (1983) *Adult Learners, Adult Education and the Community*, Milton Keynes: Open University Press.

Chickering, A. W. (ed.) (1981) *The Modern American College*, San Francisco: Jossey-Bass.

Coombs, P. H. *et al.* (1973) *New Paths to Learning*, New York: International Council for Educational Development.

Cross, K. P. (1982) *Adults as Learners*, San Francisco: Jossey-Bass.

De Sanctis, F. M. (1984) 'Problems of defining the public in the context of lifelong education', *International Journal of Lifelong Education* 3 (4), 265–78.

Erickson, E. (1968) *Identity: Youth and Crisis*, London: Faber & Faber.

Eurich, N. P. (1985) *Corporate Classrooms*, Princeton: Carnegie Foundation for the Advancement of Teaching.

Fletcher, C. and Thompson, N. (1980) *Issues in Community Education*, Lewes: Falmer Press.

Fordham, P. (1979) 'The interaction of formal and non-formal education', *Studies in Adult Education*, 11 (1), 1–11.

Freire, P. (1983) 'Education and conscientização', in M. Tight (ed.), *Adult Learning and Education*, London: Croom Helm.

Habermas, J. (1974) *Theory and Practice* (trans. J. Viertel), London: Heinemann.

Houle, C. O. (1980) *Continuing Learning in the Professions*, San Francisco: Jossey-Bass.

Kelly, T. (1970) *A History of Adult Education in Great Britain*, Liverpool: University of Liverpool.

Knowles, M. (1978) *The Adult Learner: A Neglected Species* (2nd edn), Houston: Gulf.

Knox, A. B. (1977) *Adult Development and Learning*, San Francisco: Jossey-Bass.

Kogan, N. (1976) *Cognitive Styles in Infancy and Early Childhood*, New York: Wiley.

Kohlberg, L. (1973) 'Continuities in childhood and adult moral development revisited', in P. Baltes and K. W. Schaie (eds), *Life-span Developmental Psychology: Personality and Socialization*, New York: Academic Press.

Lawson, K. H. (1975) *Philosophical Concepts and Values in Adult Education*, Nottingham: University of Nottingham.

Loevinger, J. (1976) *Ego Development: Conceptions and Theories*, San Francisco: Jossey-Bass.

Lowe, J. (1970) *Adult Education in England and Wales*, London: Michael Joseph.

Messick, S. *et al.* (1978) *Individuality in Learning*, San Francisco: Jossey-Bass.

Mezirow, J. (1983) 'A critical theory of adult learning and education', in M. Tight (ed.), *Adult Learning and Education*, London: Croom Helm.

Newman, M. (1983) 'Community', in M. Tight (ed.), *Adult Learning and Education*, London: Croom Helm.

Nottingham Andragogy Group (1983) *Towards a Developmental Theory of Andragogy*, Nottingham: University of Nottingham Dept. of Adult Education.

Perry, W. G. (1970) *Forms of Intellectual and Ethical Development in the College Years*, New York: Holt, Rinehart & Winston.

Riegel, K. F. (1979) *Foundations of Dialectical Psychology*, New York: Academic Press.

Russell, Sir Lionel (Chairman) (1973) *Adult Education: A Plan for Development* (Report of the Committee of Inquiry), London: HMSO.

Squires, G. (1980) 'Individuality in higher education', *Studies in Higher Education*, 5 (2), 217–26.

—— (1981) *Cognitive Styles and Adult Learning*, University of Nottingham: Dept of Adult Education.

Tight, M. (1985) 'Modelling the education of adults,' *Studies in the Education of Adults*, 17 (1), 3–18.

Tough, A. (1971) *The Adult's Learning Projects*, Toronto: Ontario Institute for Studies in Education.

Chapter 7

Is there any way out of the andragogy morass?

Joseph Davenport

Source: This is an edited version of an article which appeared in *Lifelong learning: An omnibus of practice and research*, vol. II, no. 3, 1987, pp. 17–20.

Andragogy continues to be an important, and quite often controversial, topic in adult education environs. True believers, including many practitioners, apply andragogical principles with fervour while critics challenge everything from andragogy's assumptions to its effectiveness. Indeed, adult education may be viewed as being trapped in an andragogy morass. One might ask if there is any way out of this dilemma.

This chapter provides a brief overview of the history and assumptions of andragogy, it views the literature base detailing the nature of the andragogy debate, and it advances a revised definition of andragogy aimed at moving adult education from the morass to a higher conceptual ground.

HISTORY AND ASSUMPTIONS

Andragogy has a most interesting history. Alexander Kapp, a German teacher, coined the term in 1833 to describe the educational philosophy of Plato (Nottingham Andragogy Group 1983). John Frederick Herbert, a fellow German, disapproved of this usage, hence andragogy vanished from educational sight for nearly a century. The term surfaced again in Europe in 1921 and became extensively used in the 1960s in France, Holland, and Yugoslavia.

While Malcom Knowles is so associated with andragogy that some persons believe he actually invented the word, most people credit Knowles with introducing the term to the United States in the late 1960s. Knowles's article, 'Andragogy Not Pedagogy', published in *Adult Leadership* in 1968 is generally acknowledged as being his earliest written pronouncements on andragogy. However, Knowles was first introduced to the word in the summer of 1967 by Dusan Savicevic, a Yugoslavian adult educator attending a summer session course (Knowles 1984). Additionally Huey Long (1986) believes that Knowles discussed andragogy during a presentation in Georgia in 1967. Whether 1967 or 1968, Knowles certainly generated a whirlwind with both his spoken and written words.

Stephen Brookfield (1984) clarified the American history of andragogy when he recently discovered that Knowles had been preceded by Martha Anderson and Eduard Lindeman. According to Brookfield, Anderson and Lindeman referred to andragogy in a volume titled *Education Through Experience* (1927a) and in the journal *Workers' Education* (1927b). David Stewart (1986) then pushed the pages of the history of American andragogy back even further by reporting that Lindeman mentioned andragogy in an 'odd' one-paragraph article in *Workers' Education* in November, 1926.

Lindeman, influenced heavily by colleague John Dewey, also laid the framework for Knowles by emphasizing a commitment to a self-directed, experiential, problem-solving approach to adult education. However, Lindeman apparently saw no great value in the term 'andragogy' since he did not use it to describe his developing philosophy and theory. In fact, Lindeman may not have referred to andragogy at all after 1927.

Knowles apparently adopted Lindeman's general philosophical and theoretical tenets and buttressed them with additional support from adult education, progressive education, developmental psychology and humanistic psychology. Moreover, he added what he thought was a new label – andragogy. Both Lindeman and Knowles must be viewed as having played an important patriarchal role in the evolution of American andragogy. Lindeman might be seen as the spiritual father of andragogy while Knowles could be seen as the putative father who nurtured the andragogical child into young adulthood (Davenport and Davenport 1985c). Knowles's public relations skills quickly made andragogy a household word in adult education circles.

Knowles's definition of andragogy was developed as a parallel to pedagogy. According to Knowles, pedagogy is derived from the Greek words *paid* (meaning 'child') and *agogos* (meaning 'leader of'); consequently pedagogy literally means 'the art and science of teaching children'. Knowles then makes a curious semantical leap when he defines andragogy. *Aner* (meaning 'man' or 'adult') and *agogos* (meaning 'leader of') would seemingly be translated as 'the art and science of teaching men or adults'. However, Knowles apparently wants to emphasize the differences between the education of children and adults so he interprets andragogy as the 'art and science of helping adults learn'.

Some of andragogy's problems may be traced to these faulty definitions. If pedagogy means 'child leader' or 'leader of children', then andragogy should refer to 'adult leader' or 'leader of adults'.

The emphasis in both cases is on the role of the teacher. Neither definition places emphasis on the role of the learner. Notwithstanding this semantical confusion, Knowles (1970) originally advanced four assumptions which undergirded his theory of andragogy:

1 As a person matures self-concept moves from dependency towards self-direction;
2 Maturity brings an accumulating reservoir of experience that becomes an increasing resource for learning;
3 As the person matures, readiness to learn is increasingly oriented towards the person's social roles;
4 As the person matures, the orientation towards learning becomes less subject-centred and increasingly problem-centred.

These assumptions, plus Knowles's original assertion that andragogy could be seen as a legitimate theory of adult education, drew considerable criticism from the time they were advanced.

THE ANDRAGOGY CONTROVERSY

Adult education journals such as *Adult Education Quarterly* and *Life-long Learning* became the sparring arena for educators contesting the merits of andragogy (Davenport and Davenport 1985b). Cyril Houle (1972), Jack London (1973), J. L. Elias (1979) and others questioned andragogy's theoretical status, general utility, and how it differed from progressive education applied to adults. They preferred to stress the oneness or unity in education as opposed to a dichotomous perspective. Knowles (1979) retreated somewhat by viewing andragogy more as an approach or method instead of a theory and by conceptualizing andragogy and pedagogy as a continuum rather than a dichotomy. He also indicated that there were occasions when andragogy could be used with children and pedagogy with adults. However, he still emphasized that andragogy was generally better for adults and pedagogy for children.

Knowles was joined by McKenzie (1977, 1979) who defended andragogy on philosophical grounds. McKenzie argued that the existential differences between children and adults required a strategic differentiation of educational practice. Carlson (1979) also supported Knowles by seeing andragogy as a legitimate theory, although he broadened the use of theory to include a political and philosophical dimension. Carlson maintained that politically a democratic society did not have the right to socialize or resocialize adults; therefore education had to be controlled and directed by the learner à la andragogy. He further argued that philosophically adult educators must possess a view of humankind consonant with the emphasis of andragogy – in other words a democratic, humanistic perspective.

Other authors entered the fray. Lebel (1978) called for a 'gerogogy' since older adults differed from younger adults while Yeo (1982) preferred 'eldergogy' for the older population. Knudson (1979) opted for 'humanagogy' which would include andragogy, eldergogy and gerogogy. Rachal (1983) and Courtenay and Stevenson (1983) called for an end to 'gogymania' fearing an educational taxonomy of infantagogy, pedagogy, adolescagogy, andragogy, and gerogogy, or possibly such specialties as Caucasiogogy or Negrogogy.

While most of these articles were relatively brief and argued over small pieces of the andragogy puzzle, the 1980s witnessed more in-depth critical analyses of andragogy. Cross (1982) questioned whether andragogy could be viewed as a unified theory of adult education and described Knowles's claim as 'optimistic'. Day and Baskett (1982: 150) concluded that:

1 Andragogy is not a theory of adult learning, but is an educational ideology rooted in an inquiry-based learning and teaching paradigm – and should be recognized as such. Though Knowles states that adult education must make optimal provision for differences in style, time, place, and pace of learning, the client-centered, problem-solving andragogical model which he presents does not do this. It is not always the most appropriate or the most effective means of educating.
2 The distinction between andragogy and pedagogy is based on an inaccurately conceived notion of pedagogy.

Hartree (1984) essentially took Knowles to task for conceptual sloppiness. She found that Knowles's work presented three basic difficulties for adult educators: a confusion between whether he is presenting a theory of teaching or one of learning; a similar confusion over the relationship which he sees between adult and child learning; and a considerable degree of ambiguity as to whether he is dealing with theory or practice.

Hartree also questioned the soundness of the basic assumptions underlying the theory or practice of andragogy. For example, she states that Knowles does not clarify whether his statements are descriptive or prescriptive. Hartree (1984: 206) points out:

As many adult tutors would recognize, the experience of school has left many adult students with both an expectation of and a 'felt need' for dependency and tutor direction (although they may experience the need to be seen as adult by others as a conflicting pressure). The view of the adult learner as self-directing, then, is often more a pious hope than a description of his or her learning. In this assumption, at least, Knowles' model is prescriptive rather than descriptive.

Clardy (1986) agreed with Hartree and further questioned what empirical base supported such a prescriptive theory. Several major studies on andragogical assumptions have failed to provide strong backing. Rosenblum and Darkenwald (1983) found that including learners in the process of course planning, diagnosis, objectives, and designs did not result in meaningful differences in either learning or satisfaction. In fact, their control group actually scored somewhat higher on learning than did the experimental group.

McLoughlin (1971) conducted a similar study and measured students in terms of attitudes and learning. The experimental group scored higher on satisfaction, but again there were no significant differences in learning, and again the control group scored slightly higher on learning.

Conti (1985) found that teaching style can affect student achievement, but that collaborative approaches were no panacea for adults. His research with twenty-nine teachers indicated that teacher-centred (pedagogical) approaches were more effective with GED[1] classes which focused on the short-term task of passing the predefined GED examination, while learner-centred (andragogical) approaches appeared more effective with basic level classes and English as a Second Language – classes which were aimed at a long-term process of acquiring skills. Conti concluded that 'These findings switch the general argument from a combative stance of which style is best to a more practical position of when is each style most appropriate.'

Goodnow (1982) voiced similar sentiments after comparing educational learning styles with leadership styles. Just as the effectiveness of leadership style may be contingent upon environmental characteristics, educational methodology may also be contingent upon external factors. Such an analogy requires that andragogy and pedagogy be viewed as different characteristics of methodologies rather than as opposites.

Elias, another critic of Knowles, concluded:

> Upon careful analysis, then, it is clear that andragogy and pedagogy describe not two distinct arts and sciences of teaching. They rather present two different approaches to the education of children and adults. Dewey called the two approaches the traditional and the progressive. In their extreme forms he rejected both of these approaches in favor of an approach that uses both experience and subject-centered, both present and future-oriented.
>
> (Elias 1979: 252)

Even Knowles conceivably might be seen as in favour of such a perspective. Knowles stated that:

> So I am not saying that pedagogy is for children and andragogy for adults, since some pedagogical assumptions are realistic for adults in some situations and some andragogical assumptions are realistic for children in some situations. And I am certainly not saying that pedagogy is bad and andragogy is good; each is appropriate given the relevant assumptions.
>
> (Knowles 1979: 53)

Nevertheless, the central thrust of Knowles's work definitely portrays andragogy as the most appropriate approach for most adults in most learning situations. And of course, Knowles's definition of andragogy has tended to muddy the educational waters.

A WAY OUT

Given the semantical problems in Knowles's definition of andragogy, the lack of clarity and specificity in his underlying assumptions, the research results which do not support and sometimes even refute it, and the mounting academic criticism of it as a legitimate theory or approach, one might ask if andragogy retains any utility or viability for the discipline of adult education. Might not adult education be better off if the word dropped back into academic oblivion for another one hundred years?

The author of this article certainly believes that adult education could survive quite nicely without andragogy. There is merit in the position of those who prefer to view all education, whether for children or adults, as a simple, unified process. However, there is also some merit in andragogy if the term could be redefined, conceptually clarified, and empirically based.

Andragogy is definitely a 'catchy' word with public relations value for adult education. The word simply begs for a second look. Many people teaching adults in other professions (for example nursing, social work) were first exposed to andragogy and through it to the larger field of adult education.

Redefining andragogy could be as simple as returning to and perhaps broadening its original definition. Knowles's definition is far from perfect and should not be viewed as sacrosanct. In fact, Knowles's inconsistency in defining pedagogy and andragogy is part of the problem which must be corrected.

If the Greek *paid* (meaning 'child') and *agogos* (meaning 'leader of') is defined literally as 'child leader', which is then interpreted as 'the art and science of teaching children', then the Greek *aner* (meaning 'adult') and *agogos* (meaning 'leader of') should be defined as 'adult leader', which is interpreted as 'the art and science of teaching adults'. Such definitions are true to their original meanings and avoid the paradox inherent in defining andragogy as the 'art and science of helping adults learn' while at the same time claiming that it may be used with children! They also escape the corollary paradox of defining pedagogy as 'the art and science of teaching children' yet also conveying that it may be used with adults!

Another advantage of the literal and original definitions is that they can allow for both teacher-centred and learner-centred activities. Who says that a child leader or adult leader has to be 100 per cent directive all of the time? That error in thought stems from Knowles's interpretation. Both a child leader and an adult leader may find occasions to be directive and non-directive, authoritative and facilitative, etc.

Pedagogy, meaning 'child leader', and previously defined as the 'art and science of teaching children', could just as easily be defined as the 'art and science of teaching and facilitating the learning of children'. Concomitantly, andragogy, meaning 'adult leader', and previously defined as 'the art and science of facilitating adult learning', could be defined as 'the art and science of teaching and facilitating the learning of adults'. Such definitions would also be consistent with the beliefs and research results of many authors who claim that selection of learning approaches has little to do with age but a lot to do with other variables such as learning style, type of content, goals of instruction-learning, and even gender (Davenport and Davenport 1985a).

After acknowledging the public relations value of the word 'andragogy', and after returning to its original definition, the next step would be to organize knowledge and theory in a systematic fashion. Assumptions, including Knowles's, would be placed in the form of hypotheses and rigorously tested. Those that survive their trial by empirical fire would become part of the theory of andragogy – a theory which would have genuine explanatory and predictive powers. Those assumptions which could not be verified would be discarded or reformulated instead of being accepted as gospel by true believers.

For example, Knowles's general assumption concerning the self-directedness of adult learners would probably not survive. Instead, Conti's findings that GED students achieved more from teacher-centred approaches while ESL[2] students achieved more from collaborative approaches might be a good example of how empirical and theoretical underpinning could be established. Andragogy would be built on fact rather than faith, fad, or fancy.

Such an approach would include the many similarities between child and adult education while providing a place for the discovery of differences. For example, research results on self-directed learning by children would be included under pedagogy; conversely, results on self-directed learning by adults would be included under andragogy.

Both young and old must deal with developmental roles and stages which have implications for education. Implications related to children or adolescents (for example, establishing autonomy) would fall within the realm of pedagogy while implications related to adults (for example, child raising) would fall within the realm of andragogy. Additionally, differences related to biological and physiological factors could be placed in their respective categories. For example, education related to children's sexual maturation would belong to pedagogy while education which considers the ageing process and its effect upon accuracy and speed would belong to andragogy. Many other examples could be given, but these should suffice for illustrative purposes.

SUMMARY

Andragogy continues to generate discussion and to capture the imagination of many adult educators. However, early critics have been joined by an increasing number of educators, researchers and practitioners who question its theoretical and practical efficacy. Knowles has perhaps added to the confusion with his paradoxical definitions of andragogy and pedagogy and with his assumptions which lack clarity and solid empirical support. Emerging research results do not appear to support Knowles's conceptualization of andragogy as a theory or proven method. Some adult educators even argue that adult education should simply drop the word from its lexicon.

Adult education could survive without andragogy, but the term does possess significant public relations value. Andragogy also has the potential of serving as a unifying framework for adult education if definitional problems can be worked out, and if old and new assumptions are rigorously tested before possible incorporation into a larger theory. This article has suggested a revised definition of andragogy aimed at eliminating definitional disorder and conceptual confusion while providing a base for the orderly development of empirically-supported theory.

NOTES

1 A form of basic education for adults.
2 English as a second language.

REFERENCES

Anderson, M. L. and Lindeman, E. C. (1927a) *Education Through Experience*, New York: Workers' Education Bureau.

―――― (1927b) 'Education through experience', *Workers' Education: A Quarterly Journal*, 4, 33–4.

Brookfield, S. (1984) 'The contribution of Eduard Lindeman to the development of theory and philosophy in adult education', *Adult Education Quarterly*, 34, 185–96.

Carlson, R. A. (1979) 'The time of andragogy', *Adult Education*, 30, 53–6.

Clardy, A. (1986) 'Andragogy: adult learning and education at its best?', Unpublished paper.

Conti, G. J. (1985) 'Assessing teaching style in adult education: how and why', *Life-long Learning: An Omnibus in Practice and Research*, 9, 7–11, 28.

Cross, K. P. (1982) *Adults as Learners*, San Francisco: Jossey-Bass.

Davenport, J. and Davenport, J. A. (1985a) 'Andragogical-pedagogical orientations of adult learners: research results and practice recommendations', *Life-long Learning: An Omnibus of Practice and Research*, 9, 6–8.

―――― (1985b) 'A chronology and analysis of the andragogy debate', *Adult Education Quarterly*, 35, 152–9.

―――― (1985c) Knowles or Lindeman: would the real father of American andragogy please stand up?' *Life-long Learning: An Omnibus of Practice and Research*, 9, 4–5.

Day, C. and Baskett, H. K. (1982) 'Discrepancies between intentions and practice: re-examining some basic assumptions about adult and continuing professional education', *International Journal of Lifelong Education*,1, 143–55.

Elias, J. L. (1979) 'Critique: andragogy revisited', *Adult Education*, 29, 252–5.

Goodnow, E. G. (1982) 'The contingency theory of education', *International Journal of Lifelong Education*, 1, 341–53.

Hartree, A. (1984) 'Malcolm Knowles' theory of andragogy: a critique', *International Journal of Lifelong Education*, 3, 203–10.

Houle, C. D. (1972) *The Design of Education*, San Francisco: Jossey-Bass.

Knowles, M. S. (1968) 'Andragogy not pedagogy', *Adult Leadership*, 16, 350–2, 386.

_____ (1970) *The Modern Practice of Adult Education: Andragogy versus Pedagogy*, New York: Association Press.

_____ (1979) 'Andragogy revisited, part II', *Adult Education* 30 (1), 52–3.

_____ (1984) *Andragogy in Action*, San Francisco: Jossey-Bass.

Lebel, J. (1978) 'Beyond andragogy to gerogogy', *Lifelong Learning: The Adult Years*, 1, 16–18.

London, J. (1973) 'Adult education for the 1970s: promise or illusion?', *Adult Education*, 24, 60–70.

Long, H. (1986) Personal discussion between Long and authors.

McKenzie, L. (1977) 'The issue of andragogy', *Adult Education*, 27, 225–9.

_____ (1979) 'A response to Elias', *Adult Education*, 29, 256–60.

McLoughlin, D. (1971) 'Participation of the adult learner in program planning', *Adult Education*, 22, 30–5.

Nottingham Andragogy Group (1983) *Towards a Developmental Theory of Andragogy*, Nottingham: University of Nottingham Department of Adult Education.

Rachal, J. (1983) 'The andragogy-pedagogy debate: another voice in the fray', *Lifelong Learning: An Omnibus of Practice and Research*, 6, 14–15.

Rosenblum, S. and Darkenwald, G. C. (1983) 'Effects of adult learner participation in course planning on achievement and satisfaction', *Adult Education Quarterly*, 33, 147–53.

Stewart, D. W. (1986) 'Perspectives', *Life-long Learning: An Omnibus of Practice and Research*, 9, 2.

Yeo, G. (1982) 'Eldergogy: a specialized approach to education for elders', *Lifelong Learning: The Adult Years*, S, 4–7.

Chapter 8

Adult development

Mark Tennant

Source: This is an edited version of a chapter in M. Tennant, *Psychology and Adult Learning*, London, Routledge, 1988.

Adult educators, who in many respects are critical consumers of ideas about teaching and learning, seem to have a weakness when it comes to critically evaluating theory and research in adult development. This weakness is perhaps due to the belief that the identity of adult education is premised on the identity of the adult. Hence the literature on adult development is attractive because it offers (however illusory the offer may be) the promise of a distinct and coherent theory of adult learning.

Published accounts of the adult learning process nearly always make reference to life-span developmental stages, the life cycle or the 'phases' of adult life. In a similar way many policy documents in adult and continuing education stress the importance of addressing the needs associated with adult development and growth. Allman (1982) sets out the case for this interest in adult development. She observes that studies of adult life reveal it to be a period of change and development, much like that of childhood and adolescence. She argues that the results of such studies serve notice on the prevailing assumptions about adulthood – that it is a long period of stability where previously learned capacities, skills, attitudes and values are applied to one's activities at work, in the family, in leisure and in civic life. These assumptions need to be challenged because they 'clearly affect decision makers in the field of politics, education and social policy' (Allman 1982: 42). In education they are linked to the conventional view that the period of initial education equips young adults for the remainder of their working lives – a view which continues to inform political debate on educational priorities.

[. . .] Arguments like these are convincing and we do need to revise our outmoded views about adult life. But, as I shall argue we need to proceed with caution, otherwise there is a risk of replacing one set of false beliefs with another equally false (albeit more palatable) set of beliefs about adult development.

The first part of this chapter reviews some of the connections which have been made between adult development and adult education. The second part focuses on evaluating the adequacy of existing theory and research in this area.

A question commonly posed by those with an interest in adult learning is: 'What are the implications of adult development for adult and continuing education practitioners?' Knox outlines three possible implications:

1 To predict and explain success in education: 'Practitioners are typically interested in developmental generalizations regarding performance or personality in order to predict and explain successful participation in educative activity'.
2 To help people adapt to changing adult roles: 'Adult life cycle trends in performance in family, occupational and community roles suggest ways in which continuing education participation might facilitate adaptation and growth related to each role area'.
3 To improve the effectiveness of marketing and instructional activities: 'From time to time, the stability of adulthood is punctuated by role change events such as the birth of the first child, a move to another community or retirement . . . Such change events typically produce heightened readiness to learn which, if recognized, can contribute to the effectiveness of marketing and instructional activities'.

(Knox 1979: 59–60)

The whole tenor of the above implications indicates a view about adult development and an attitude to adult education. That is, that the various 'roles' of adult life are inevitable and people must learn to cope with them as they arise; and that adult education agencies, if they wish to be successful, should gear their marketing and instructional activities to cater for the different needs of adults at different life-stages. There is no sense in which adult roles are portrayed as arbitrary or even oppressive, or that alternative roles and options are possible for a given life period. In this sense adult education contributes towards the maintenance of social norms and structures.

One need not look very far to find other instances of this type of approach. A significant example can be found in McCoy's tabulation of 'Adult life cycle tasks and educational program responses' which is reproduced in Chickering's influential volume *The Modern American College* (Chickering 1981). McCoy identifies seven developmental stages, each of which is characterized by a set of common tasks. For example, the 'leaving home' stage has the associated tasks of 'break psychological ties', 'choose career', 'enter work', 'manage time' and so on. Each stage is then related to an appropriate range of programme responses, with a final column indicating the outcomes sought from the educational programme. The table is too lengthy to reproduce here but a cross-section of one stage only will be sufficient to illustrate the general strategy. Table 8.1 shows the 'tasks' and 'program responses' appropriate for the developmental stage 'becoming adult'.

Table 8.1 Educational responses to life-cycle tasks

Task	Programme responses
1 Select mate	Marriage workshops
2 Settle in work, begin career ladder	Management, advancement training
3 Parent	Parenting workshops
4 Become involved in community	Civic education; volunteer training
5 Consume wisely	Consumer education; financial management training
6 Home-own	Home-owning, maintenance workshops
7 Socially interact	Human relations groups, translation analysis
8 Achieve autonomy	Living alone, divorce workshops
9 Problem-solve	Creative problem-solving workshops
10 Manage stress accompanying change	Stress management, biofeedback, relaxation, workshops

Source: McCoy (1977).

A casual glance at the list of tasks and how each of them relates to specified programmes confirms my general point about adult education supporting the *status quo*. Even a non-specific 'task' such as 'achieving autonomy', is interpreted in the most narrow sense possible – that is, as the capacity to 'live alone successfully'. It is unnecessary to elaborate further, the tabulation speaks for itself. What is surprising, and disappointing, is that anyone in adult education would take such an analysis seriously as anything other than a narrow descriptive exercise.

Yet there is a strongly held view among adult educators that the everyday reality of learners should be acknowledged, no matter how culturally specific that reality may be. The reader may remonstrate that McCoy is simply following this precept – what, then, is so objectionable? As I see it, there are two objections. The first of these is that there is no acknowledgement of the narrow culturally specific 'tasks' which are identified. Quite the opposite, the 'tasks' are presented as a generalizable framework to be used by adult education agencies in formulating their programmes. There is no sense in which McCoy is using her analysis as a case study of a process for others to emulate in a different cultural context. The second objection, already mentioned in relation to Knox, is that the response of adult education is depicted as solely adaptive. There is no scope for questioning and challenging the tasks – they constitute the taken for granted reality of the learners and the adult educators.

There are many adult educators who, being dismissive of the above approach, nevertheless subscribe to the view that adult development is a central concept in adult education. An interest in adult development stems quite naturally from a commitment to the notion of lifelong learning and the associated concepts of 'lifelong education', 'recurrent education' and 'education permanente'. The policy and research documents of UNESCO, the OECD and the Council of Europe, which are the major sponsoring bodies of these concepts, frequently cite adult development as a central concern of any lifelong learning strategy. However, they do not understand adult development to be an immutable sequence of stages through which people pass at more or less predictable ages. Indeed, they challenge the concept of the 'typical' life cycle and support their view with an analysis of contemporary social and economic change. This is particularly apparent in the literature on recurrent education, and the following extract, taken from an article by one of its chief proponents, Jarl Bengtsson, typifies this approach:

> significant changes are taking place in the relationship between work and non-work time seen over the individual's whole life cycle in terms of increased education, earlier retirement, longer holidays, etc. It has also been made clear that these changes affect social groups according to their hierarchical position in working life, as well as the way their work is being scheduled, i.e. full-time, part-time, shiftwork, long spells of employment, etc.
>
> The claim is not that more non-work time is or will be used for education, although that certainly remains a strong possibility. Rather it is that to look at recurrent education from this perspective provides a very useful point of departure for placing it in the broader context of emerging new life-styles and life cycles. Most likely, the crucial factors behind changes in the individual's lifecycle pattern will be the economic and employment conditions that the industrialized countries will face during coming years.
>
> (Bengtsson 1979: 26)

Recurrent education, and its closely related concepts, accepts the diversity of life-cycle patterns and the need for educational institutions to respond to and foster this diversity through a diversity of provision. It supports the notion that individual options should be extended, especially the way in which paid work, unpaid work, education and leisure are combined. The principles espoused can be seen as a response to the effects of social, economic and technological change. Changes in demographic patterns, the sexual division of labour, the length of working life, hours spent at work, retirement age and so on, are all seen as relevant to the proposition that educational opportunities should be distributed, in a recurring way, across the life-span. Recurrent education also embodies the notion of social justice, and its evolution as a concept from the late 1960s has been linked with a host of terms implying broad social reforms: industrial democracy, participation in planning, social equity, decentralization, links between education and work and between younger and older generations, and concern with the disadvantaged. An underlying value in all this is a humanistic concern for the individual. The idea of self-development, which is based on notions of individuality and growth, is contrasted with the opposing notions of enslavement, alienation and stagnation – which are the psychological consequences of clinging to an outmoded conception of the 'normal' life cycle. [. . .]

There are two persistent problems which are a feature of adult developmental psychology. The first is that there are insurmountable methodological difficulties in establishing 'phases' or 'stages' of adult life. The second is that much of the literature is historically and socially rooted and lacks any worthwhile generalizability.

METHODOLOGICAL DIFFICULTIES

[. . .] Not all adult development studies adopt a stage-sequence approach; nevertheless, they usually have a stake in making comparisons between different 'ages', 'phases' or 'stages' of life. Leaving aside the problem of deciding what type of data to gather, the common methodological problem is to construct a research design which generates comparative data (on whatever dimension) which indicates the effects of age changes only (where the effects of other factors, such as 'history' and 'time of measurement' are neutralized). Many of the most influential studies in adult development use research designs which fail to do this. Three basic research designs are the 'cross-sectional', 'longitudinal' and 'time-lag' designs. These are illustrated in Figure 8.1. The cross-sectional design is represented by each of the columns. It is where two or more age cohorts are investigated at one time of measurement. The hypothetical example in the table appears in the left hand column, where at one time of measurement (1970) data are gathered from four age cohorts (people born in 1930, 1940, 1950, 1960). Perhaps the best known example of this technique is to be found in the research of Gould (1972). In an initial study Gould observed and recorded the concerns expressed by a number of psychiatric outpatients. He hypothesized that these concerns differed among different age groups. He then used these expressed concerns to construct a questionnaire which contained 160 questions divided into ten areas of life. This questionnaire was then administered, in a later study, to a sample of 524 non-patients, who were white middle-class men and women aged 16–50 years. [. . .]

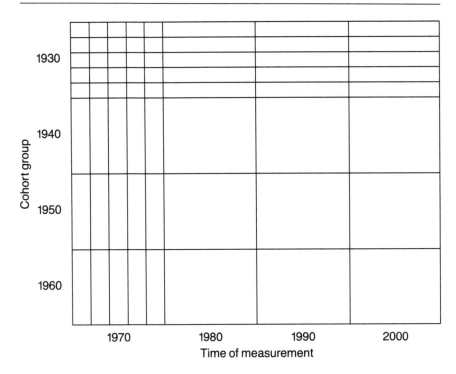

Figure 8.1 Adult development: basic research designs

The difficulty with a research design such as this is that the observed differences in 'concerns' may be due to the different life experiences of the different age cohorts. For example, the life history of a 50-year-old in 1972 would necessarily include the 'great depression' of the 1930s and the experience of the Second World War. This would be quite different from the life history of a 22-year-old in 1972 who would have experienced (as a child and youth) the economic boom of the post-Second World War years and the social changes of the 1960s. It seems reasonable to assume that such historical events and trends affect people's 'concerns'. Indeed they may be more significant in explaining the different concerns of different age cohorts than any hypothesized notion of the life cycle.

One way to avoid making comparisons between different cohorts is to investigate a single age cohort over a number of years. This is referred to as a longitudinal design and is represented by the rows in Figure 8.1. The horizontal lines on the top row provide a hypothetical example. A sample of people born in 1930 could be studied at different times, in 1970 (40 years), 1980 (50 years), 1990 (60 years) and 2000 (70 years). The Grant Study (Vaillant 1977) provides a good example of this type of research design. Ninety-four college graduates from the early 1940s were followed through until 1969. They were part of an initial study of 268 male under-

graduates who were given extensive physiological and psychological examinations early in their college years. After graduation the sample of 94
graduates completed annual questionnaires until 1955, and every two years
after that date. They were interviewed in their homes twice, between 1950
and 1952 and in 1969. Vaillant (1977) reports the results in detail, but his
thesis is simple: that ego defence mechanisms mature through the life cycle
and that healthy adults progress through a hierarchy of adaptive mechanisms as shown in Table 8.2.

Table 8.2 Hierarchy of adaptive mechanisms

Level I: Psychotic mechanisms (common in psychosis, dreams, childhood)
  Denial (of external reality)
  Distortion
  Delusional projection

Level II: Immature mechanisms (common in severe depression, personality dis-
    orders and adolescence)
  Fantasy (schizoid withdrawal, denial through fantasy)
  Projection
  Hypochondriasis
  Passive–aggressive behaviour (masochism, turning against the self)
  Acting out (compulsive delinquency, perversion)

Level III: Neurotic mechanisms (common in everyone)
  Intellectualization (isolation, obsessive behaviour, undoing, rationalization)
  Repression
  Reaction formation
  Displacement (conversion, phobias, wit)
  Dissociation (neurotic denial)

Level IV: Mature mechanisms (common in 'healthy' adults)
  Sublimation
  Altruism
  Suppression
  Anticipation
  Humour

Source: Vaillant 1977, p. 80

There are some well-documented problems with longitudinal studies,
such as experimental mortality (where participants drop out of the study)
and practice effects (where the participants become overly familiar with
the style of the questionnaire and the structure of the interview) and time-
of-measurement effects (where measurements, because they are taken at
different times, may only reflect changed social and cultural conditions).
A significant problem, and one often overlooked, is that over, say, a 30-
year period, there are bound to be shifts in the theoretical perspective of
the theory upon which the research is based. This often means that the
initial questions and modes of analysis become obsolescent and are

replaced by more contemporary techniques. This certainly happened in Vaillant's study:

> Unfortunately, the work of four other innovative students of personality in the 1930s was ignored. I say unfortunately because the work of these four men and women has affected my interpretation of the results of the Study. Erik Erikson, Anna Freud, Harry Stack Sullivan and Heinz Hartmann all significantly influenced modern understanding of personality; but in 1937–1942 their work was still too novel to shape the early design of the Grant Study.
>
> By 1940 Harry Stack Sullivan had begun to revolutionize the psychodynamic theory of personality. Slowly, Sullivan and his British counterpart, Melanie Klein, led psychiatrists to realize that interpersonal, relations played as important a role in shaping personality as did the intrapersonal relations between ego, conscience and instinct, but not before the Grant Study was well under way. For example, although in college the psychiatric interviews had included a careful history of adolescent sexual development, the Study psychiatrists did not inquire into the boys' friendship patterns, or their efforts at heterosexual intimacy. Not until 1950, really, did the Grant Study begin to pay close attention to the men's relationships with older men and women.
>
> In 1937 Anna Freud first published in English 'The Ego and The Mechanisms of Defense' and Heinz Hartmann had presented in German 'Ego Psychology and the Problem of Adaptation'. Not until 1967 did the Grant Study focus on these men's styles of psychological adaptation.
>
> In the late 1930s at the University of California Erikson had begun the work that in 1950 was to culminate in 'Childhood and Society' – providing convincing evidence that adults mature as well as children. During the same period, the Grant Study staff, like their colleagues elsewhere, saw psychodynamic maturation as being largely completed by adolescence.
>
> (Vaillant 1977: 43–4)

Even though longitudinal studies overcome the problems of comparing different cohorts, they nevertheless remain historically bound. This means that generalizations to different cohort groups can only be made on the assumption that historical variation is unimportant.

Is it possible to avoid the influence of historical variation? The answer to this question rests heavily on one's analysis of how history and culture influence the psychological make-up of individuals. From a research design point of view it is certainly possible to control for historical effects by using some combination of longitudinal and cross-sectional designs. For example, combining the first two vertical columns in Figure 8.1 would represent a cross-sectional sequence where all four cohort groups are investigated twice, once in 1970 and again in 1980. Similarly, combining the bottom two rows would represent a longitudinal sequence, where two cohort groups are investigated simultaneously over a number of years (1970–2000). Through such techniques it is possible to obtain data about the effects of cohort differences, time-of-measurement differences and age differences. For example, the differences between 20-year-olds (1970–80) can be compared with the differences between 30-year-olds (1980–90) in order to gauge the effect of cohort membership on the general difference between 20- and 30-year-olds. This, in effect, is a way of 'controlling' for historical variation. But the control gained through such a practice is very limited. First, it depends on whether the changes being monitored are easily quantifiable. In fact, most of the studies of this kind have been developed by those with an interest in measuring the development of human abilities, especially intellectual development (for example, Schaie 1979). The research designs employed were initially intended to partial out the historical effects of improvements in educational provision during (longitudinal) or between (cross-sectional) the lifetimes of the subjects being studied. This is easy to do when it is simply a matter of comparing test scores, but it is a dubious task to make such comparisons with qualitative data of the kind found in adult personality development. Second, there is an assumption that the impact of history is linear and cumulative. But this is an untenable assumption (for example, a 20-year-old in 1975 may be quite different from a 20-year-old in 1970 or 1980).

Another way of minimizing the impact of historical variation on developmental research is to gather 'data' of a high level of generality. [...] For example, Lowenthal et al. (1977) used a cross-sectional technique to investigate the adaptive processes of men and women across the life-span. In their study they documented such general psychological qualities as complexity, self-image, expressiveness and perceptions in continuity of value structure. The biographical interview technique of Levinson (1978) was primarily aimed at elucidating changes in the relationship between self and world throughout the life course. Loevinger (1976) was also concerned with the rather abstract notion of ego as a central frame of reference for understanding self and others. However, a closer look at this research will still reveal its social and historical specificity.

SOCIAL AND HISTORICAL BIAS

In the immediately preceding section on methodological difficulties I outlined some of the research design problems when comparing different people of different ages at a given time (cross-sectional) or when comparing the same people at different ages (longitudinal). I argued that historical events either confound the results of any comparison or they limit the generalizability of the results.

[...] Unfortunately, research in adult development, especially the genre concerned with life 'stages' or 'phases', seems prone to social and historical bias. This is evident in four ways; the existence of purely descriptive inventories of life 'tasks', the selection of subjects for research, the data gathering techniques, and the way in which the concept of the 'healthy' personality is constructed.

Descriptive inventories

This approach, whereby an inventory of life tasks is constructed, has its origins in Havighurst's (1972) *Developmental Tasks and Education* which was written in the early 1940s. Table 8.3 is a modified version of Havighurst's original set of developmental tasks. It is similar to the inventory of McCoy (1977) and the same objections apply here. It is worthwhile noting, however, Havighurst's comments on his original inventory.

> The tasks the individual must learn – the developmental task of life – are those things that constitute healthy and satisfactory growth in our society. They are the things a person must learn if he is to be judged and to judge himself to be a reasonably happy and successful person. A developmental task is a task which arises at or about a certain period in the life of the individual, successful achievement of which leads to his happiness and to success with later tasks, while failure leads to unhappiness in the individual, disapproval by the society, and difficulty with later tasks.
>
> (Havighurst 1972: 2)

Thus the developmental tasks of life amount to a socially approved timetable for individual growth and development. In a pluralistic society this timetable will differ between social groups. While it may be useful to identify the developmental tasks of particular social or community groups, as Tucker and Huerta (1987) have done in their study of Mexican-American females, it is dangerous to generalize about the developmental tasks of society as such.

Sample selection, data gathering techniques

Table 8.4 sets out the sample, method and developmental processes identified by each of six well-known adult developmental psychologists. Five of these gathered data prior to formulating their views about adult development. An impressionistic description of the samples used is that they consisted of North American, white, middle class, better educated, predominantly male subjects.

The techniques for gathering data were the structured interview, questionnaire, self-rating checklist, standard psychological test and observer

Table 8.3 Developmental tasks of the adult years

16–23 Late adolescence and youth	23–35 Early adulthood	35–45 Midlife transition	45–57 Middle adulthood	57–65 Late adult transition	65+ Late adulthood
Achieving emotional independence Preparing for marriage and family life Choosing and preparing for a career Developing an ethical system	Deciding on a partner Starting a family Managing a home Starting in an occupation Assuming civic responsibilities	Adapting to a changing time perspective Revising career plans Redefining family relationships	Maintaining a career or developing a new one Restabilizing family relationships Making mature civic contributions Adjusting to biological change	Preparing for retirement	Adjusting to retirement Adjusting to declining health and strength Becoming affiliated with late-adult age groups Establishing satisfactory living arrangements Adjusting to the death of a spouse Maintaining integrity

rating. But one should be wary of accepting reported results without a detailed knowledge of how these techniques were applied in each case.

Conceptions of the healthy personality

Development implies growth and progress, not merely change. But growth and progress towards what end? The answer to this question is often the starting point for theories of adult development, and it is the conception of the end point of development, the 'mature' or 'healthy' personality which frequently governs how progress and growth is monitored and explained within a given theory. For Kohlberg, growth is towards autonomous and principled morality, for Erikson, towards inner unity, and for Maslow it is towards self-actualization with its increased sense of self and autonomy. Many developmental psychologists construe the end point of development with terms like 'individuality', 'autonomy' and the 'integrated self'.

But do such descriptions represent a particular way of looking at the world which excludes certain cultures or sections of the population? A closer look may help to resolve this issue. Levinson, for example, makes the following remarks about the 'individuation' process:

> Throughout the life cycle, but especially in the key transition periods such as infancy, pubescence and the Mid-life Transition, the developmental process of individuation is going on. This term refers to the changes in a person's relationship to himself and to the external world. [...]
> These changes are part of the individuation process. In successive periods of development, as this process goes on, the person forms a clearer boundary between self and world. He forms a stronger sense of who he is and what he wants, and a more realistic, sophisticated view of the world: what it is like, what it offers him and demands from him. Greater individuation allows him to be more separate from the world, to be more independent and self-generating. But it also gives him the confidence and understanding to have more intense attachments in the world and to feel more fully a part of it.
>
> (Levinson 1978: 195)

This emphasis on 'separateness', 'independence' and 'self-generation' is the language of the ethic of individualism, [...] it is worthwhile noting the claims of at least one commentator, Gilligan (1979), that the emphasis on the development of individual identity among developmental theories is an aspect of gender bias which pervades the literature. She begins her analysis by referring to the work of Chodorow (1978), who observes that, in general, girls are parented by a person of the same gender while boys are parented by a person of the opposite gender. The significance of this

Table 8.4 Some methods and views on the developmental process

Theorist	Sample	Method	Developmental process
Levinson (1978) The life cycle of men	• Forty men, 35–45 years old in 1968–70. All American born. 10 biologists, 10 blue-collar workers, 10 novelists, 10 business executives • Social class: varied • Race, ethnicity: mixture • Education: 70% completed college • Marital status: all had been married at least once	• Biographical interviewing 10–20 hours each. Test as part of interview • Task was to construct the 'story' of each man's life • Interview protocols provided basis for generalizations about the life cycle	• Building and modifying life structures (basic pattern of a person's life) • Alternation of stable and transitional periods in life structure • Individualization proceeds throughout the course of life – this refers to the relationship between self and the external world
Gould (1978) Stages in the development of adult consciousness	• 125 psychiatric residents • unspecified number of psychiatric out-patients • non-patients, 524, 16–50 years, white and middle class men and women	• Cross-sectional • Questionnaire and therapeutic observations • Questionnaire contained statements based on expressed concerns of psychiatric patients: 160 questions on 10 areas of life – each area requiring a forced ranking of statements according to personal applicability (self-rating)	• People strive for a fuller, more independent, more conscious self-definition and overcoming childhood consciousness • Growth implies reformulating our self-definition and overcoming childhood consciousness • Growth implies shedding the unconscious and restrictive set of protective devices which form the safety boundary of childhood – that is, overcoming major false assumptions
Lowenthal (1977) Four stages of life	• 216 urban men and women, largely Caucasian, middle and lower-middle class • Four groups: High School mean age 17 Newly wed mean age 24 Middle aged mean age 50 Pre-retirement mean age 60	• Cross-sectional • Interviews (8 hours): – structural interview schedule and – measures and rating related to adaptation	• No global theoretical framework – but uses a range of theoretical concepts to understand adaptive processes across the life-span – for example, complexity, expressiveness, self-image, life satisfaction, perspectives on past and future, perceived stress, perceptions of continuity in value structure

Chickering and Havighurst (1981) Adult developmental tasks	• No direct research reported	• Relies on a range of developmental phase studies	Three sources of developmental tasks: 1 physical/biological 2 social/cultural life 3 personal values and aspirations of the individual
Loevinger (1976) Ego development	• A number of studies using undergraduate students	• Systematic comparison of her stages with those of other stage theorists – for example, Erikson, Fromm, Piaget, Sullivan, Kohlberg, Perry • Projective tests requiring sentence completion (for example, education is . . .)	• Ego is a central frame of reference for understanding self and others • There is a developmental movement from simple stereotyped thinking and perceptions to a more complex and differentiated view of self and world.
Vaillant (1977) Hierarchy of adaptive mechanisms	• Initially 268 male undergraduates (39–44) • 94 male graduates followed up in 1969 – average age 47	• Longitudinal (Grant Study) interviews and annual questionnaires • Initially extensive physical, physiological and psychological examinations	• Ego defence mechanisms mature through the life cycle – especially for those who were psychosocially mature in Erikson's sense

is that the identity of boys is built on the perception of contrast and separateness from their primary caregiver, while the identity of girls is built upon the perception of sameness and attachment to their primary caregiver. Gilligan remarks:

> Consequently, relationships, and particularly issues of dependency, are experienced differently by women and men. For boys and men, separation and individuation are critically tied to gender identity since separation from the mother is essential for the development of masculinity. For girls and women, issues of femininity or feminine identity do not depend on the achievement of separation from the mother or on the progress of individuation. Since masculinity is defined through separation while femininity is defined through attachment, male gender identity is threatened by intimacy while female gender identity is threatened by separation. Thus males tend to have difficulty with relationships, while females tend to have problems with individuation. The quality of embeddedness in social interaction and personal relationships that characterizes women's lives in contrast to men's, however, becomes not only a descriptive difference but also a developmental liability when the milestones of childhood and adolescent development in the psychological literature are markers of increasing separation. Women's failure to separate then becomes by definition a failure to develop.
>
> (Gilligan 1979: 8–9)

Gilligan then proceeds to cite evidence of the undervaluing of female characteristics – the concern with relationships and responsibilities, empathy and attachment – among developmental theories. For example, Freud considered the persistence of women's pre-Oedipal attachment to their mother to be linked with their failure to resolve completely their Oedipal feelings and their consequent failure to develop a strong superego. This developmental failure in women results (in Freud's view) in their having little sense of justice:

> The fact that women must be regarded as having little sense of justice is no doubt related to the predominance of envy in their mental life . . .
>
> (Freud 1973: 168)

Another example comes from Jean Piaget, who observed sex differences in the way children engage in games. Girls, because of their more flexible attitude towards rules and their enforcement were considered to have a less developed legal sense than boys – which is the cornerstone of moral development.

> [for boys and girls] . . . the rule is no longer an imperative coming from an adult and accepted without discussion, it is a means of agreement resulting from co-operation itself. But girls are less explicit about this

agreement and this is our reason for suspecting them of being less concerned with legal elaborations. A rule is good so long as the game repays it.

(Piaget 1977: 78)

Kohlberg too is open to the same criticism. Gilligan observes that his empirical work, which led to the formulation of moral development stages, was based on a sample of boys only. Not surprisingly, women tend to score lower on Kohlberg's scale than men. According to Gilligan, this is because the higher stages of Kohlberg's scale are constructed from what are traditionally 'male' qualities – the concern with justice and rights (premised on individuation) rather than with responsibilities and relationships.

The thrust of Gilligan's argument is that womanhood is rarely equated with mature healthy adulthood in much of the adult developmental literature. This is because the healthy personality is too often portrayed from a male perspective, with an emphasis on individuation and autonomy.

The elusive mystery of women's development lies in its recognition of the continuing importance of attachment in the human life cycle. Woman's place in man's life cycle is to protect this recognition while the developmental litany intones the celebration of separation, autonomy, individuation, and natural rights.

(Gilligan 1979: 23)

DEVELOPMENT AS A DIALECTICAL PROCESS

An alternative to documenting the 'stages' and 'phases' of adult life is to understand development as an ongoing dialectical process (see Riegel 1976, Buss 1979, Wozniak 1975, Basseches 1984). The basic notion here is that there is a constant 'dialectic' between the changing or developing person and the changing or evolving society. That is, the person creates, and is created by the society in which he/she lives. Accompanying this notion is the rejection of those psychological approaches which search for stability, equilibrium and balance in the life course. The person is construed as a changing person in a changing world, and the dialectical approach is very much concerned with the dynamics of change:

The preference for an equilibrium model in the behavioural sciences has been as firmly established as has the preference for abstract traits or competencies. Without any debate it has been taken for granted that a state of balance, stability, and rest is more desirable than a state of upheaval, conflict and change. Thus we have always aimed for a psychology of satisfaction but not of excitement. This preference has found expression in balance theory, equilibrium theory, steady state theory, and indirectly in the theory of cognitive dissonance. With the possible exception of the latter, these interpretations fail to explore the fact that every change has to be explained by the process of imbalance which forms the basis for any movement. Once this prerequisite is recognized, stability appears as a transitory condition in the stream of ceaseless changes.

(Riegel 1976: 690)

One source of such change is the historical change in one's culture (or sub-culture), the other source is the change associated with one's age-related social category (for example, child, youth, young adult, elder). Such changes are primarily mediated through people interacting in everyday life – thus an investigation of developmental change will entail an analysis of common, everyday interactions and the dialogues contained in them.

Riegel's position has much in common with Berger and Luckmann's (1967) exposition of how personal identity is shaped, maintained and transmitted within a given social order. Their analysis offers a powerful account of how personal identity is a social construction which, especially in a modern pluralistic society, is constantly open to change and transformation. What is meant by the proposition that personal identity is a social construction? Put simply, the idea is as follows:

1 We do not have biologically determined identities;
2 We are all born into a particular social world which has been constructed by humans;
3 We develop a notion of who we are from the way 'significant' others (for example, parents) treat us (interact with us);
4 These 'significant' others represent the social world and mediate it to us.
5 We take on the roles and attitudes of significant others, internalize them and make them our own;
6 We extend our identification with significant others to an identification with society as whole: 'Only by virtue of this generalised identification does his own self-identification attain stability and continuity. He now has not only an identity vis-à-vis this or that significant other, but an identity in general . . .'

(Berger and Luckmann 1967: 153).

Identity, as a social construction, needs to be maintained through social interaction. The routines of everyday life serve to confirm the reality of the world and our place in it. In particular, the language used in everyday conversations confirms for us the silent, taken-for-granted world that forms the foundation of our personal identity. In modern pluralistic society, however, there is a multiplicity of world views or realities. Because there is no common social reality there is (after primary socialization) no socially produced stable structure of personal identity. This means that achieving a stable personal identity in modern society becomes an individual, private enterprise. Moreover, the possibility of transforming one's identity is always present. Indeed, one could argue that many life events require a change or re-orientation of identity (for example, retirement, caring for children, the death of a spouse).

Berger and Luckmann (1967) maintain that any transformation of identity requires a process of re-socialization. In extreme cases, such as with religious conversion, there may be a complete dismantling of one's former identity. This would require the following:

1 Affiliation with the new community;
2 Segregation of the individual from the inhabitants of other 'worlds', especially those from the 'world' being left behind (at least at the initial stages);
3 A reinterpretation of the old 'reality' in terms of the new 'reality' (for example, 'Now I understand the purpose of my doing such and such . . .).

Each of these steps can be recognized as extreme versions of what happens to many adults as they develop new personal, family, work and leisure pursuits. The difference between this analysis and the life-span development literature is that transformation does not imply a move towards some state of maturity – it simply means change, not improvement. Also, there are no propositions about the regularity and predictability of change – only that personal identity is open to change, subject to the existence of a community of others who maintain the change through discourse in everyday life.

The idea of the malleability of personal identity is both a source of hope and an occasion for despair. Hope, because it means that change is always possible; despair, because it implies that a belief in the real, true, authentic self is a fanciful indulgence.

The studies cited in this chapter represent only a sampling of a rich and diverse field of enquiry. They were chosen to reveal some of the pitfalls in theory and research in adult development. Adult development is, in principle, germane to anyone with an interest in adult education. Too often, however, people with an applied intent will latch on to an easily assimilated theory, one which clearly differentiates and orders the 'phases' or 'stages' of life and which advances an unambiguous account of the process and end point of development. Adult educators may find such theories useful but they need to be wary of the methodological and conceptual difficulties. They also need to be mindful of the impact such theories have on shaping and maintaining conventionally held views about what it means to be a mature, healthy adult.

REFERENCES

Allman, P. (1982) 'New perspectives on the adult, an argument for lifelong education', *International Journal of Lifelong Education* 1 (1), 41–52.

Basseches, M. (1984) *Dialectical Thinking and Adult Development*, New Jersey: Ablex Publishing.

Bengtsson, J. (1979) 'The work/leisure/education life cycle', in T. Schuller and J. Megarry (eds), *Recurrent Education and Lifelong Learning*, London: Kogan Page.

Berger, P. and Luckmann, T. (1967) *The Social Construction of Reality*, Hardmondsworth: Penguin.

Buss, A. R. (1979) 'Dialectics, history and development: the historical roots of the individual – society dialectic', in P. Baltes and O. Brim (eds), *Life-span Development and Behaviour* (vol. 2), New York: Academic Press.

Chickering, A. W. (ed.) (1981) *The Modern American College*, San Francisco: Jossey-Bass.

——— and Havighurst, R. (1981) 'The life cycle', in A. W. Chickering (ed.), *The Modern American College*, San Francisco: Jossey-Bass.

Chodorow, N. (1978) *The Reproduction of Mothering: Psychoanalysis and the Sociology of Gender*, Berkeley: University of California Press.

Freud, S. (1973) *New Introductory Lectures on Psychoanalysis*, Harmondsworth: Penguin.

Gilligan, C. (1979) *In a Different Voice*, Cambridge, Mass.: Harvard University Press.

Gould, R. (1972) 'The phases of adult life', *The American Journal of Psychiatry* 129 (5), 521–31.

——— (1978) *Transformations: Growth and Change in Adult Life*, New York: Simon & Schuster.

Havighurst, R. J. (1972) *Developmental Tasks and Education* (3rd edn), New York: McKay.

Knox, A. (1979) 'Research insights into adult learning', in T. Schuller and J. Megarry (eds), *Recurrent Education and Lifelong Learning*, London: Kogan Page.

Levinson, D. (1978) *The Seasons of a Man's Life*, New York: Knopf.

Loevinger, J. (1976) *Ego Development*, San Francisco: Jossey-Bass.

Lowenthal, M., Thurnher, M. and Chiriboga, D. (1977) *Four Stages of Life*, San Francisco: Jossey-Bass.

McCoy, V. (1977) 'Adult life cycle change: how does growth affect our education needs?',*Lifelong Learning: The Adult Years*, 31, 14–18.

Piaget, J. (1977) *The Moral Judgement of the Child*, Harmondsworth: Penguin.

Riegel, K. F. (1976) 'The dialectics of human development', *American Psychologist*, October, 689–99.

——— and Rosenwald, G. (eds) (1975) *Structure and Transformation*, New York: Wiley.

Schaie, K. (1979) 'The primary mental abilities in adulthood: an exploration in the development of psychometric intelligence', in P. Baltes and O. Brim (eds), *Lifespan Development and Behaviour* (vol. 2), New York: Academic Press.

Tucker, B. and Huerta, C. (1987) 'A study of developmental tasks as perceived by young adult Mexican–American females', *Lifelong Learning* 10 (4), 4–7.

Vaillant, G. (1977) *Adaptation to Life*, Boston: Little, Brown & Co.

Wozniak, R. H. (1975) 'Dialecticism and structuralism: the philosophical foundation of Social psychology and Piagetian cognitive developmental theory', in K. Riegel and G. Rosenwald (eds), *Structure and Transformation*, New York: Wiley.

Chapter 9

The process of experiential learning

David A. Kolb

Source: This is an edited version of a chapter in D. A. Kolb, *Experiential Learning*, Englewood Cliffs, N.J., Prentice-Hall, 1984.

> We shall not cease from exploration
> And the end of all our exploring
> Will be to arrive where we started
> And know the place for the first time.
> T. S. Eliot, *Four Quartets*[1]

Experiential learning theory offers a fundamentally different view of the learning process from that of the behavioural theories of learning based on an empirical epistemology or the more implicit theories of learning that underlie traditional educational methods, methods that for the most part are based on a rational, idealist epistemology. From this different perspective emerge some very different prescriptions for the conduct of education, the proper relationships among learning, work, and other life activities, and the creation of knowledge itself.

This perspective on learning is called 'experiential' for two reasons. The first is to tie it clearly to its intellectual origins in the work of Dewey, Lewin, and Piaget. The second reason is to emphasize the central role that experience plays in the learning process. This differentiates experiential learning theory from rationalist and other cognitive theories of learning that tend to give primary emphasis to acquisition, manipulation, and recall of abstract symbols, and from behavioural learning theories that deny any role for consciousness and subjective experience in the learning process. It should be emphasized, however, that the aim [. . .] is not to pose experiential learning theory as a third alternative to behavioural and cognitive learning theories, but rather to suggest through experiential learning theory a holistic integrative perspective on learning that combines experience, perception, cognition, and behaviour. This chapter will describe the learning models of Lewin, Dewey, and Piaget and identify the common characteristics they share – characteristics that serve to define the nature of experiential learning.

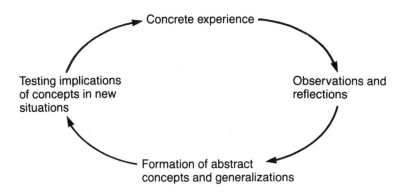

Figure 9.1 The Lewinian experiential learning model

THREE MODELS OF THE EXPERIENTIAL LEARNING PROCESS

The Lewinian model of action research and laboratory training

In the techniques of action research and the laboratory method, learning, change, and growth are seen to be facilitated best by an integrated process that begins with here-and-now experience followed by collection of data and observations about that experience. The data are then analysed and the conclusions of this analysis are fed back to the actors in the experience for their use in the modification of their behaviour and choice of new experiences. Learning is thus conceived as a four-stage cycle, as shown in Figure 9.1. Immediate concrete experience is the basis for observation and reflection. These observations are assimilated into a 'theory' from which new implications for action can be deduced. These implications or hypotheses then serve as guides in acting to create new experiences.

Two aspects of this learning model are particularly noteworthy. First is its emphasis on *here-and-now concrete experience* to validate and test abstract concepts. Immediate personal experience is the focal point for learning, giving life, texture, and subjective personal meaning to abstract concepts and at the same time providing a concrete, publicly shared reference point for testing the implications and validity of ideas created during the learning process. When human beings share an experience, they can share it fully, concretely, *and* abstractly.

Second, action research and laboratory training are based on *feedback processes*. Lewin borrowed the concept of feedback from electrical engineering to describe a social learning and problem-solving process that generates valid information to assess deviations from desired goals. This information feedback provides the basis for a continuous process of goal-directed action and evaluation of the consequences of that action. Lewin and his followers believed that much individual and organizational ineffectiveness could be traced ultimately to a lack of adequate feedback processes. This ineffectiveness results from an imbalance between observation and action – either from a tendency for individuals and organizations to emphasize decision and action at the expense of information gathering, or from a tendency to become bogged down by data collection and analysis. The aim of the laboratory method and action research is to integrate these two perspectives into an effective, goal-directed learning process.

Dewey's model of learning

John Dewey's model of the learning process is remarkably similar to the Lewinian model, although he makes more explicit the developmental nature of learning implied in Lewin's conception of it as a feedback process by describing how learning transforms the impulses, feelings, and desires of concrete experience into higher-order purposeful action.

> The formation of purposes is, then, a rather complex intellectual operation. It involves: (1) observation of surrounding conditions; (2) knowledge of what has happened in similar situations in the past, a knowledge obtained partly by recollection and partly from the information, advice, and warning of those who have had a wider experience; and (3) judgment, which puts together what is observed and what is recalled to see what they signify. A purpose differs from an original impulse and desire through its translation into a plan and method of action based upon foresight of the consequences of action under given observed conditions in a certain way ... The crucial educational problem is that of procuring the postponement of immediate action upon desire until observation and judgment have intervened ... Mere foresight, even if it takes the form of accurate prediction, is not, of course, enough. The intellectual anticipation, the idea of consequences, must blend with desire and impulse to acquire moving force. It then gives direction to what otherwise is blind, while desire gives ideas impetus and momentum.
>
> (Dewey 1938: 69)

Dewey's model of experiential learning is graphically portrayed in Figure 9.2. We note in his description of learning a similarity with Lewin, in the emphasis on learning as a dialectic process integrating experience and concepts, observations, and action. The impulse of experience gives ideas their moving force, and ideas give direction to impulse. Postponement of immediate action is essential for observation and judgement to intervene, and action is essential for achievement of purpose. It is through the integration of these opposing but symbiotically related processes that sophisticated, mature purpose develops from blind impulse.

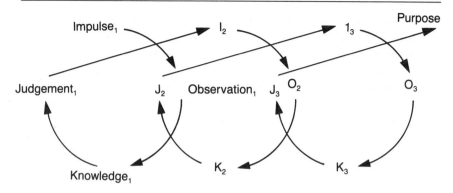

Figure 9.2 Dewey's model of experiential learning

Piaget's model of learning and cognitive development

For Piaget, the dimensions of experience and concept, reflection, and action form the basic continua for the development of adult thought. Development from infancy to adulthood moves from a concrete phenomenal view of the world to an abstract constructionist view, from an active egocentric view to a reflective internalized mode of knowing. Piaget also maintained that these have been the major directions of development in scientific knowledge (Piaget 1970). The learning process whereby this development takes place is a cycle of interaction between the individual and the environment that is similar to the learning models of Dewey and Lewin. In Piaget's terms, the key to learning lies in the mutual interaction of the process of *accommodation* of concepts or schemas to experience in the world and the process of *assimilation* of events and experiences from the world into existing concepts and schemas. Learning or, in Piaget's term, intelligent adaptation results from a balanced tension between these two processes. When accommodation processes dominate assimilation, we have imitation – the moulding of oneself to environmental contours or constraints. When assimilation predominates over accommodation, we have play – the imposition of one's concept and images without regard to environmental realities. The process of cognitive growth from concrete to abstract and from active to reflective is based on this continual transaction between assimilation and accommodation, occurring in successive stages, each of which incorporates what has gone before into a new, higher level of cognitive functioning.

Piaget's work has identified four major stages of cognitive growth that emerge from birth to about the age of 14–16. In the first stage (0–2 years), the child is predominantly concrete and active in his learning style. This stage is called the sensory-motor stage. Learning is predominantly enactive through feeling, touching, and handling. Representation is based on action – for example, 'a hole is to dig'. Perhaps the greatest accomplishment of this period is the development of goal-oriented behaviour: 'The sensory-motor period shows a remarkable evolution from non-intentional habits to experimental and exploratory activity which is obviously intentional or goal oriented' (Flavell 1963: 107). Yet the child has few schemes or theories into which he can assimilate events, and as a result, his primary stance towards the world is accommodative. Environment plays a major role in shaping his ideas and intentions. Learning occurs primarily through the association between stimulus and response.

In the second stage (2–6 years), the child retains his concrete orientation but begins to develop a reflective orientation as he begins to internalize actions, converting them to images. This is called the representational stage. Learning is now predominantly iconic in nature, through the manipulation of observations and images. The child is now freed somewhat from his immersion in immediate experience and, as a result, is free to play with and manipulate his images of the world. At this stage, the child's primary stance towards the world is divergent. He is captivated with his ability to collect images and to view the world from different perspectives. [...]

In the third stage (7–11 years), the intensive development of abstract symbolic powers begins. The first symbolic developmental stage Piaget calls the stage of concrete operations. Learning in this stage is governed by the logic of classes and relations. The child in this stage further increases his independence from his immediate experiential world through the development of inductive powers [...] Thus, in contrast to the child in the sensory-motor stage whose learning style was dominated by accommodative processes, the child at the stage of concrete operations is more assimilative in his learning style. He relies on concepts and theories to select and give shape to his experiences.

Piaget's final stage of cognitive development comes with the onset of adolescence (12–15 years). In this stage, the adolescent moves from symbolic processes based on concrete operations to the symbolic processes of representational logic, the stage of formal operations. He now returns to a more active orientation, but it is an active orientation that is now modified by the development of the reflective and abstract power that preceded it. The symbolic powers he now possesses enable him to engage in hypothetico-deductive reasoning. He develops the possible implications of his theories and proceeds to experimentally test which of these are true. Thus his basic learning style is convergent, in contrast to the divergent orientation of the child in the representational stage [...] This brief outline of Piaget's cognitive development theory identifies those basic developmental processes that shape the basic learning process of adults (see Figure 9.3).

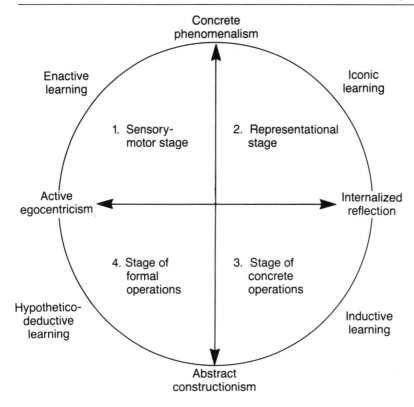

Figure 9.3 Piaget's model of learning and cognitive development

CHARACTERISTICS OF EXPERIENTIAL LEARNING

There is a great deal of similarity among the models of the learning process discussed above. Taken together, they form a unique perspective on learning and development, a perspective that can be characterized by the following propositions, which are shared by the three major traditions of experiential learning.

Learning is best conceived as a process, not in terms of outcomes

The emphasis on the process of learning as opposed to the behavioural outcomes distinguishes experiential learning from the idealist approaches of traditional education and from the behavioural theories of learning created by Watson, Hull, Skinner, and others. The theory of experiential learning rests on a different philosophical and epistemological base from behaviourist theories of learning and idealist educational approaches. Modern versions of these latter approaches are based on the empiricist philosophies of Locke and others. This epistemology is based on the idea that there are elements of consciousness – mental atoms, or, in Locke's term 'simple ideas' – that always remain the same. The various combinations and associations of these consistent elements form our varying patterns of thought. It is the notion of constant fixed elements of thought that has had such a profound effect on prevailing approaches to learning and education, resulting in a tendency to define learning in terms of its outcomes, whether these be knowledge in an accumulated storehouse of facts or habits representing behavioural responses to specific stimulus conditions. If ideas are seen to be fixed and immutable, then it seems possible to measure how much someone has learned by the amount of these fixed ideas the person has accumulated.

Experiential learning theory, however, proceeds from a different set of assumptions. Ideas are not fixed and immutable elements of thought but are formed and re-formed through experience. In all three of the learning models just reviewed, learning is described as a process whereby concepts are derived from and continuously modified by experience. No two thoughts are ever the same, since experience always intervenes [...] Learning is an emergent process whose outcomes represent only historical record, not knowledge of the future.

When viewed from the perspective of experiential learning, the tendency to define learning in terms of outcomes can become a definition of non-learning, in the process sense that the failure to modify ideas and habits as a result of experience is maladaptive. The clearest example of this irony lies in the behaviourist axiom that the strength of a habit can be measured by its resistance to extinction. That is, the more I have 'learned' a given habit, the longer I will persist in behaving that way when it is no longer rewarded. Similarly, there are those who feel that the orientations that conceive of learning in terms of outcomes as opposed to a process of adaptation have had a negative effect on the educational system. Jerome Bruner, in his influential book, *Toward a Theory of Instruction*, makes the point that the purpose of education is to stimulate enquiry and skill in the process of knowledge getting, not to memorize a body of knowledge: 'Knowing is a process, not a product' (Bruner 1966: 72). Paulo Freire calls the orientation that conceives of education as the transmission of fixed content the 'banking' concept of education:

> Education thus becomes an act of depositing, in which the students are the depositories and the teacher is the depositor. Instead of communicating, the teacher issues communiques and makes deposits which the students patiently receive, memorize, and repeat. This is the 'banking' concept of education, in which the scope of action allowed to the students extends only as far as receiving, filing, and storing the deposits. They do, it is true, have the opportunity to become collectors or cataloguers of the things they store. But in the last analysis, it is men

themselves who are filed away through the lack of creativity, transformation, and knowledge in this (at best) misguided system. For apart from
inquiry, apart from the praxis, men cannot be truly human. Knowledge
emerges only through invention and reinvention, through the restless,
impatient, continuing, hopeful inquiry men pursue in the world, with
the world, and with each other.

(Freire 1974: 58)

Learning is a continuous process grounded in experience

Knowledge is continuously derived from and tested out in the experiences
of the learner. William James (1890), in his studies on the nature of human
consciousness, marvelled at the fact that consciousness is continuous. How
is it, he asked, that I awake in the morning with the same consciousness,
the same thoughts, feelings, memories, and sense of who I am that I went
to sleep with the night before? Similarly for Dewey, continuity of experience was a powerful truth of human existence, central to the theory of
learning: 'the principle of continuity of experience means that every experience both takes up something from those which have gone before and
modifies in some way the quality of those which come after . . . (Dewey
1938: 35).

Although we are all aware of the sense of continuity in consciousness
and experience to which James and Dewey refer, and take comfort from
the predictability and security it provides, there is on occasion in the
penumbra of that awareness an element of doubt and uncertainty. How
do I reconcile my own sense of continuity and predictability with what
at times appears to be a chaotic and unpredictable world around me? I
move through my daily round of tasks and meetings with a fair sense of
what the issues are, of what others are saying and thinking, and with ideas
about what actions to take. Yet I am occasionally upended by unforeseen
circumstances, miscommunications, and dreadful miscalculations. It is in
this interplay between expectation and experience that learning occurs
[. . .]

The fact that learning is a continuous process grounded in experience
has important educational implications. Put simply, it implies that all
learning is *relearning*. How easy and tempting it is in designing a course
to think of the learner's mind as being as blank as the paper on which
we scratch our outline. Yet this is not the case. Everyone enters every
learning situation with more or less articulate ideas about the topic at
hand. We are all psychologists, historians, and atomic physicists. It is just
that some of our theories are more crude and incorrect than others. But
to focus solely on the refinement and validity of these theories misses the
point. The important point is that the people we teach have held these
beliefs whatever their quality and that until now they have used them

whenever the situation called for them to be atomic physicists, historians, or whatever.

Thus, one's job as an educator is not only to implant new ideas but also to dispose of or modify old ones. In many cases, resistance to new ideas stems from their conflict with old beliefs that are inconsistent with them. If the education process begins by bringing out the learner's beliefs and theories, examining and testing them, and then integrating the new, more refined ideas into the person's belief systems, the learning process will be facilitated. Piaget has identified two mechanisms by which new ideas are adopted by an individual – integration and substitution. Ideas that evolve through integration tend to become highly stable parts of the person's conception of the world. On the other hand, when the content of a concept changes by means of substitution, there is always the possibility of a reversion to the earlier level of conceptualization and understanding, or to a dual theory of the world where espoused theories learned through substitution are incongruent with theories-in-use that are more integrated with the person's total conceptual and attitudinal view of the world. It is this latter outcome that stimulated Argyris and Schon's inquiry into the effectiveness of professional education:

> We thought the trouble people have in learning new theories may stem not so much from the inherent difficulty of the new theories as from the existing theories people have that already determine practices. We call their operational theories of action *theories-in-use* to distinguish them from the *espoused* theories that are used to describe and justify behavior. We wondered whether the difficulty in learning new theories of action is related to a disposition to protect the old theory-in-use.
>
> (Argyris and Schon 1974: viii)

The process of learning requires the resolution of conflicts between dialectically opposed modes of adaptation to the world

Each of the three models of experiential learning describes conflicts between opposing ways of dealing with the world, suggesting that learning results from resolution of these conflicts. The Lewinian model emphasizes two such dialectics – the conflict between concrete experience and abstract concepts and the conflict between observation and action. For Dewey, the major dialectic is between the impulse that gives ideas their 'moving force' and reason that gives desire its direction. In Piaget's framework, the twin processes of accommodation of ideas to the external world and assimilation of experience into existing conceptual structures are the moving forces of cognitive development. In Paulo Freire's work, the dialectic nature of learning and adaptation is encompassed in his concept of *praxis*, which he defines as 'reflection and action upon the world in order to transform it'

(Freire 1974: 36). Central to the concept of praxis is the process of 'naming the world', which is both active (in the sense that naming something transforms it) and reflective (in that our choice of words gives meaning to the world around us). This process of naming the world is accomplished through dialogue among equals, a joint process of inquiry and learning that Freire sets against the banking concept of education described earlier:

> As we attempt to analyze dialogue as a human phenomenon, we discover something which is the essence of dialogue itself: *the word*. But the word is more than just an instrument which makes dialogue possible; accordingly, we must seek its constitutive elements. Within the word we find two dimensions, reflection and action, in such radical interaction that if one is sacrificed – even in part – the other immediately suffers. There is no true word that is not at the same time a praxis. Thus, to speak a true word is to transform the world.
>
> An unauthentic word, one which is unable to transform reality, results when dichotomy is imposed upon its constitutive elements. When a word is deprived of its dimension of action, reflection automatically suffers as well; and the word is changed into idle chatter, into *verbalism*, into an alienated and alienating 'blah.' It becomes an empty word, one which cannot denounce the world, for denunciation is impossible without a commitment to transform, and there is no transformation without action.
>
> On the other hand, if action is emphasized exclusively, to the detriment of reflection, the word is converted into *activism*. The latter – action for action's sake – negates the true praxis and makes dialogue impossible. Either dichotomy, by creating unauthentic forms of existence, creates also unauthentic forms of thought, which reinforce the original dichotomy.
>
> Human existence cannot be silent, nor can it be nourished by false words, but only by true words, with which men transform the world. To exist, humanly, is to *name* the world, to change it. Once named, the world in its turn appears to the namers as a problem and requires of them a new *naming*. Men are not built in silence, but in word, in work, in action-reflection.
>
> But while to say the true word – which is work, which is praxis – is to transform the world, saying that word is not the privilege of some few men, but the right of every man. Consequently, no one can say a true word alone – nor can he say it for another, in a prescriptive act which robs others of their words.

(Freire 1974: 75–6)

All the models above suggest the idea that learning is by its very nature a tension- and conflict-filled process. New knowledge, skills, or attitudes are achieved through confrontation among four modes of experiential learning. Learners, if they are to be effective, need four different kinds of abilities – *concrete experience* abilities (CE), *reflective observation* abilities (RO), *abstract conceptualization* abilities (AC), and *active experimentation* (AE) abilities. That is, they must be able to involve themselves fully, openly, and without bias in new experiences (CE). They must be able to reflect on and observe their experiences from many perspectives (RO). They must be able to create concepts that integrate their observations into logically sound theories (AC), and they must be able to use these theories to make decisions and solve problems (AE). Yet this ideal is difficult to achieve. How can one act and reflect at the same time? How can one be concrete and immediate and still be theoretical? Learning requires abilities that are polar opposites, and the learner, as a result, must continually choose which set of learning abilities he or she will bring to bear in any specific learning situation. More specifically, there are two primary dimensions to the learning process. The first dimension represents the concrete experiencing of events at one end and abstract conceptualization at the other. The other dimension has active experimentation at one extreme and reflective observation at the other. Thus, in the process of learning, one moves in varying degrees from actor to observer, and from specific involvement to general analytic detachment.

In addition, the *way* in which the conflict among the dialectically opposed modes of adaptation get resolved determines the level of learning that results. If conflicts are resolved by suppression of one mode and/or dominance by another, learning tends to be specialized around the dominant mode and limited in areas controlled by the dominated mode. For example, in Piaget's model, imitation is the result when accommodation processes dominate, and play results when assimilation dominates. Or for Freire, dominance of the active mode results in 'activism', and dominance of the reflective mode results in 'verbalism'. [. . .]

Learning is an holistic process of adaptation to the world

Experiential learning is not a molecular educational concept but rather is a molar concept describing the central process of human adaptation to the social and physical environment. It is a holistic concept much akin to the Jungian theory of psychological types (Jung 1923), in that it seeks to describe the emergence of basic life orientations as a function of dialectic tensions between basic modes of relating to the world. To learn is not the special province of a single specialized realm of human functioning such as cognition or perception. It involves the integrated functioning of the total organism – thinking, feeling, perceiving, and behaving.

This concept of holistic adaptation is somewhat out of step with current research trends in the behavioural sciences. Since the early years of this century and the decline of what Gordon Allport called the 'simple and sovereign' theories of human behaviour, the trend in the behavioural sciences has been away from theories such as those of Freud and his followers that proposed to explain the totality of human functioning by focusing on the interrelatedness among human processes such as thought, emotion, perception, and so on. Research has instead tended to specialize in more detailed exploration and description of particular processes and subprocesses of human adaptation – perception, person perception, attribution, achievement motivation, cognition, memory – the list could go on and on. The fruit of this labour has been bountiful. Because of this intensive specialized research, we now know a vast amount about human behaviour, so much that any attempt to integrate and do justice to all this diverse knowledge seems impossible. Any holistic theory proposed today could not be simple and would certainly not be sovereign. Yet if we are to understand human behaviour, particularly in any practical way, we must in some way put together all the pieces that have been so carefully analysed. In addition to knowing how we think and how we feel, we must also know when behaviour is governed by thought and when by feeling. In addition to addressing the nature of specialized human functions, experiential learning theory is also concerned with how these functions are integrated by the person into a holistic adaptive posture towards the world.

Learning is *the* major process of human adaptation. This concept of learning is considerably broader than that commonly associated with the school classroom. It occurs in all human settings, from schools to the workplace, from the research laboratory to the management board room, in personal relationships and the aisles of the local grocery. It encompasses all life-stages, from childhood to adolescence, to middle and old age. Therefore it encompasses other, more limited adaptive concepts such as creativity, problem-solving, decision-making, and attitude change that focus heavily on one or another of the basic aspects of adaptation. Thus, creativity research has tended to focus on the divergent (concrete and reflective) factors in adaptation such as tolerance for ambiguity, metaphorical thinking, and flexibility, whereas research on decision-making has emphasized more convergent (abstract and active) adaptive factors such as the rational evaluation of solution alternatives.

The cyclic description of the experiential learning process is mirrored in many of the specialized modes of the adaptive process. The common theme in all these models is that all forms of human adaptation approximate scientific inquiry, a point of view articulated most thoroughly by the late George Kelly (1955). Dewey, Lewin, and Piaget in one way or another seem to take the scientific method as their model for the learning process; or to put it another way, they see in the scientific method the highest philosophical and technological refinement of the basic processes of human adaptation. The scientific method, thus, provides a means for describing the holistic integration of all human functions.

Figure 9.4 shows the experiential learning cycle in the centre circle and a model of the scientific inquiry process in the outer circle (Kolb 1978), with models of the problem-solving process (Pounds 1965), the decision-making process (Simon 1947), and the creative process (Wallas 1926) in between. Although the models all use different terms, there is a remarkable similarity in concept among them. This similarity suggests that there may be great payoff in the integration of findings from these specialized areas into a single general adaptive model such as that proposed by experiential learning theory. Bruner's work on a theory of instruction (1966) shows one example of this potential payoff. His integration of research on cognitive processes, problem-solving, and learning theory provided a rich new perspective for the conduct of education.

When learning is conceived as a holistic adaptive process, it provides conceptual bridges across life situations such as school and work, portraying learning as a continuous, lifelong process. Similarly, this perspective highlights the similarities among adaptive/learning activities that are commonly called by specialized names – learning, creativity, problem-solving, decision-making, and scientific research. Finally, learning conceived holistically includes adaptive activities that vary in their extension through time and space. Typically, an immediate reaction to a limited situation or problem is not thought of as learning but as *performance*. Similarly at the other extreme, we do not commonly think of long-term adaptations to one's total life situation as learning but as *development*. Yet performance, learning, and development, when viewed from the perspectives of experiential learning theory, form a continuum of adaptive postures to the environment, varying only in their degree of extension in time and space. Performance is limited to short-term adaptations to immediate circumstance, learning encompasses somewhat longer-term mastery of generic classes of situations, and development encompasses lifelong adaptations to one's total life situation.

Learning involves transactions between the person and the environment

So stated, this proposition must seem obvious. Yet strangely enough, its implications seem to have been widely ignored in research on learning and practice in education, replaced instead by a person-centred psychological view of learning. The casual observer of the traditional educational process would undoubtedly conclude that learning was primarily a personal, internal process requiring only the limited environment of books, teacher, and classroom. Indeed, the wider 'real-world' environment at times seems to be actively rejected by educational systems at all levels.

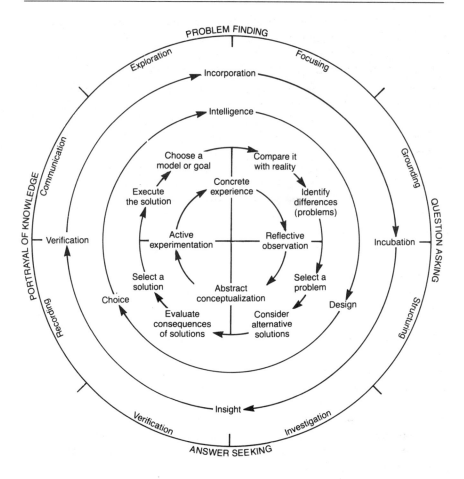

Figure 9.4 Similarities among conceptions of basic adaptive processes: inquiry/research, creativity, decision-making, problem-solving, learning

There is an analogous situation in psychological research on learning and development. In theory, stimulus-response theories of learning describe relationships between environmental stimuli and responses of the organism. But in practice, most of this research involves treating the environmental stimuli as independent variables manipulated artificially by the experimenter to determine their effect on dependent response characteristics. This approach has had two outcomes. The first is a tendency to perceive the person-environment relationship as one-way, placing great emphasis on how environment shapes behaviour with little regard for how behaviour shapes the environment. Second, the models of learning are essentially decontextualized and lacking in what Egon Brunswick (1943) called ecological validity. In the emphasis on scientific control of environmental conditions, laboratory situations were created that bore little resemblance to the environment of real life, resulting in empirically validated models of learning that accurately described behaviour in these artificial settings but could not easily be generalized to subjects in their natural environment. It is to me not surprising that the foremost proponent of this theory of learning would be fascinated by the creation of Utopian societies such as Walden II (Skinner 1948); for the only way to apply the results of these studies is to make the world a laboratory, subject to 'experimenter' control.

Similar criticisms have been made of developmental psychology. Piaget's work, for example, has been criticized for its failure to take account of environmental and cultural circumstances (Cole 1971). Speaking of developmental psychology in general, Bronfenbrenner states, 'Much of developmental psychology as it now exists is *the science of the strange behavior of children in strange situations with strange adults for the briefest possible periods of time*' (Bronfenbrenner 1977: 19).

In experiential learning theory, the transactional relationship between the person and the environment is symbolized in the dual meanings of the term *experience* – one subjective and personal, referring to the person's internal state, as in 'the experience of joy and happiness', and the other objective and environmental, as in, 'He has 20 years of experience on this job.' These two forms of experience interpenetrate and interrelate in very complex ways, as, for example, in the old saw, 'He doesn't have 20 years of experience, but one year repeated 20 times.' Dewey describes the matter this way:

> Experience does not go on simply inside a person. It does go on there, for it influences the formation of attitudes of desire and purpose. But this is not the whole of the story. Every genuine experience has an active side which changes in some degree the objective conditions under which experiences are had. The difference between civilization and savagery, to take an example on a large scale, is found in the degree in which previous experiences have changed the objective conditions under which subsequent experiences take place. The existence of roads, of means of rapid movement and transportation, tools, implements, furniture, electric light and power, are illustrations. [...]
>
> The word 'interaction' assigns equal rights to both factors in experience – objective and internal conditions. Any normal experience is an interplay of these two sets of conditions. Taken together ... they form what we call a situation.
>
> The statement that individuals live in a world means, in the concrete, that they live in a series of situations. And when it is said that they live *in* these situations, the meaning of the word 'in' is different from its meaning when it is said that pennies are 'in' a pocket or paint is 'in'

a can. It means, once more, that interaction is going on between an individual and objects and other persons. The conceptions of situation and of *interaction* are inseparable from each other. An experience is always what it is because of a transaction taking place between an individual and what, at the time, constitutes his environment, whether the latter consists of persons with whom he is talking about some topic or event, the subject talked about being also a part of the situation; the book he is reading (in which his environing conditions at the time may be England or ancient Greece or an imaginary region); or the materials of an experiment he is performing. The environment, in other words, is whatever conditions interact with personal needs, desires, purposes, and capacities to create the experience which is had. Even when a person builds a castle in the air he is interacting with the objects which he constructs in fancy.

(Dewey 1938: 39, 42–3)

Although Dewey refers to the relationship between the objective and subjective conditions of experience as an 'interaction', he is struggling in the last portion of the quote above to convey the special, complex nature of the relationship. The word *transaction* is more appropriate than *interaction* to describe the relationship between the person and the environment in experiential learning theory, because the connotation of interaction is somehow too mechanical, involving unchanging separate entities that become intertwined but retain their separate identities. This is why Dewey attempts to give special meaning to the word *in*. The concept of transaction implies a more fluid, interpenetrating relationship between objective conditions and subjective experience, such that once they become related, both are essentially changed. [. . .]

Learning is the process of creating knowledge

To understand learning, we must understand the nature and forms of human knowledge and the processes whereby this knowledge is created. It has already been emphasized that this process of creation occurs at all levels of sophistication, from the most advanced forms of scientific research to the child's discovery that a rubber ball bounces. Knowledge is the result of the transaction between social knowledge and personal knowledge. The former, as Dewey noted, is the civilized objective accumulation of previous human cultural experience, whereas the latter is the accumulation of the individual person's subjective life experiences. Knowledge results from the transaction between these objective and subjective experiences in a process called learning. Hence, to understand knowledge, we must understand the psychology of the learning process, and to understand learning, we must understand epistemology – the origins, nature, methods, and limits of knowledge. Piaget makes the following comments on these last points:

> Psychology thus occupies a key position, and its implications become increasingly clear. The very simple reason for this is that if the sciences of nature explain the human species, humans in turn explain the sciences of nature, and it is up to psychology to show us how. Psychology, in fact, represents the junction of two opposite directions of scientific thought that are dialectically complementary. It follows that the system of sciences cannot be arranged in a linear order, as many people beginning with Auguste Comte have attempted to arrange them. The form that characterizes the system of sciences is that of a circle, or more precisely that of a spiral as it becomes ever larger. In fact, objects are known only through the subject, while the subject can know himself or herself only by acting on objects materially and mentally. Indeed, if objects are innumerable and science indefinitely diverse, all knowledge of the subject brings us back to psychology, the science of the subject and the subject's actions.
>
> ... it is impossible to dissociate psychology from epistemology... how is knowledge acquired, how does it increase, and how does it become organized or reorganized? ... The answers we find, and from which we can only choose by more or less refining them, are necessarily of the following three types: Either knowledge comes exclusively from the object, or it is constructed by the subject alone, or it results from multiple interactions between the subject and the object – but what interactions and in what form? Indeed, we see at once that these are epistemological solutions stemming from empiricism, apriorism, or diverse interactionism.
>
> (Piaget 1978: 651)

It is surprising that few learning and cognitive researchers other than Piaget have recognized the intimate relationship between learning and knowledge and hence recognized the need for epistemological as well as psychological inquiry into these related processes. In my own research and practice with experiential learning, I have been impressed with the very practical ramifications of the epistemological perspective. In teaching, for example, I have found it essential to take into account the nature of the subject matter in deciding how to help students learn the material at hand. Trying to develop skills in empathic listening is a different educational task, requiring a different teaching approach from that of teaching fundamentals of statistics. Similarly, in consulting work with organizations, I have often seen barriers to communication and problem-solving that at root are epistemologically based – that is, based on conflicting assumptions about the nature of knowledge and truth.

The theory of experiential learning provides a perspective from which to approach these practical problems, suggesting a typology of different knowledge systems that results from the way the dialectic conflicts between adaptive modes of concrete experience and abstract conceptualization and the modes of active experimentation and reflective observation are characteristically resolved in different fields of inquiry. This approach draws on the work of Stephen Pepper (1942), who proposes a system for describing the different viable forms of social knowledge. This system is based on what Pepper calls world hypotheses. World hypotheses correspond to metaphysical systems that define assumptions and rules for the development of refined knowledge from common sense. Pepper maintains that all knowledge systems are refinements of common sense based on different assumptions about the nature of knowledge and truth. In this process of refinement he sees a basic dilemma. Although common sense is always applicable as a means of explaining an experience, it tends to be imprecise. Refined knowledge, on the other hand, is precise but limited in its application or generalizability because it is based on assumptions or world hypotheses. Thus, common sense requires the criticism of refined knowledge, and refined knowledge requires the security of common sense, suggesting that all social knowledge requires an attitude of partial scepticism in its interpretation.

SUMMARY: A DEFINITION OF LEARNING

Even though definitions have a way of making things seem more certain than they are, it may be useful to summarize this chapter on the characteristics of the experiential learning process by offering a working definition of learning. *Learning is the process whereby knowledge is created through the transformation of experience.* This definition emphasizes several critical aspects of the learning process as viewed from the experiential perspective. First is the emphasis on the process of adaptation and learning as opposed to content or outcomes. Second is that knowledge is a transformation process, being continuously created and recreated, not an independent entity to be acquired or transmitted. Third, learning transforms experience in both its objective and subjective forms. Finally, to understand learning, we must understand the nature of knowledge, and vice versa.

NOTE

1 From 'Little Gidding' in *Four Quartets*, © 1943 by T. S. Eliot; renewed 1971 by Esme Valerie Eliot. Reprinted by permission of Harcourt Brace Jovanovich, Inc.

REFERENCES

Argyris, S. and Schon, D. (1978) *Organizational Learning: A Theory of Action Perspective*, Reading, Mass.: Addison-Wesley.

Bronfenbrenner, U. (1977) 'Toward an experimental ecology of human development', *American Psychologist*.

Bruner, J. (1966) *Toward a Theory of Instruction*, New York: W. W. Norton.

Brunswick, E. (1943) 'Orgasismic achievement and environment probability', *Psychological Review*, 50, 255–72.

Cole, M. V. (1971) *The Cultural Context of Learning and Thinking* New York: Basic Books.

Dewey, J. (1938) *Experience and Education*, Kappa Delta Pi.

Flavell, J. (1963) *The Development Psychology of Jean Piaget*, New York: Van Nostrand Reinhold Co.

Freire, P. (1974) *Education for Critical Consciousness*, New York: Continuum.

Jung (1923) *Theory of Psychological Types* (vol. 6 in *Collected Works*, trans. R. F. C. Hull, 1977), Princeton, N.J.: Princeton University Press.

Kelly, G. (1955) *The Psychology of Personal Constructs* (vols I and II), New York: W. W. Norton.

Kolb, D. A. (1978) 'Applications of experiential learning theory to the information sciences', Paper delivered at the National Science Foundation Conference on Contributions of the Behavioural Sciences to Research in Information Science, December.

Pepper, S. (1942) *World Hypothesis*, Berkeley, Calif.: University of California Press.

Piaget, J. (1970) *Genetic Epistemology*, New York: Columbia University Press.

_____ (1978) 'What is psychology?', *American Psychologist*, pp. 648–52.

Pounds, W. (1965) *On Problem Finding*, Sloan School Working Paper, 145–65.

Simon, H. A. (1947) *Administrative Behaviour*, New York: Macmillan.

Skinner, B. F. (1948) *Walden II*, New York: Macmillan.

Wallas, G. (1926) *The Art of Thought*, New York: Harcourt Brace.

Part 3

Learners' experience and facilitating learning

Chapter 10

Access: towards education or miseducation?

Adults imagine the future

Susan Warner Weil

Source: This is an edited version of a chapter in O. Fulton (ed.), *Access and Institutional Change*, Milton Keynes, Society for Research into Higher Education/Open University Press, 1989.

INTRODUCTION

The issue of wider access is but one of many driving forces putting the impact and process of higher education under scrutiny. The following kinds of questions are now the subject of frequent speculation and, more recently, research:

- What are students learning and why?
- In what kinds of learning processes are they engaging?
- What is the quality of their experience?
- How effectively and efficiently are resources being deployed to develop the potential of new kinds of students?
- What kinds of qualities and competences are being developed and assessed, and for what purposes?
- To what extent do flexibility, openness and choice obtain with regard to learning structures and opportunities?
- Do different kinds of students experience the education on offer as 'relevant, useful and enabling'? (Ball 1988)
- Are students being helped to 'learn how to learn', for a changing world in which social relations are more complex, professional authority and the effectiveness of traditional structures are being challenged, and knowledge and information increase at a rapid pace?

[...] In this chapter, students, an increasingly influential group of stake-holders but heretofore often invisible in such debates, consider the impact, process and structures of higher education. Their reflections on issues such as quality and responsiveness derive from their experience of having returned to academic learning programmes. The voices represented in this chapter come largely from those adults who are often at issue in access debates. The literature on adults as learners in higher and continuing education tends to reflect the experience of largely white middle-class adults, often North American, who as students or educators have experienced a great deal of previous formal education (for example, Brookfield 1986, OECD 1987, Woodley *et al.* 1987). The majority who speak in this chapter, however, are adults who have demonstrated their 'ability to benefit' from higher education (National Advisory Body 1984, University Grants Committee 1984) but who have spent most of their lives believing that such an opportunity would never be available for the 'likes of them'. In this, they may be similar to other younger adults who have spent most of their school years feeling like this, and who remain under-represented in British higher-education institutions.

The views represented here come from a multi-site qualitative research study. I have investigated the perspectives of adults who have returned to do some kind of higher or continuing education course (diploma, degree, post-graduate degree, continuing professional development course) after an interval of generally at least five years following the end of their initial education. In this study I was concerned to know if and how their prior learning, within and outside formal education, had a bearing on their expectations and experiences of returning to a formal learning context. Through largely individual depth interviews, supported by participant observation and group interviews and discussions, I enquired into meanings about being a learner and learning during the course of these adults' lives in different kinds of situations within and outside formal education.

Broadly, 32 different kinds of learning situations provide the basis from which these adults reflect on their experiences as learners. Overall, 48 learners participated in the study over the course of 8 research cycles, each involving a different formal learning context. Twenty-three of the total 32 who were interviewed individually, and who therefore provided in-depth learning histories, left school with few or no qualifications. Only 7 in the study had experienced higher education previously.

Thirty-seven in the study were women; 6 were black (Asian and Afro-Caribbean). Thirty identified themselves as clearly working class, 12 as clearly middle class, with 3 unknown. Nine found it difficult to make a distinction, but of this group, 5 felt more working class than middle class.

Six women were followed up, after they completed the diploma at Hillcroft College about which they were first interviewed, and had moved on to university or polytechnic degree courses. At the end of these second interviews, they had the opportunity to reflect upon the transcript of our previous meeting, at which they had anticipated their experiences of higher education. [. . .]

I begin by summarizing the key issues that have emerged from the study. These have mainly been organized around the conceptual formulation of disjunction and integration in lifelong learning, and I focus on these adults' experience of disjunction and integration as it relates to their expectations and experiences of returning to formal learning contexts. I then draw upon a particular aspect of the data, in which participants imagined the future from the perspective of their past needs and experiences as learners. They spoke about the kinds of relationships, learning processes, structures and higher-education systems that, in their experience, would help to enhance quality and responsiveness in higher education, in relation to new kinds of students such as themselves; and these themes are discussed in turn. In the last section I consider some of the implications for those concerned with widening access and suggest that not only structures and processes but preconceptions need to be reassessed.

DISJUNCTION AND INTEGRATION AND THE RETURN TO FORMAL LEARNING CONTEXTS: EMERGENT THEMES

Disjunction and the possibility for miseducation

Disjunction refers generally to a sense of feeling at odds with oneself, as a learner learning in a particular set of circumstances. It is not the result of a cause-and-effect relationship but rather emerges out of mutually interacting influences, as well as past and present experiences of being a learner in different kinds of learning contexts (formal, non-formal, informal; see Weil 1986). A sense of disjunction can be felt to be associated with who one is, where one is, and how one's present experience as a learner relates to previous or concurrent experiences, within and outside the formal learning context. Disjunction can be associated with feelings of alienation, anger, frustration and confusion. In this study it always refers to a sense of fragmentation and involves issues of both personal and social identity.

Disjunction sets up the potential for education and for miseducation (Dewey 1938, Jarvis 1987), depending upon mitigating circumstances from the past and in the current situation. When miseducation results, thus 'arresting or distorting the growth of further experience', the overall sense of identity as a learner (incorporating notions of personal and social identity) can be fundamentally undermined. Certain kinds of social conditions can lead to the damaging effects of such an experience becoming internalized.

Alternatively, by chance, design or conscientious planning on the part of educators, disjunction can be constructively 'made sense of' and managed. This is especially true when various partners in the learning context become more responsible and accountable for what is occurring. This creates the possibility of future actions that can simultaneously compensate for, anticipate and manage disjunction.

There are, however, academic learning situations that, by design, intent, or tradition, afford little or no possibility for individual or collective structured reflection on what it means to learn in that situation or on how the situation might be made more effective. The management of disjunction under such circumstances may be more challenging for some learners. The extent to which adults feel able and willing to cope with disjunction, and the concomitant feelings of isolation and lowered self-worth that can be generated, seems to be tied up with many factors. These include the influences of previous learning and assumptions about education at home and school; experiences of learning and being a learner as an adult within and outside higher education; one's self-concept and overall sense of self-esteem at that time in one's life; the quality of the support and relationships available within and outside the education situation; and the kinds of compensating experiences available at the time in the overall learning environment.

In this study, adults described experiences characterized by a sense of disjunction in relation to the following:

- their expectations of and their initial encounter with the formal learning context (including the level and quality of support offered);
- the degree of continuity between the new learning experience and prior ones, both within and outside formal education;
- their experience of the assumptions and approaches operating with regard to teaching and learning, and the extent to which these jarred with prior expectations and assumptions about learning, based on experience elsewhere;
- the ways in which social differences and power relations were experienced and managed in the learning environment;
- the extent to which core aspects of their personal and social identity felt threatened or at risk in that environment;
- the management of multiple and often conflicting roles (especially for women in the study);
- the impact of contradictions between tutors' private and public stances;
- the kinds of knowledge that were allowed or disallowed as a focus for critical reflection and analysis (for example, experiential, intuitive, practical, propositional; dualistic or contextual and relativistic (Perry 1981, see also Weil 1986));
- the ways in which it was expected that knowledge and knowing could be legitimately explored in that learning situation (such as through logical argument, supported by evidence, or through building and creating knowledge, drawing on sources including learners' experience):
- the nature of the dialogue, relationships and learning processes experienced in the formal learning context;
- the ways in which personal development and change were occurring:

in spite of or because of what was occurring in a particular learning situation.

Integration as equilibrium

On the other hand, integration within this conceptual formulation implies that one's sense of personal and social identity does not feel itself to be fundamentally at issue, or at risk, in a particular learning environment. Integration tends to be associated with a sense of equilibrium, or an 'all of a piece feeling'. Integration does not necessarily give rise to learning itself, but rather helps to create the conditions conducive to an individual learner being able and willing to learn in a particular learning situation. In other words, there is potential for benefit, and for education. Integration thus need not be associated with intensely positive feelings.

For example, adults who have moved in and out of formal learning contexts throughout the course of their lives, and who experience little discontinuity in the assumptions and expectations about learning operating across those various situations, can feel a sense of integration upon entry and in their overall experience of subsequent comparable learning environments. What they achieve in that situation is tied in with other kinds of influences within that context and within themselves (see, for example, Entwistle and Ramsden 1983, Marton *et al.* 1984, Richardson *et al.* 1987, Ramsden 1988).

Integration as heightened self-validation

Integration can also refer to heightened feelings of self-validation, arising out of a particular learning situation. In this study, this sense of integration arose out of the extent to which a new situation compensated for prior experiences of disjunction elsewhere. Alternatively, it emerged as a resolution to disjunction involving some kind of invalidation of previously held beliefs, ideas or meanings. It is within this context that disjunction can be experienced as a constructive starting point for learning. The critical difference between the experience of disjunction as an enabling rather than a disabling experience lies in the kinds of values, purposes and relationships which obtain in the learning situation. A critical factor is the nature of the support available to guide the learner through the sense of confusion and fragmentation generated by the experience of disjunction and which enables him or her to steer a path through it towards significant learning and change. (See also Mezirow 1978, 1985; Perry 1981; Taylor 1986; Jarvis 1987.) In this study, such situations tended to be characterized by the adults concerned as feeling valued for who they were as people, and for their prior experience. Learning entailed active involvement and interrelating. Conditions associated with cycles of disjunction and integration, and indeed an overall sense of integration itself in connection with academic learning programmes, included the following: the active use and appreciation of different forms of knowledge (for example, experiential, tacit, practical, propositional), the making of connections across disciplinary boundaries, and a positive valuing and use of personal and social differences within a group. For many learners in this study, to experience learning situations characterized by such conditions and an overall sense of integration, often served to repair severely damaged confidence and self-esteem, and to compensate for prior experiences of education.

Compensating influences

Alternatively, a relationship with a particular tutor could positively mediate an overall sense of disjunction with regard to that course or learning context as a whole. Others found that experiences of disjunction on a course could be positively mediated by prior experiences (such as access courses, or 'returning to learning programmes') in which confidence had been built, and self-esteem with regard to one's learner identity and potentiality began to develop. Relationships with peers and spouses also played a vital role in enabling learners to make sense of and manage experiences of disjunction. None the less, many of the learners in this study seemed to have required repeated experiences of integration to enable them to feel sufficiently resilient and able to withstand and indeed manage forces which could otherwise damage them. Even then, the path of the development of such resilience and confidence was by no means linear. Certain situations could spiral the learner back into feeling the scars of prior experiences, although in this study no one experienced the feeling of going back to 'square one': earlier experiences that had given rise to a sense of integration had created an internal store upon which to draw when necessary. To survive, and thrive, in academic contexts, however, it seemed that some of these experiences needed to have occurred within formal education.

IMAGINING: EXPERIENCING LEARNING AS 'ALL OF A PIECE'

It would be well beyond the scope of a single chapter to illustrate the many ways in which the concepts of disjunction and integration are grounded in the data. Here, however, I shall draw upon a specific block of material from the study, which was generated in one of two ways. During the course of the initial research cycles, I would often ask participants directly about what they wanted and needed from teachers in higher and continuing education. In later cycles of the study, however, I began to use a role-play approach to get at these needs from another angle. I would ask participants to imagine that I had just finished my Ph.D., was an expert in a particular subject, and that my first teaching job was with adults such as themselves, many of whom had left school with no qualifications and had been away from education for some time. I suggested they advise me as to how I might best approach this challenge, basing their advice on their own experience as a learner in higher education.

Each of these approaches involved participants in a particular kind of imagining process in relation to their needs and previous expectations. In undertaking it, they teased out the kinds of learning situations and relationships that they saw as conducive to integration and thus to the possibility of education rather than miseducation. The role-play approach, especially, helped to draw out issues which most mattered to these adults if they were to feel willing and able to learn in academic learning situations.

The following main themes emerged from the data elicited by these two techniques: the notion of personal stance in teaching and learning; recognizing and respecting differences; 'unlearning to not speak'; the role of relationships in mediating disjunction; and 'learning-in-relation'. Each of these is dealt with below, illustrating from a particular angle various aspects to the disjunction-integration formulation.

The notion of personal stance in teaching and learning

We often speak about teaching and learning as if they were simply a function of subject expertise, skill and method. These adults' accounts, however, illustrate the extent to which for them, the quality of teaching, and indeed of learning, is mediated by the 'personal stance' of the teacher. I use this term in the sense of Salmon (1988, 1989) who suggests that 'the *material* of learning has traditionally been viewed in different terms from those that define the learner' (1989: 231). For Salmon, the metaphor of personal stance lays emphasis on the personal positions of teachers and learners, and how they give meaning to their learning:

> How we *place ourselves*, within any learning context, whether formal or informal, is fundamental. This is not just a matter of 'attitude', in so far as it defines our own engagement with the material; it represents the very stuff of learning itself . . . how we position ourselves towards [each other] in any educational setting . . . is what governs the limits and possibilities of our engagement together, what shapes and defines the material we construct out of that engagement.
>
> (Salmon 1989: 231)

In the accounts which follow, these adults' perceptions and experiences of teachers' personal stances towards them as adult learners are seen as vital to their feeling able to enter into the possibility of education.

For example, Gaynor was a working-class woman in her mid-fifties who returned to do an academic diploma which would enable her to go on to a degree course. She had worked largely inside her home for many years and had little confidence and low self-esteem when she entered Hillcroft College. Speaking within the context of the role-play described above, she implores me (the new teacher) to

> remember what it is like to have no knowledge of that subject at all. I have found that here. I think it is very difficult for the tutor to put themselves in the position of the student who has no knowledge whatsoever, so I think it needs a fairly gentle introduction. . . .

SWW: Anything as to how I introduce. How I relate to students?
Gaynor: I suppose attitude. Not to be patronizing. That's an obvious thing but I think they can slip into that attitude. I suppose that's the same thing as patronizing. Not to stand back as the great authority! —— is very good at it . . . She is marvellous. I don't know quite what it is, but her manner is very good. I think also because she is very prepared to talk about her own inadequacies.
SWW: To show a bit of herself?
Gaynor: Yes and it means she is more someone you can relate to.

[. . .] Rhoda, long unemployed and with little sense of self-esteem or direction, stresses the negative impact of tutors who position themselves towards their material, rather than towards the student. She is describing here the extent to which she had felt progressively silenced by what she had experienced from certain tutors.

Rhoda: They have to be hearing what *they* have to say. I constantly get interruptions which makes me feel, 'Should I be here?' . . . And they are always so busy. I always feel I'm taking up his time.
SWW: What about attitudes?
Rhoda: I always have the feeling with my tutor that he's 'in the know'. He does most of the talking. He should be more laid back and draw me out more.

Frank was a lower working-class man and previously a labourer who read 12–15 books a week, across at least six subject areas. He re-encountered a former teacher whose previous attempts to encourage him at school had been 'too little, too late'. She persuaded him to return as a mature student to an FE college to do O-levels. He did A-levels there also and, after an interval, went on to a polytechnic course. He had, however, consistently encountered structural and attitudinal barriers in his attempts to engage with formal learning contexts. He felt that, during those years of struggle, it was only in political groups that he was able to find the intellectual stimulation and dialogue that he actively craved. Here, he too emphasizes the importance of a personal and social dimension in his interactions with teachers. Unlike many of the women in the above accounts and those that follow, however, he communicates a certain resilience and autonomy in his expressed wish for confrontation and challenge.

> *Frank*: Their responsibility is to point out the central core of the basic theory, to confront you as an individual. You can then decide if you agree or not . . . But they must draw people out. Reach for their potential. Help you to engage with central theory. It is an interactive relationship. This requires knowledge, skills and personal qualities. Also, they must be sensitive to personal problems because these will distort the learning process.
>
> *SWW*: What skills?
>
> *Frank*: An intellectual grasp. A degree of lucidity with which they can explain. Must be evaluated on the extent to which they can facilitate people's interest in and ability to deal with knowledge and their capacity to incorporate within the learning situation the views of the students. Especially the older ones. Which may be in *direct contradiction* and which may *not* be supported with six million academic references, but practical experience.

Fran was a working-class woman who throughout her initial schooling aimed to be a hairdresser. She eventually became a lecturer and teacher in this field, to the amazement of her family, since they had always seen her sister as the 'academic one' and Fran as the 'practical one'. The ways Fran strived to use her intelligence and creativity in each work situation, however, often seemed to put her at odds with colleagues. One summer, after she had left an unsatisfactory work situation, by chance she came upon information about the local polytechnic's willingness to accept adults without A-levels. She enquired, out of curiosity, and was offered a place. She describes running all the way home, in panic and disbelief. She spent the entire summer trying to persuade officials that, if they were willing to give her a grant to study for three years, they could give her one-third that money to set up her own business as a hairdresser. Failing in this, she began at the local polytechnic in the autumn.

Fran speaks about the need for someone 'with communication skills' and for tutors who can 'break into a language that you can understand.'

> *Fran*: If I could understand what they were saying it would be lovely. They need to talk to me and explain it to me. I would expect them to be positive and encouraging. Usually, if you ask a question, you end up with a negative . . . They don't

SWW: use a reinforcing way of learning. They just sit there and rub
up their own ego . . . One thing they need to know is how
to be a teacher. That's the one thing they *don't* know.

SWW: What does that mean to you?

Fran: If I have to sit and take notes for an hour, which is far too
long, I need something that is constructed in a sane pattern.
So when I read my notes afterwards, they make sense to
me . . . They ought to be able to use experience, and break
into the lecture, without feeling you are taking them off at
a tangent . . . They can't convey what they know . . . They
don't connect it with anybody else's subject matter.

I believe Fran and the others highlight the divide that adults can feel
between themselves and their expectations of academic learning situations.
Moreover, her own experience as a hairdressing lecturer, after years of
apprenticeship and training, led her to feel incredulous that teachers in
higher education had preparation only in their subject area.

Recognizing and respecting differences

Adults in the study continually spoke about the importance of being
acknowledged and respected for their differences. The interview questions
constantly revealed ways in which a failure – in actions, not just words – to
recognize and respect their differences could prove a source of disjunction.

Connie was a middle-class woman who had worked entirely inside her
home and had taken primary responsibility for parenting. She reached a
point where she bought an IQ book, because she felt no better than a
'cabbage'. She returned to higher education via an FE college that catered
particularly for mature women returners. This experience had been characterized largely by integration, with continual discovery and challenge
emerging out of the quality of the relationships with peers and tutors. She
found her transition to the polytechnic unsettling in many ways. Here she
emphasizes the effect of different kinds of personal stances of tutors upon
her as a learner. In particular, she highlights a confusion she elaborates in
other parts of our interview: namely, that tutors are adult learners too,
and therefore *how* can they not understand the differences? She speaks
about the need for tutors to

remember that they *too* are mature students and to use that as a way
of relating to mature students. They come with experience. How they
see us affects how they interact. They must be helped to see that. [But
they imply], 'If you're motivated, you'll get it.' Your pressures are seen
as a testing ground. For example, 'You'll be a good [names occupation]'
rather than *realizing* the pressures you are under. I wouldn't want the
structure and the knowledge to be changed. Just to have more time,

and more emphasis on motivation. But sometimes, I just cannot cope. There must be a positive discrimination towards older people.

Todd, a working-class man, had struggled all through initial schooling, feeling out of place in terms of his artistic interests. Throughout his education he had felt pressured to be someone he was not, symbolized by the efforts of teachers to turn him from left-handedness to right-handedness. He left school with no qualifications and went to work in the markets. Before returning to do a degree, he had been both unemployed and a musician, having discovered a relationship with another musician through which he could develop these interests and talents. Here he elaborates on the differences cited by Connie and, like her, stresses the pressures on him in terms of the complexity of his life: in this case, as a musician, as a parent, as one of many in this situation who were not well-heeled financially, and who had anything but the prior learning and life histories of more traditional students. He asserts the need for tutors to recognize

> that we're not just students. We have an outside life too. We suffer the same problems. We're not purely a brain. We're human beings. That's the way it is with normal education. It's not right. But they think they can group us in a lump. Shows a lack of responsibility. Here, they still teach you like you were secondary school. It's the same process: socialize, work, see tutor. But they *must* know about people like when they are starting to flag. Like this guy who was living in a squat and had to take casual work for four weeks. They have to have skills of working with people: diverse people. People who were delinquent, mentally ill. It's not so much they are misfits. There are lots of really clever people. It's just that they should not be treated as if they were academics . . . No one here has asked me what I am going to do, much less what I have done.

Recognizing differences for a number in the study also meant recognizing previous damage and actively repairing confidence, particularly in the case of women. Sally is another working-class woman who experienced redundancy and separation before her return to study at Hillcroft. Initial education for her had been fraught with one trauma after another [. . .] Here she speaks out of her experience of returning to formal education in a women's college where small groups were a key feature of the learning environment. She stresses the importance of recognizing differences in women's pacing and patterning in group dialogue. Once again, the relational aspect of teaching and learning emerges as a central feature:

> I think that is one of the pivots of adult education. *Don't* have too big a group. They will be overawed. If so, some will be quite vocal. You must use them, take their ideas, but don't let them overawe the others.

Encourage those who are quiet. You've got to encourage people to speak, those who are quiet. Don't bully or say, 'What do you think?' I would need time to think about that, but I am sure that there are subtle ways in which you can include people in small group discussion. But the women I know, the women are quite enthusiastic. But the more they get to know you, the more they will open up. I think they are also very afraid of examination situations and formal learning and they have to be very *gently* introduced to this.

Unlearning to not speak

Sally experienced considerable disjunction arising from the contrast between her experiences at Hillcroft, and her university science-based course. In the latter context, she felt an acute sense of fragmentation with regard to the treatment of the discipline, the process of learning, and the underlying assumptions about knowledge and research operating in that environment. Although there was an essential coherence across the latter three, it none the less made Sally feel fundamentally at odds with herself and that environment. The disjunction and subsequent anxiety generated by this situation focused her attention on whether and how she could cope, at the expense of academic achievement. Here she describes the other kinds of forces that can diminish or enhance resilience in a learning situation. She reinforces the findings of previous research (for example, Aslanian and Brickell 1980) that women often return to higher or continuing education at a time of trauma or transition in their lives. Here she speaks again about the need to 'repair confidence'. Her conviction indicates how much she too had spiralled back into self-doubt in her new learning situation (see also Weil 1988):

> I have realized, being at university, young people nowadays are much more confident, but when women get to my age and are returning to learning, usually and not always, it is for a good reason. They've lost their husband through divorce or illness, and they have suffered some kind of traumatic experience and need to make a living and they are very very traumatized. In a delicate state. The only way you can describe it is that. And they need not only the ability to learn, but their confidence building. They need to be able to talk about their worries and fears and they need, perhaps, extra time given to them, because they might find it harder to learn after a big gap.

For Sally, integration entails being actively engaged in a learning process which involves actively relating to others, building on their contributions, and gently nurturing confidence. However, she and others often referred to the ways in which they could feel silenced by an intervention, often male – although few conceptualized it in gender terms, and virtually none in feminist terms. But the sense conveyed is that of feeling 'stopped in one's tracks'. Often accounts of such situations awoke memories of being negatively reinforced for being assertive and speaking with conviction. Such forces had taken their toll on women's sense of self-worth and of possibility as a learner.

Karen is a working-class woman who had worked largely in secretarial jobs, and had eventually found her way to Hillcroft. [. . .] She implies how easily tutors can, even unintentionally, abuse their power to the detriment of the learner. Later, at university, Karen experienced considerable disjunction in the form of a major writing block on a humanities course. Although the method of teaching was largely in small groups, she felt severely silenced by certain attitudes and stances on the part of some male tutors and later a male counsellor. Here, speaking from the perspective of Hillcroft, before moving into this learning situation, she talks about the need for tutors to approach people, 'on a one-to-one basis, a personal basis, not as teacher–pupil':

SWW: What would I need to know about people?

Karen: To be able to assess personalities. To know who can take harsh criticism and the people who need drawing out more. To know the things that draw them out. Know people's names [laughter]. That sounds silly, but if you call people by their names, you get this sort of bridge. But the main thing is to treat people as an adult, rather than teacher–pupil . . . Don't be too harsh in your criticism in certain situations. Not to be patronizing, but put yourself in their position. These women have gone through the same situations as you have. You should approach them on an equal footing, although you are 'imparting the knowledge'. You're sharing it, not dictating it.

Godfrey and Janice also consider the kinds of learning situations that promote their development and learning to fuller potential. For them, issues of personal and social identity, and the experience of differences, are central to the possibilities of education or miseducation. In their learning situation, and in the wider world, the majority group wields a great deal of power and control over opportunity for them and other black people.

Godfrey's description contrasts to some extent with the accounts of the women above, in the sense in which he stresses his autonomy and strength in the face of adversity. None the less, he conveys how a respect for differences and a recognition of the complex social arena within which learning is taking place can be fundamentally at issue for some adult learners. As such, he elaborates themes introduced above. Here, in the context of a group interview, he and Janice talk about what they need to feel able and willing to learn. They describe what they experience when they learn with other black people in comparison with how it feels in an academic situation, where different kinds of judgement and power are operating, especially when they are in a room full of white people.

Godfrey: When I am challenged and criticized by anyone, I feel every part of me is learning. When cornered, for example, on a platform, giving a speech, 1 am all angry and aggressive when I'm at my height. If I'm in a group of people and everyone's against me, I learn most. When I must challenge myself and assimilate what I've learned. Give different interpretations to things. Why, I enjoy people not agreeing with me. Find it beneficial, useful.

SWW: Does it matter who the person is?

Godfrey: I never feel comfortable in a room full of whites. Never relaxed. Always on guard. Automatic. Immune to it. Unconscious. I speak in a particular manner. More passive in the way I present myself. Not if in a group of black people. [Changed body posture, language, phrasing] Whaa . . . [laughed]. More relaxed. It's *me*! [Smiled.] Can curse, do anything. Like when you're angry, revert to your past experience. To learn fully, to be total, must be amongst black people.

Janice: Certainly think you have to be on guard when you are with [white people]. Depends, on position, authority. Must think of that. Must infringe on you as a person, depending on the group you are in . . .

Godfrey: I need respect in my environment for me to learn. Plus a stable psychology!

Janice: I feel much more relaxed with a black community group. Because there, constantly raising other people's consciousness.

Godfrey: Also, at these times, when black people challenge you with something. But if *they* [i.e. white people] challenge you, that is *your* view and this is my view. Just leave it. No drive, no push, no encouragement to continue ongoing dialogue. With group of black people, if someone says, black people are inferior to white, you will argue, say, 'No, no, no.' But in terms of their point of view, will read about it to see where they are coming from. But if white person, will ignore it.

In this account, they engage centrally with dimensions of learning that are at the heart of disjunction and integration. They speak about 'to feel total', 'to learn fully', 'you as a person', 'It's *me*'. They convey the extent to which a certain sense of integration in their personal and social identity must be felt, in a context of constructive support and challenge. They talk about needing 'a stable psychology' in order to derive maximum benefit from a learning situation. Here they suggest the extent to which they have felt it necessary to always be 'on guard' in the learning situation.

Godfrey and Janice experienced a great deal of disjunction on their course, but this was mediated by a number of influences: their opportunities to reflect on their experiences with other black people, both within and outside that learning situation; their relationships with some significant-other peers on their course who could help them to keep in perspective what they were experiencing; their determination to get the piece of paper and more power, whereby they could influence the situation of other black people; and finally, the extent to which at the end of their course, tutors began to engage with them in a constructive process of reflection and showed themselves to be valuing actively the perspectives and experiences they brought to the course. Both were involved in advising on issues of process and curriculum, in order to enhance possibilities for education, rather than miseducation. [. . .]

In these accounts, from those who, not just in terms of age, but also in terms of gender, class and race, have traditionally been under-represented in higher and continuing education, the complexities and struggles in 'unlearning to not speak' become manifest. The possibilities for experiences of disjunction, rather than integration, for miseducation, not education, become clearer.

Mediating disjunction

The possibilities for disjunction can be significantly heightened when some of the sources of disjunction remain invisible to, or are actively denied by, tutors. [. . .] Ethel is another working-class woman who never associated learning with school (see also Weil 1986). She, like many others in the study, found herself on a course at her local polytechnic more as the result of chance rather than design. She experienced considerable disjunction throughout her course, particularly with regard to the emphasis placed on what she regarded as 'knowledge for knowledge's sake' and the extent to which she experienced higher education as an arena where 'they are playing intellectual ping-pong with other people's ideas' rather than creating, originating. Her project work created a kind of oasis for integration, thus playing a significant role in compensating for the disjunction she was experiencing overall: 'My only original work on this course was my research. I loved that . . . From June to March I worked non-stop.' A particular tutor also played a key role in enabling her to manage what she was experiencing.

[. . .] She acknowledges the personal and institutional power that tutors have, and the extent to which this can feel enhanced by the ways in which they choose to use their intelligence. Her account suggests the potentially destructive impact of such power when, for example, the norms of a course, department or institution favour attack and competitive argument as the primary means for 'building people up' intellectually. Alternatively, as in the case of Godfrey or Janice above, such different kinds of power can also combine with social power, something that was at issue for many on the course – particularly when they were confronted with learning situations where there were few people with whom they could socially identify, amongst their peers or the staff. [. . .]

Learning in relation

Women's voices predominate in this study, and in their accounts there seem to be fundamental assumptions about learning that can be at odds with the kinds of assumptions about knowledge or teaching and learning that can predominate in academic learning environments. The themes of 'learning in relation' and learning as a process of making connections recur again and again. For many adults in the study, there seemed to be a vital need to make connections: with one's life, with other disciplines, with issues that personally mattered, and with experience that was both prior to and had also emerged out of that course.

For example, Fran (quoted above) talked about how, in her experience, '[teachers in higher education] don't connect [their subject matter] with anybody else's'. For Fran, subject matter is as much 'in her' and in her experience, as it is in books or in academics' heads. There is nothing in her experience that has taught her to discriminate between these forms of knowledge, or to elevate one form above another. To deny the validity of her forms was to deny the validity of her personal and social identity, and her prior experiences of learning particularly outside formal education. [. . .]

Sally speaks here also from the context of her university course where, as a result of the disjunction she was experiencing she has a heightened sense of the kinds of conditions in which the probability of integration, and therefore of education, is increased:

> I think that one of the first things I would say to a student is that *everything connects*. I had no idea until I came here . . . So if I were a lecturer here, I would ask others what they were teaching so I could make the connections in my mind and then put it over to the students. Because that is one of the first things that amazed me. That no subject is an island. All interconnect and interrelate. And same with the students: they all interconnect and react with each other and need to bounce ideas off each other.

The theme of interweaving – across ideas, subject boundaries and in the context of one's relationships with peers and tutors – is vivid here.

For many of the women, not to learn in relation, and in ways t̖ enabled them to work from and build upon their existing strengths an understandings, was to put at risk a fragile sense of self-esteem. Those kinds of conditions seemed to nurture trust in one's own voice, without feeling that powerful forces would intervene either to silence that voice, tell it it was *wrong*, or revive the feeling that to speak, to write, to create and have access to knowledge in higher education was not really for 'the likes of them'. [. . .]

CONCLUSION

Adult learners do not bring their experience with them into education; they *are* their experience (Knowles 1978). But the answers to the real complexities and challenges of this idea do not seem to lie simply in modular programmes, access courses, distance- or open-learning initiatives, experiential learning or andragogy. They lie in much finer nuances of expressing respect, concern and care for individuals, and in giving priority to the need for adults to build upon and make sense of their experiences within the context of their own and others' 'life worlds' (Wildemeersch 1989).

Issues crucial to wider access – such as impact and process, boundaries and partnerships and institutional structures – gain in meaning when they are examined from the perspective of learners who, in their bones, can feel the interrelatedness of these dimensions to their experience of learning in higher and continuing education. Moreover, probably better than any of us they can see if and when the Emperor has no clothes:

> People may find it hard to accept that their personal models are not the world as it is but are constructed realities and they are not soundly based in absolute truths. When faced with the challenge of [alternative views], people may be unwilling to accept the responsibility which goes along with the acknowledgement that it is *they* that construct their own world views. For many, it is more acceptable to believe that their worlds are imposed upon them by the way things really are.
>
> (Pope 1985: 5)

[. . .] These adults present us with the opportunity to raise fundamental questions about quality and responsiveness from perspectives entirely different from those that usually figure in such debates. For example, to what extent and why do we feel able to assure new kinds of learners of the possibility of education, not miseducation? How do we *know* if we offer to new kinds of students an education that enables, rather than compounds, previous disabling forces: What more do we need to do, and which of our many strengths do we most need to build upon? [. . .]

In these adults' stories, we find the clues as to the kinds of issues we need to address if we are to ensure that wider access remains concerned with more and different students (not just more and the same) and quality for all. By reframing the problems, and by exploring alternative solutions, we may very well create new kinds of pathways to enable those of us in higher education to move with integrity and greater clarity through what may now seem only a tangled thicket of demands from too many stake-holders. And in so doing, many other adults may approach our doorways, confident that here we do not just imagine the future, but here the future is lived.

REFERENCES

Aslanian, C. B. and Brickell, H. M. (1980) *Americans in Transition: Life Changes as a Reason for Learning*, Princeton, New Jersey: College Entrance Examination Board.

Ball, C. (1988) 'What is the use of higher education?', Address delivered at University of St Andrews, 23 February.

Brookfield, S. (1986) *Understanding and Facilitating Adult Learning*, Milton Keynes: Open University Press.

Dewey, J. (1938) *Experience and Education*, New York: Collier.

Entwistle, N. and Ramsden, P. (1983) *Understanding Student Learning*, London: Croom Helm.

Jarvis, P. (1987) *Adult Learning in the Social Context*, London: Croom Helm.

Knowles, M. (1978) *The Adult Learner: A Neglected Species*, Houston, Texas: Gulf Publishing Company.

Marton, F., Hounsell, D. and Entwistle, N. (1984) *The Experience of Learning*, Edinburgh: Scottish Academic Press.

Mezirow, J. (1978) 'Perspective transformation', *Adult Education* (US) 38 (2), 100–10.

_____ (1985) 'Concept and action in adult education', *Adult Education Quarterly* (US) 35 (3), 142–51.

National Advisory Body (1984) *Report of the Continuing Education Group*, London: National Advisory Body.

Organization for Economic Co-operation and Development (OECD) (1987) *Adults in Higher Education*, Paris: Centre for Educational Research and Innovation.

Perry, W. (1981) 'Cognitive and ethical growth: the making of meaning', in A. Chickering (ed.), *The Modern American College*, San Francisco: Jossey-Bass.

Pope, M. (1985) 'Constructivist goggles: implications for process in teaching and learning', Paper presented at BERA Conference, Sheffield.

Ramsden, P. (ed.) (1988) *Improving Learning: New Perspectives*, London: Kogan Page.

Richardson, J., Eysenck, M. W. and Warren Piper, D. W. (eds) (1987) *Student Learning*, Milton Keynes: SRHE and Open University Press.

Salmon, P. (1988) *Psychology for Teachers: An Alternative Approach*, London: Hutchinson.

_____ (1989) 'Personal stances in learning', in S. W. Weil and I. McGill (eds), *Making Sense of Experiential Learning: Diversity in Theory and Practice*, Milton Keynes: SRHE and Open University Press.

Taylor, M. (1986) 'Learning for self-direction in the classroom: the pattern of a transition process', *Studies in Higher Education* 11 (1), 55–72.

University Grants Committee (1984) *Report of the Continuing Education Working Party*, London: HMSO.

Weil, S. W. (1986) 'Non-traditional students in traditional higher education institutions: discovery and disappointment', *Studies in Higher Education* 11 (3), 219–35.

—— (1988) 'From a language of observation to a language of experience: studying the perspectives of diverse adults in higher education', *Journal of Access Studies* 3 (1), 17–43.

Wildemeersch, D. (1989) 'The principal meaning of dialogue for the construction and transformation of reality', in S. W. Weil and I. McGill (eds), *Making Sense of Experiential Learning: Diversity in Theory and Practice*, Milton Keynes: SRHE and Open University Press.

Woodley, A., Wagner, L., Slowey, M., Hamilton, M. and Fulton, O. (1987) *Choosing to Learn: Adults in Education*, Milton Keynes: SRHE and Open University Press.

Chapter 11

Black students in higher education

Verna Rosen

Our picture of our own individuality is built up by our own assessments of others' pictures of us.

D. Bannister and F. Fransella,
Inquiring Man: The Psychology of Personal Constructs

For the last twenty years there has been growing attention given to the low proportion of black people in professional and managerial jobs and to the wide gulf between the measured achievements of white and black students in schools. Concern has been expressed at the under-representation of black students in universities and polytechnics and in 1975, as part of a conscious attempt to improve equality of opportunity at higher education (HE) level, the Access movement began in this country.

THE DEVELOPMENT OF ACCESS

The North London Polytechnic and City and East London College of Further Education, concerned about the lack of applications from Caribbeans for social work training, combined forces. They planned to provide entry into the polytechnic for West Indians and others from ethnic minority groups who showed potential for professional training but lacked the educational qualifications required for admission. The Further Education (FE) College was to provide a year's intensive preparation in the communication and study skills required for academic work and an introduction to the subjects of the higher education course. The students, all black, were to be integrated into the polytechnic from the start with some courses being taught at the polytechnic and by its staff. There was to be no further academic hurdle before entry to the professional course. This first course became the model for a number of Access courses which followed after it, both linked with the Polytechnic of North London and with many other polytechnics and universities throughout the country. Later courses have diverged in form, subject and target group, but all have the same aim of providing access to HE alternative to the conventional school route.

During its development, this access course produced a much more complex picture of the interaction between students and institution than expected and this might provide some clues as to the shortage of black students entering HE. The focus in the preparatory year shifted from study skills training to education/socialization for students, while staff had to learn to adapt fast to a much more challenging group of students than they had known before. It became apparent that people from backgrounds where it had not been the custom to enter into HE had not only to deal, as adults, with a host of practical and family issues and had, as consumers, a more evaluative stance towards their education, but were also locked in intense personal conflict in relation to expectations of the course. There was a powerful hidden curriculum which influenced the way in which people took advantage of the education offered.

Their assumptions about the nature of teaching and learning, based on their most recent schooling – often many years before, possibly not in this country and rarely requiring abstract conceptualization – were all confounded. There was an apparently limitless gap between their starting point and the level required for HE. In addition, they had to deal with a number of ambivalences.

Eurocentric social work content frequently attacked many of their fundamental values, particularly those relating to the family and the very childcare they sought to enter. They sometimes identified with the pathology in the subject matter of the course. Personal counselling was wanted, but suspicion of the power of the white institution held people back from seeking it out. Tutorials, an opportunity to gain some individual tuition, were also a source of anxiety. Who could they trust with their uncertainties without being labelled as failing?

However, in an all-black group, they found themselves able to speak freely amongst themselves in an educational setting for the first time. In mixed-race classes at school they had learned not to explore ideas, especially aloud. On the Access course they began to argue and discover their own powers. They perceived teachers prepared to listen to them and take their ideas seriously. They found themselves changing profoundly and in the process they began to express fear, grief and a new sense of self, but most of all they allowed themselves to vent anger.

The degree and level of anger nonplussed (and sometimes frightened) the staff, who expected initially to devote themselves to the students' 'learning' needs. In fact, tutors were forced to acknowledge the extent to which cognitive and emotional factors interweave by transforming the course to take account of this as much as possible. Experiential learning took a larger part, and space was provided for students and staff together to engage in sensitivity group meetings. Black history and social work issues, including projects in which students presented aspects of their own cultural background became part of the syllabus. Students kept a weekly log of their personal learning development which for many became an essential part of the course. The importance of black role models was recognized and the tutor group began to include non-white teachers.

During the Access course the white staff had begun to get a glimpse of the effects of racism on self-image, and realized that a one-year course could not obliterate those effects. The hope was that students would learn a few more survival strategies and that they could provide mutual support when they entered the less nurturing environment of the polytechnic.

THE RESEARCH

How these students experienced their Access course and their later course of professional training at the Polytechnic of North London was the subject of two sets of interviews:

1 In 1982 when in-depth open-ended interviews were carried out with 21 students, 14 currently on the Access to Social Work course, and 7 from previous cohorts who were currently studying on the professional course (Rosen 1982).
2 Between 1987 and 1989 when a follow-up study of 86 former students, nearly all qualified and in employment, from several different Access courses at the North London Polytechnic (including students from the original Social Work Access course) was set up under the auspices of the North and East London Open College Network and Access to Learning for Adults (ALFA) at the North London Polytechnic (Rosen 1990).

Not all the students in the later research, *Beyond Higher Education* (Rosen 1990), were black but, as mature students, they all had similar experiences of coping with major and often unexpected adjustments to their lives which became integrally involved with the academic process. The method of conducting open-ended in-depth interviews was continued to enable people to raise whatever subjects they wished. The purpose of the interviews was not to focus specifically on the black experience in HE, but rather on what it meant to have arrived in the polytechnic via an Access course. Where race and racism arose they did so because they were raised as issues by the interviewee. Most black ex-students reported racism; few white students mentioned it.

The majority of people interviewed were working-class black women. They talked freely about their expectations and their experiences of higher education and, in doing so, were similar to the students on the Social Work Access course in presenting a picture of domestic, institutional and emotional factors inextricably involved with the learning process.

Most had qualified. All reported similar experiences, describing the return to education as having been exciting, stimulating, 'the best four years of my life', but few said it had been without pain.

A theoretical perspective

What came through strongly from interviews was, first, that it was impossible to separate what people were feeling from what they were learning as they progressed through Access and the polytechnic. Second, the 'aggressive/demanding' stance of students, identified by tutors in both FE and HE was interpreted very differently by students: rather than aggression, they saw it as a reflection of their keen desire to 'get things right', 'to understand the rules', 'to find out what the teacher really wanted', and a reaction to racist teachers. This clash of perceptions caused dissonance and much time was spent by staff trying to identify and deal with the reasons for the anger and depression experienced by many students, the 'hidden curriculum' which could block or enhance academic progress (Snyder 1970).

In *The Hidden Curriculum*, Synder (1970) described:

the dissonances that are created by the distance between . . . formal rules and informal responses . . . and the way that professors and students work out, clarify and discuss the conflicts and issues that are often concealed.

Students must, he suggested:

develop a series of stratagems, of ploys and adaptive techniques to deal with the choices that confront them.

He proposed that:

a hidden curriculum determines, to a significant degree, what becomes the basis for all participants' sense of worth and self esteem. It is this hidden curriculum, more than the formal curriculum, that influences the adaptation of students and faculty.

How students reacted to the hidden curriculum is illuminated by George Kelly's 'theory of personal constructs' (Kelly 1963), which explicitly refuses to differentiate between cognition and emotion and suggests that the self is identified by what it can understand of others. For example, when a person interprets another's behaviour as labelling, the label may be accepted and acted on or may be rejected and fought against. He distinguishes between 'aggression' – 'the active elaboration of one's perceptual field' – which he saw as a creative force, and 'hostility', which he viewed as a block to learning because it makes a 'continued effort to extort validational evidence in favour of a type of social prejudice which has already been recognized as a failure'. This might come about as an 'aware-ness of an imminent comprehensive change in one's core structures', – that is as a result of a threat to one's basic beliefs and values.

How ex-Access students construed the events and attitudes they encountered depended on what they had brought with them onto their courses. Previously, most had experienced either poverty, family disturb-ance or ill-health. Many had constructed a negative self-image for them-selves from being labelled non-achieving, but also were aware of an inner force which compelled them to challenge that label. Black students, in addition, had had to cope with education interrupted by immigration and direct racial prejudice which they had perceived as identifying them as inferior from first childhood encounters with non-black people. Their constructs of those who traditionally entered higher education was of beings capable of almost infinite intellectual facility, but antagonistic towards any outsider entering the white citadel. They had acquired a distrust of white institutions which shackled their progress, however much they wanted education. They were entering unknown territory and feeling their way blindfolded through what they understood to be a minefield, intended to explode their aspirations at the first chance.

Although there were many similarities between the responses of both black and white ex-students (they were mainly both women and working class), in what follows I have used only the 'voices' of black ex-students in order to explore their perspective in particular.

MASKS

First, how the hidden curriculum operated for one 'typical' black ex-student is exemplified in her description of her progress through British education.

Pearl was 5-years-old when she arrived in this country to join her mother and stepfather living in one room in London. By the age of 6 she was taking the baby to the nanny, buying the paraffin, washing the nappies after school to help her mother (soon to have four more children) who was doing a cleaning job to help buy a house. Of her education she says:

> For people in my age group the whole thing was to survive in the system. This led to your being aggressive (because of kids calling you 'nigger' and so on) and then being punished for it. School was very much an escape for me, but for the major part of my primary education I was faced with a lot of hostility from classmates. We lived in a white area. Later we moved to Brixton where I had a peer group to identify with like the foundation year at [the FE college].

> At home you were expected to do well at school but nobody ever

sat with you to help you and say, 'Let's look at what you are doing at school.'

My mother and I were constantly moving – my parents didn't have a very good relationship – so school was a place where I could be a kid really and laugh with my friends. I didn't pay much attention to learning until I left school and entered nursery nursing.

After four CSEs of 'not very good grade', and an NNEB course, she worked as a nursery nurse until she 'felt the need to go on' to train as a social worker. The shock she received on seeing how many O- and A-levels were needed for social work training affected her strongly. 'It suddenly hit me that I had failed and I needed a lot more than I had.'

She entered the Access course and was assessed by staff and the placement supervisor as being an able student, demonstrating new strengths as the Access year progressed.

For Pearl the reality was not so simple. She had found school easy. She explained how, 'a liberal system like this doesn't give school the same importance after a taste of West Indian schooling'. She had been to a Dame school in Jamaica where, at 5, she was beaten for not being able to spell 'carrot'. By contrast, in the London schools:

There was never any follow up except school reports, and mine all said I was a pleasant girl to have in the class. So I didn't get a walloping and told to do better next year as I would if they had said that I wasn't doing well.

On the Access course and at the polytechnic she found the abstract thinking very demanding after what had been expected at her comprehensive school. At the same time she was gaining an exposure to knowledge that revised her whole view of herself. It:

opened up ways of looking at the world that hadn't occurred to me. Psychology went into much greater depth than on the Nursery Nurse course. There was much more going on around me. Before, I had just gone to work, come home, watched television or went to a party, and that was all there was to life. I developed other ways of looking at things, but it cost me. I lost a lot of friends who hadn't the same interests. I compensated with new friends I made on the course. I don't regret it, but there were moments when I nearly left. I felt for months there was a battle going on inside of me between the old me and the new. I had a problem knowing who was what. I began to ask myself which was the real me. It sounds as if I'm going of my head, doesn't it? But especially at the Polytechnic I felt my phantasy was – I was performing – speaking with the right academic language, etc. At home I performed on a different level to my own little world.

At the same time the Access year presented the opportunity to be with like-minded people and to talk about issues that concerned them as black people on a level very different from the superficial conversations with previous friends.

> I shared experiences as never before. I started to watch documentaries instead of *Coronation Street*, and became more conscious of the world. My outlook broadened. In a way it's quite devastating. You wake up suddenly and realize that there are a lot of things going on. Life isn't simple anymore. Sometimes I wanted to turn it all off and revert to my old self-centred little world. You feel as though you have the burden of the whole world on your shoulders.

The FE college had provided:

> a small, nurturing environment in which I felt more confident than in the tutorial groups or lecture halls at [the polytechnic]. Every morning, every time I entered the poly I felt I had to put on a mask. I didn't have that feeling at the FE college. I suppose it was because of the dispersal of the group and suddenly being thrown into various different groups of people from different backgrounds. I remember one incident in the first lecture at the poly. All of us from [the Acess course] sat together. A student, raising a question, used the word 'dichotomy'. None of us knew what it meant. I felt, 'Christ, can I really cope?' How did I cope? Mostly by wearing a mask. You see, the course was about acquiring a certain body of knowledge but also about re-socializing us.

Somewhere around the middle of the second year 'the mask faded'. Until then, the group had remained a coherent unit whose members, 'stuck to each other and didn't make much effort to get to know others', except for two of the three direct-entry black students who had 'gravitated towards our group'. Pearl did not make relationships with any of the non-black students on the course until the second year and then around course information issues, not ever anything personal such as doubts about succeeding with an essay. It was only at this time that she got over the impact of 'dichotomy'. The other students' wider vocabulary had dazzled her. However, as the pressure of work developed, they were asking her for help.

> This tore down the sort of superhuman image we had of them and we saw them as not necessarily any cleverer than us and as having the same problems.

The foundation year group was important in other ways:

> We felt that as a group we had to succeed. There was no question of failing. Therefore we took the course a lot more seriously than white

students. I couldn't understand them sitting in the bar, missing lectures. I couldn't see that as part of college life. Now I feel I missed out – on the wider socialization and wider issues; on the exchange of ideas with people from other courses, other countries. We just focused on getting through. You've got to succeed because this is your chance. We also felt, because it was an experimental course, the course might depend on us.

For that reason too we always felt watched. We always felt we had to turn up to lectures whereas we noticed large numbers of other students didn't.

Initially, although almost overwhelmed by the prospect before her, Pearl had attempted the course, not because she was sure of succeeding, although her previous success in nursery nursing had given her some confidence, but 'out of desperation' for further education. She believed that 'black children are not programmed to succeed' and that while research continued to show black children failing, there would continue to be need for second chance compensatory courses such as the Access course.

In spite of her original lack of qualifications, Pearl's sense of purpose, expressed by her as 'desperation to succeed' had enabled her to become, at the time of her second interview, an Educational Welfare Officer who saw the black children she worked with as 'very much as I was at their age'.

STRATAGEMS, PLOYS AND ADAPTIVE TECHNIQUES

Pearl's story expresses the essence of what most black students experienced. Having responded to the hostility of racism she was early in life branded as aggressive in its negative sense. Her first schools did not meet her needs since they did not understand that the culture of her childhood allowed her to construe school in a way that did not prepare her to reach her potential. The blandness of the school's construct of her as 'a pleasant girl' did not recognize her potential and, like the 'able student' of the Access course, did not enable her to recognize what she needed for herself.

The way her family interpreted her school reports prevented her from receiving the home support she required. The hidden curriculum for her even at that stage was to obtain release from the too early responsibilities that kept her from being 'a kid', laughing with her friends. It is not surprising that she turned to nursery nursing as her first career since it continued her caring role and allowed her to finish her growing up in contact with childhood.

When she perceived that she might now be labelled as a 'failure', her own inner strength, perhaps the 'aggression' she had demonstrated so early, enabled her to respond by action. She sought out education and was fortunate that the Access course, in its second year, was within reach.

The impact of new knowledge transformed her. As she, in Kelly's words, 'actively elaborated her perceptual field' she faced with fear and anxiety the threat both of people who seemed superior and hostile and of changes in the basic constructs she had of herself. The adaptive techniques she used to deal with this situation were 'aggressively' responsive. In spite of temptation, she did not retreat. Her strategy for coping was to put on 'a mask' and to stick close within the protection of the Access group whose shared values provided security in the transition from further to higher education. The importance of the need to relate with people familiar to her is demonstrated by the attraction of the group to other solitary black students who had not entered the polytechnic via Access and who, presumably, felt less comfortable in white groups. Her recognition that the language of white students which had so overawed her was also a mask afforded her some sort of kinship with these alien beings and also an improved self-image, able to compete openly.

However, since masks often covered other masks she could not be sure enough of what she perceived to allow herself complete familiarity. Racism had made an early and lasting impression. She could not permit herself the risk of indulging in wider learning. She had to take what she perceived to be her chance and qualify. Her sense of responsibility also forced her to make sure that entry to higher education should remain open for other black students. The group had a constraining as well as a supporting force.

THE SCENE FOR OTHER BLACK STUDENTS

What then did other black students have to add about their experiences in further and higher education? Largely, they corroborated what Pearl described. Interviews stressed their survival strategies in the face of racism and the importance of having a group of other black students with whom to relate. It is not coincidental that the polytechnic department first to receive Access students now has a very large proportion of black direct entrants.

Personal change

Although people initially expressed a desire to improve life for themselves or their children, or to help improve the black community, the strongest of all motivating factors was, as for Pearl, the 'need to go on' and this became hunger for learning which led many to further degrees after qualifying.

However, most people were not prepared for the changes that internalizing learning would have on them as people. Changing constructs often put strain on family relationships.

> My family told me since I've started social work I've changed. I was annoyed. I didn't feel changed. What was happening was that I was able to explain and talk about things in a different way. My sister was bitter. She said I sounded like a text book. It nearly broke us up and we were very close. I moved (I was staying with her) and since then its been better. My views have changed on women's role in the home and even though I knew I shouldn't say things I did because I felt it was wrong for her to live the way she does. It's probably too late for her to meet these new ideas. She resented the little sister telling her what to do.

This 'adaptive choice' was not easy, but demonstrates the drive for self-development of this student.

Another issue was that of 'going over to the other side', to that establishment towards which they and their communities felt distrust. They feared that they were commmitting a disloyalty, and that this might lead to them being isolated. Perhaps the course would be:

> telling me, a black person, how to become a white middle-class person with that person's way of thinking. I'm not sure where these changes are leading.

Those things which provided their sense of basic identity were under attack by that same education they had seen as bringing them personal fulfilment. A student described her anxiety as the feeling of 'being between two worlds – an inner struggle which no one can help you with'.

Anger

Like Pearl, many wore masks to hide the inner conflict, but some expressed their frustration in the anger which, invading the curriculum both on the Access course and at the polytechnic, overturned course demands for rational analysis. One student recalled how, 'anger about what happens to black kids in court led to a lot of people being upset'. When this anger appeared as hostility, progress was hampered. Students expressed fury at 'racist' staff who, in turn, responded either constructively or with hostility. The latter response compounded the problem.

The assault on personal confidence which racism makes appears a major force to be reckoned with, the effect both on self and others being devastating to the learning process. Thus, how people perceived their reception by staff at the polytechnic was of great importance.

Positive discrimination

Some interviewees accepted (albeit reluctantly) the need for all-black Access courses, after much heart-searching discussion and a degree of resentment at this form of positive discrimination. Here are several of the views expressed:

> If it's the only way in for blacks, we'll take it to get into the system. You can't do anything until you get in and so you might as well use the system as it is set up.

> I wish they had a course like this that was compulsory for black students on all courses. You have time to sort out amongst yourselves all sorts of sensitive areas.

> There's a bond, a commonness amongst us which means you don't have to explain yourself all the time. In a mixed group you have to defend yourself from all different angles, and that is where confusion comes about.

They knew from growing up in this country that there were things they would have, 'to contend with on [any] . . . course. Racial prejudice is not imaginary. It's there and a black skin is not going to disappear.'

Race and authority

Probably most difficult of all for students to handle was the sort of institutionalized racism described by a senior hospital social worker (with a first-class degree in Applied Sociology):

> I'm sure people don't even know they're racist sometimes. For example, if I'm in the department with two junior people talking with someone from outside, I'm talking from management, but instead of going through me the outsider talks to the two junior people until they can't cope and turn to me for answers. The outsider doesn't address me.

Only a person with a strong sense of her own worth must be able to withstand such an attack on her self-image. In this student's case, perhaps it was that she came from a financially secure, loving, professional family and a good education in the West Indies before arriving here to be 'relegated' (she was sure for racist reasons) to the Access course.

Without some strong defence, to be perceived as irrelevant must have a powerful impact on a person's ability to function which may explain why the quality of personal contact with tutors was so important for people who had come from an environment which had largely ignored them.

One student felt that not only was 'learning made easier by friendlier relations with teachers than I had know before', but that this was related to his:

> becoming less frightened of authority . . . I was literally shaking and sweating at interviews, really getting bogged down by the presence of authority which interfered with my exposing my thoughts. Now I'm more open. I'm getting over it. Is this just getting used to the tutors on the course? I was able to have a long conversation with the magistrate after visiting the juvenile court. Before I never would have accepted the invitation into the back room.

He then gave an example of how course and personal life can interweave:

> I'm better able to cope with meeting new people. Even with my own father I'm geting better able to talk to him. He always came over as an authority figure.

Personal tutoring

Students' views on the help they received from tutors came over strongly: it was very positive when referring to the preparation year which had been specially designed for them; often more negative when discussing the need to adapt to the bigger, more impersonal professional course which held sway over their future. Of the Access course one person said:

> I was helped by most staff . . . I felt they were concerned with our getting ahead, [and] did not treat us as a bunch of idiots. This probably helped me to be in a better frame of mind about taking in the academic side of the course by removing a block.

The deep-rooted suspicion of all established British institutions dogged every move, so that what seemed a simple step to those within the system presented mountainous obstacles. This social worker was inhibited from seeking much-wanted tuition:

> I didn't use tutors because . . . I feel as though some of the tutors are really racialist. Their stand towards blacks makes me uneasy. I've got that feeling that they look on blacks as being inadequate, needing a foundation year, and therefore the Poly is doing them a favour . . . It kept me back from going to the tutor to express fears and anxieties, even though I wanted to. I did use the tutors sometimes, but not enough. I [went] to my tutor . . . but I [didn't] feel I [could] confide in her. You can't trust the confidentiality of tutorials – they might use it against you. Because we're at a disadvantage already, this might be increased by their saying we as a group can't cope and this might affect our work.

Such a reaction, paranoid and hypersensitive though it may seem, was common and demonstrated the fragile nature of the trust between staff and students.

However, some did demonstrate trust where there seemed a positive acceptance of their blackness:

> I don't remember most tutors, except those who could understand me as a person, as a black person, and who didn't want to turn me into a white person, who thought what I had to say was important.

The need for personal contact to facilitate learning was often expressed:

> Except for personal tutors there is no one to ask questions of and here the onus is entirely on you. You can be quite depressed if you're not able to ask questions – it can't be conducive to good learning.

Remedying racism

Multicultural and race awareness programmes did not always have the desired effect. Black students who had subsequently become teachers had been frustrated by the missed opportunity of the multicultural input on the B.Ed. course:

> It didn't provide any answers or explain what was happening.

> It should not have been an elective.

> I hoped the multicultural thread would run through everything.

> It shouldn't be separately hived off.

Several commented that a valuable resource had not been made use of, that their 'experience was not taken into account'. One teacher talked of being moved to tears at the waste.

In race awareness sessions, white students, perceiving themselves under threat, disappointed the black students by reacting strongly against the notion that they might be racist (even unconsciously). They had not comprehended that without explicit acknowledgement of black people and their values those people experience a sense of 'not being' while they are with white people. Alienation from the society which does this can follow.

Group support

These students, however, armed themselves against alienation. Collectively they made demands that there be references for them in the polytechnic course. The strategy that they adopted towards the larger, more impersonal institution was to turn to their Access course for support and this became an essential factor in their education. It had provided a learning and emotional resource.

We all help each other find books for essays and start each other off, share notes and so on.

When we went to PNL we met stigma from the staff. We clung to the college group for support throughout, both for course work and for private matters – family break ups, for quite a lot.

It had been a disciplinary force.

If we as individuals don't achieve we'll never hear the last of it from the rest of the group.

It had also been a reinforcing element in bringing difficulties before authority:

We prop each other. I didn't feel I needed the tutor so much . . . only when nobody knew what was going on we went to the tutor . . . one of us went in first and if we still didn't understand somebody else went in and asked. Sometimes the group as a whole went in.

It had, however, been problematic when it hindered self-expression and this had often arisen from focus on the black issue.

I sometimes feel pressured by the group not to speak when I find myself in opposition to others' views. For example when we talk about how black people are prevented by the system from being social workers I think this itself is prejudice. I haven't yet the courage to stand up and say this to the group although I'd dearly love to do so. I don't want to be called white-minded.

On the all-black Access courses students had gained from having confronted their own blackness, impossible to achieve in a mixed group. They had had only other blacks to compete with and had needed to reckon on the responsibilities of their own strengths and face up to learning difficulties in terms of their own individual powers. They had developed new self-constructs.

What it has done is make me more aware of who I am and what I believe and given me a chance to look at other people as well.

When the group had reached the polytechnic, however, it had become a coherent unit protecting individuals from external threat.

We're all responsible for each other now. There's a lot of competition on this course and we don't want anyone to fail from [Access].

Membership of the group not only defended those within it but also endowed its individuals with benevolent power, which, as Pearl discovered, promoted self-growth. Access students were able to act as a chain of information between groups, sharing knowledge and resources with others.

RACE OR ACCESS AS STIGMA?

In talking to these past students it has been difficult to tease out how much their negative experiences have been related to race and how much to the other factors which have affected all students. The same events interpreted in the light of different past experiences were construed differently. Where white students perceived Access stigma, black students saw racism. That institutional racism was indeed present was illustrated by non-Access black students being assumed to be from Access courses by some staff and white students. Those same staff and students were also inclined to construe white Access students as poor performers. Since 'a black skin doesn't go away', black students felt unable to shake off a negative stereotype.

The experience of two African post-graduate science students, not female, with no families to support and not from Access, illustrated that where prejudice exists blackness is indeed an issue. The group construct that identifies black students as low achievers makes them invisible as people. They commented on their isolation as solitary blacks and on the lack of encouragement from former white educators:

> [I was] the only black guy in a class of sixty. Two guys, students, picked on whatever I said or did. It took a while for them to accept me. When I was the only guy with a distinction in Chemistry they realized, 'This guy's brilliant' and we became friends. They were not racist, they didn't know how to react to me. I was the first black guy they'd come in contact with.

> The careers teacher who didn't teach me any subject, was a racist. He said, 'Don't even bother to apply for HE because you won't make the grades in medicine or organic chemistry.' For careers officers it seems that black guys end up in factories and the white guy in the office.

The last speaker had had the assurance to ignore the advice of the careers teacher and was currently working on a Ph.D. at London University.

A social worker, without the personal confidence of the previous speaker whose schooling in an all-black environment had given him a clear idea of his own worth, expressed the difficulty of separating racism from other issues.

> The real evil of prejudice is that it causes confusion in your mind. You've met so many occasions when your own judgement doesn't fit with what happens – in banks or going for jobs and so on – that you

can't always immediately tell when you're thinking straight even about things which aren't to do with being black, so you either keep quiet and go away or you keep asking questions and then you look a fool.

Perhaps what non-traditional students experience on entering higher education is a sense of otherness which is similar for all groups, but the intensity of feeling and reaction demonstrated depends on the degree of intransigence of both staff and students. For some of the staff who express hostility, in Kelly's sense of the word, the threat to their own 'core structures' may be too great for them to be able to perceive the strengths of non-traditional learners very quickly. The evidence from the growth in the Access movement and the success of its graduates suggest that the conventional notion of who is an acceptable and promising candidate for higher education should start to change. If institutions have the will to recognize the force of the hidden curriculum operating for these students, and sufficient resources to implement changes, the students might be able to satisfy their desire for learning without having to experience such pain and anger.

REFERENCES

Kelly, G. A. (1963) *A Theory of Personality: The Psychology of Personal Constructs*, London: Norton.

Rosen, V. (1982) 'The adaptation of students on a special Access course to the demands of a further educational institution', and 'Evaluation of the Diploma in Social Work, including a foundation year of study', MA Dissertations, University of Sussex.

—— (1990) *Beyond Higher Education: A Survey and Analysis of the Experience of Access Students Proceeding Through the Polytechnic of North London and into Employment*, London: ALFA (Access to Learning for Adults. The North and East London Open College Network).

Snyder, B. (1970) *The Hidden Curriculum*, Massachusetts Institute of Technology.

Chapter 12

Teaching learning
Redefining the teacher's role

M-J. Gremmo and D. Abé

Source: This is an edited version of a chapter in P. Riley (ed.), *Discourse and Learning*, London and New York, 1985.

The operations of any teaching and/or learning system involve a number of different tasks and roles which have to be shared out between the different components which make up the system. In systems based on a traditional structure (teacher and group) it is the teacher who performs the majority of the tasks and who takes on most of the roles: he is, therefore, the main component in the teaching/learning situation. However, recent research into applied linguistics, into the psychology of learning and into psycholinguistics has underlined the importance of the *learning* process as such, serving as a useful reminder of the fact that it is really the learner who is the essential component in any pedagogical event. If we accept, therefore, that we should now try a more learner-centred approach, what happens as regards the distribution of the various tasks and roles?

Instead of studying the activities of the teacher and those of the learner as separate realms, we thought it would be more worth while to try to investigate in detail just what the tasks are which have to be carried out in a teaching/learning situation and what the roles are which cluster around the two poles of the system: in other words, the nature of the tasks and their importance in the learning situation should help us define the respective roles of teacher and learner. To do this, we will use as examples three types of learning system, all of which are in operation at present at the Centre de Recherches et d'Applications Pédagogiques en Langues (CRAPEL) at the University of Nancy.

The first, and best known, of these systems is the *traditional course*: at the CRAPEL this is often referred to as 'evening classes' simply because they are given to adults who come to study English in the evenings after work. The point being made here is that evening classes take place at regular intervals and involve a group in a classroom with a teacher. It is this organizational structure which is traditional.

The second system we will be talking about is the *self-directed group*.

This system was an experiment run as part of the activities of the Université du Troisième Age et du Temps Disponible de l'Université de Nancy II (a 'university' within our university, for people who are retired or who simply have some spare time). In this case, the learners are provided with classrooms, equipment and material, but no teacher is present during their working sessions.

The third system we operate is that of *self-directed learning with support*. In this system, the learners do not belong to a group: they mostly work alone or, occasionally, in pairs. The teacher provides them with documents when they have none of their own and discusses their learning programme with them. Because this system tends towards the acquisition of autonomy, we call these learners *autonomes* (independent learners) and, to simplify matters, we will use the term *autonomy* when discussing the tasks and roles in all three of these systems.

In what follows, we are going to try to list the various tasks which have to be performed in any learning programme under three headings: the first section will deal with those tasks which have to be performed during the *planning* or *preparatory* stage of the learning programme. The second section will discuss the operations carried out during the actual learning sessions. Finally, we will touch on the psycholinguistic or psychological aspects of learning.

PREPARING TO LEARN

This first section deals with tasks which have to be performed before undertaking any teaching/learning programme. Four such tasks will be discussed here:

1 Collecting information about the learners' motivations and about those aspects of the external situation which incite them to learn a language;
2 The analysis of these data, to determine learning objectives and the content of the learning programme;
3 Information concerning the facilities provided by the institution;
4 Decisions concerning contents, methodologies and modalities.

Information concerning needs

One of the first tasks is to obtain information concerning the needs, expectations and linguistic knowledge of future learners. This information has to be reasonably exact, because it will be used as a basis for determining the learners' programme of action. It will concern those factors which incite the participants to learn a language. These needs can be of several types: 'professional' needs, such as looking after a foreign visitor to one's firm; 'personal' needs, such as a journey abroad; 'psychological' needs, such as wishing to get out of a rut; or 'social' needs, such as wanting to meet people or do something.

Before establishing a learning plan, it is also interesting to know the learners' linguistic history: whether they have already studied the foreign language and, if so, in what circumstances; whether they have already learnt a foreign language and, if so, what they thought of that way of learning, etc.

A further type of information to be sought is in clues concerning the learners' image of the language which they are going to learn: do they see it as a stock of words, as a set of grammatical rules, or as a tool for communication in real situations?

Analysing the learners' needs

Once the learners' needs and their conception of them has been elicited, they have to be analysed, to decide on learning objectives and on the content of the learning programme. It is rare for all members of a group to have the same needs: even if one manages to group together all the people having the same apparent need – travelling abroad, for example – one finds that some are going to England, others to the United States, some will stay in hotels, others with friends, some will go by plane, others by car, etc. We therefore need a set of categories which will allow a more detailed analysis. These are provided by functional criteria, which allow us to break down the long-term objective into a series of intermediate objectives. For example, an analysis of the needs of all the learners we have just spoken about will probably show that they all need to ask for information, to thank, to ask people to repeat what they have said or to speak more slowly when they have trouble understanding them, etc.

Information about the learners' needs, about the facilities made available by the institution and about criteria for bringing the two into line makes it possible to tackle the essential phase in preparing a teaching/learning programme: decision-making. The choices will include short- and long-term objectives; which skills to practise (written/spoken comprehension, written/spoken expression), the type of language to be studied ('specialized' or 'general'); registers and levels of language to be studied; the type of competence aimed at (linguistic and grammatical or communicative competence); methodology (will a particular progression be followed or will activities of different degrees of difficulty be mixed?; will just one course be used or several?; will there be structural drills or more creative activities?, etc.). A choice has also to be made of materials and documents (will they be authentic or not, will they be related to the real-life situations in which the learners are going to find themselves?) and of the types of evaluation to be employed.

Information about the institution

If the teaching/learning process is seen as an interaction between the two essential elements, teacher and learner, it seems natural to expect an exchange of information between these two elements. It should be possible, therefore for the learner to obtain detailed information about the facilities made available within the teaching institution. Generally, learners who are taking up some course of study want to know how many hours of classes there are per week, what the total length of the course is and when and where it will take place. Only relatively rarely do they ask questions about how their learning programme will be realized: is it going to be a highly structured course, or a miscellany of exercises and activities in 'general' English? Is the course grammatical rather than functional? Are authentic materials used, or have the documents and recordings presented in the course been specially created for language-learning purposes? Does the system provide the possibility of conversations with native speakers, or are all the models non-natives?

Decisions, decisions

There are a considerable number of decisions which have to be taken before beginning any learning programme. Until recent years, it was the teacher who performed this task. This is true of our evening classes, for example, where the decisions are taken *before* the learners arrive. We offer them a course in general English, which is advertised as such. Naturally, at the beginning of each course the teacher discusses their needs, motivations and objectives with the members of the group; but this is done to see if any members of the group are there under a false impression, to make everyone aware that a compromise involving some sort of common core is necessary in such a situation and to describe the CRAPEL's methodology. The teacher leads the discussion as and where he wants (indeed, the description of the methodology usually comes as quite a surprise for the majority of the participants).

However, our experience with the Université du Troisième Age and the independent learners has shown that learners can carry out this investigation themselves if given the chance. In the case of the independent learners, in fact, this is vital, since the system is centred on them. Some independent learners only have to be asked 'Why do you want to learn English?' for them to give a detailed analysis of what we in our jargon call needs, motivation, priorities, level of competence, etc. Of course, not all of them are ready to make all these analyses; their previous experience of learning has conditioned them to the idea that all this is part of the teacher's domain, which is why few of them ask questions about the teaching methods to which they are going to be exposed. This is above all because they lack the necessary information; some of them have no criteria for analysis whatsoever. The teacher's role in such a situation is to provide those criteria. This is usually done in the course of interviews with them, though it is perfectly possible to imagine it being done in writing, using informative questionnaires, lists of suggestions, etc. The aim of this operation is to make the learner aware of his own motivations, to help him determine his objectives and thereby to integrate him further into the teaching/learning process.

What, then, are the roles of the teacher during these opening phases? In the traditional approach, exemplified here by our evening classes, his role is one of *producer*. He is the person responsible for carrying out the different steps we have just mentioned, constructing his programme on the basis of the various kinds of information which he obtains. But this information is only one of his sources: he also has his own ideas as to what makes a 'good' course, a 'good' teaching method, a 'good' teacher and as to what type of language to deal with first. All this helps him to accomplish the task of decision-taking that we have looked at: the methodology or methodologies, timetables, programmes, etc. He is the one who organizes, who decides.

What happens, though, if these tasks are performed, even if only partially, by the learners, as is the case in the other learning systems available at the CRAPEL? The role of the teacher becomes that of consultant expert. Instead of taking the decisions himself, that is, he gathers as many tools as possible to enable the learners themselves to take these decisions in the most favourable conditions. For example, he will gather questionnaires, checklists etc. to help learners identify their objectives. He thus plays the role of a research officer whose job is to make available the greatest possible variety of methods (in the widest sense) so that the learner can choose. He also makes himself available to the learner so that he can help him make his choice.

THE LEARNING SESSIONS

In this section we are going to discuss those tasks which are performed during the sessions when the teaching/learning actually takes place.

Material tasks

As any teacher knows, an hour's work with a group can be very demanding: we distribute handouts, set up equipment and operate it, write on the blackboard, distribute more handouts, go back to the blackboard, get out the tape recorder – we hardly stop. It is rare for one of the participants to offer to work the tape recorder, for example. In the Université du Troisième Age, though, the participants do all these things without the slightest problem: they collect their equipment and their materials and operate the equipment without any help from a teacher, except, perhaps, at the beginning when the teacher may have explained how to use the equipment or have given a few suggestions as to the different ways of using a tape (for example, learners do not always realize that they can rewind several times to help clear up comprehension problems).

In our evening classes, it is not unusual for the teacher to ask one or more members of the group to operate the equipment: he may also stop writing on the blackboard, leaving this to the members who wish or feel the need to do so. This is an admittedly naïve but none the less fairly effective way of inviting the learners themselves to take part in the material tasks, so that the teacher goes from being a sort of head technician to being just one operator among others.

Transmission of knowledge or a skill

Apart from the purely material tasks, a certain amount of knowledge (or a skill) has to be transmitted. As it is usually the teacher who possesses the necessary linguistic and methodological knowledge, he is the one who has the privilege of playing the roles of linguistic informant and methodological expert. In a traditional course the teacher is the one who knows the target language best; he is the one who is supposed to speak it best and he is also the one who knows the tricks of the trade for sharing this knowledge. Not only the teacher, but also the learners see things this way: this is doubtless the reason why learners often regard the teacher as a walking dictionary or grammar, asking him for the equivalents of words in one language or the other and getting him to spell out and explain the rules of syntax of the target language.

There used to be some justification for this attitude. When there were no tape recorders, the only linguistic informants available to learners were the teacher and the textbook. Between them, these two were the only sources of the target language with which learners were ever confronted, and for this reason the learners naturally took the teacher as their model. Nowadays, however, the teacher is not the only one to give out linguistic information: the mass media often publish or broadcast in foreign languages, and exchanges, journeys abroad or contacts with foreigners are frequent, so that learners have a wide variety of sources available to them. Neither is the teacher the only informant available as regards vocabulary: information concerning the workings of the target language can be obtained not only by listening to a teacher's explanations but also by studying authentic materials and using them to locate unknown elements of grammar or vocabulary. The teacher's role changes from knowing everything and explaining everything to showing where the information can be found and how to obtain it: he is no longer the sole linguistic model; he is a *guide* to different types of discourse. In a sense, his role is teaching people how to use a dictionary.

Obviously, the teacher will continue, where necessary, to give out grammatical, lexical or functional information. But he is no longer the only informant, he is one among many. In those learning systems where the teacher is not always present, it is obvious that he is there as a last resort when all the learners' other attempts to solve their problems have failed; but even in these cases, the learner will use a native speaker as his informant where possible.

Another of the teacher's 'traditional' tasks is to arrange for learners to practise using what has been or is to be acquired: he therefore uses all sorts of exercises to encourage his learners to express themselves in the foreign language. His objective is to get his learners to 'communicate', that is, to simulate real life as it exists outside the classroom. But as Riley (1977) has shown, almost all classroom interaction and communication goes via the teacher and even those learners who were supposed to be practising or inventing their own dialogue addressed the teacher, not one another, so that the teacher was even obliged to manage their turn-taking for them. In such circumstances, it can hardly be claimed that the teacher stimulates communication between the members of the group: in fact, his presence along is enough to short-circuit it, because he is seen as a leader and because the learners keep turning to him.

To free himself from this role, the teacher can either use a large number of authentic materials as 'informants' or he can arrange for the participation of native speakers with whom the learners can practise under more realistic conditions. A third possibility is to form subgroups, he himself withdrawing from the group and leaving the members to practise directly with one another. This is how the members of the Troisième Age groups and our 'autonomous' learners manage to communicate without the help of a teacher (who simply is not present) but with the aid of documents and native speakers. The teacher's physical presence has been replaced by other factors so that satisfactory communicative exchanges can take place.

The second task which has to be carried out in the construction phase of a teaching/learning programme is to choose a set of working methods. The initial exercise has to be chosen; a choice of materials has to be made; the pace of the exercises has to be decided on. What proportions of the work will be devoted to studying documents and to memorization, or to the use of authentic materials and processed documents? How will the time available be distributed in terms of rest and work periods? Will any time and work be given over to revision, or will it be a matter of ploughing straight on?

Here, again, it is usually the teacher who makes these decisions. But things can be ordered otherwise. For example, the autonomous learners and the Troisième Age groups are able to choose their materials and methods themselves. In self-directed group learning, the learners usually study documents provided by the teacher, some of which have been processed, some not, different groups having different preferences in these matters. Some groups bring along their own documents. Work on authentic documents, whether provided by the teacher or not, calls for a choice of working technique, which, in turn, may or may not be copied from the teacher or from teaching materials. Autonomous learners, on the other hand, almost always take these decisions for themselves; if they use materials recommended by the helper, they also use their own. And, of course, they also decide when they are going to work, how long for, how often and the progression which they are going to follow. This choice is made on the basis of two essential criteria: their own personal tastes, and efficiency as regards the achievement of the objective in question. They usually proceed by trial and error. The teachers' role here involves helping with the identification of analytic criteria, advising on methodology and providing materials.

Evaluation

Different aspects of the teaching/learning programme have to be evaluated while it is actually under way in order for the necessary steps to be taken for the following part of the programme. It is not enough just to plan a programme, or even to carry it out: there also has to be a continuing process of assessment, to see whether or not objectives are being achieved.

In what ensues, we will be following Holec (1980) who argues that the evaluation process includes two different operations: the first is evaluation of the quality of the learner's performance in the foreign language; is it correct or incorrect with respect to the objectives originally chosen? For example, if the objective in question is to be able to ask for information on the phone, the learner needs to be able to assess his performance once it has been realized, using criteria such as 'Was I reasonably fluent? Were my sentences grammatical? Did the person I was speaking to understand what I was asking? Was I polite enough?', etc.

The second kind of operation involved in evaluation is the interpretation of this assessment. Here, criteria such as satisfactory/unsatisfactory come into play: 'Can I improve my performance, or is that my limit for the moment? Do I want to be able to speak like an Englishman, or will that do for me, even if it wasn't perfect?'

If the performance is judged to be satisfactory with respect to the objective in view, the learner can consider that that part of his learning programme is complete and move on to the next point. If not, he has to decide whether to go back and start again. If he does go back, he is then faced with the choice of working method: is he going to work in the same way as before, or choose another? When the teacher is present during the learning sessions, he decides what is and what is not satisfactory: it is the teacher who makes the learner repeat, go back and start again when something does not seem to have been properly learnt – and the learner is quite content to let him do so. Often enough, though, the teacher does it without knowing if the learner is satisfied with his performance or not (and the learner then accepts the teacher's judgement).

Now, clearly, it is the learner and *only* the learner who can decide if *his* objective has been achieved or not. The criteria for evaluation in terms of correct/incorrect can be provided by his interlocutor's behaviour: 'Did he ask me to repeat what I was saying? Did he seem impatient? Did I get an adequate reply? Did he seem to think that I'd got a word or sentence wrong?' By basing his judgements on the reactions of his interlocutor the learner becomes an evaluator. Obviously, self-evaluation means that the learner must have certain points of reference.

The role of the teacher is not to be the one and only point of reference, but to provide the means of comparison. As we have already mentioned, native speakers (who are not teachers) or other members of the group can also help in discussing these matters. Similarly, the teacher can also provide criteria of analysis for the learners' performances: the rhythm, speed, intelligibility, communicability, grammaticality acceptable to the interlocutor as regards expression. For comprehension, the criteria for analysis would probably include: global or detailed comprehension; ability to understand the main words or get the gist; understanding at first hearing or after several attempts; whether a script was needed or not; having recourse to an outside form of evaluation (using the script, for example) or relying on a subjective impression.

To sum up this section, then, we can say that the teacher's contribution is not necessarily limited to participation in the learning activities. His role is to create conditions which are favourable to the learners' being able to take over those different operations which are necessary in any learning programme.

PSYCHOLOGICAL FACTORS

In this section we will be discussing psychological and psycholinguistic aspects of the learning/teaching programme. In addition to the tasks which have already been discussed, there remain a number which, by their very nature, are more difficult to observe. They include the learning process itself, the stimulation which is necessary if learning is to take place and the encouragement which is given at certain points during the learning programme. Finally, we will be discussing group dynamics.

Psycholinguistic factors

First let us consider the psycholinguistic factors. The aim of the numerous tasks which have been mentioned above is to create the conditions necessary if the learner is to be able to learn. The ultimate task of any teaching/learning situation must be the acquisition of knowledge. Only the learner can carry out this final operation. Previously, it used to be believed that, provided the teacher gave a good lesson, the learner would learn the information it contained. Research in psycholinguistics has shown, though, that this is anything but the case; in fact, between the moment when the teacher provides the information (input) and the moment when it is assimilated by the learner (intake), a number of cognitive phenomena occur about which we still know very little.

This problem is aggravated by the fact that the only way in which we can measure the intake is by measuring the output, that is, the information which the learner returns. As we have little idea what actually goes on in the human brain, it is difficult to know exactly what information should be given in order to achieve a satisfactory intake and, therefore, a satisfactory output. In any traditional course, obviously, the teacher makes use of an approach which he believes will facilitate this acquisition or intake. If the learner's way of learning does not correspond to the methodology envisaged by the teacher, however, he either learns nothing at all or spends a great deal of time trying to understand and to acquire the teacher's techniques. One way in which this problem can be solved is by offering the learner a wider variety of choice. As he proceeds by trial and error, the learner is more likely to come across the method which suits him best. This is how the autonomous learning scheme works: not only is there methodological variety, but there is also a variety of materials and English speakers. Most learners choose to try out a number of different materials and methods of working during the same period.

In self-directed group learning and the evening classes, a wide variety of authentic materials of every kind (tapes, slides, video, etc.) is used. The structure of the class also varies, as do the exercises, and the teacher makes sure that this variety is kept up. We have also noticed that, in the intensive courses we organize, the learners usually enjoy the fact that there is a great diversity of materials, teachers, methods, etc., even though they may be rather wary of this approach to start with.

Here, again, the teacher sees his role changed: if he is a believer in one particular methodology, he has to accept the fact that certain learners are just not going to 'click' with him. On the other hand, if he wants to be able to deal with a wide variety of learners he has to become an adviser on methodology.

Psychological factors

Other more specifically psychological phenomena are also encountered in a teaching/learning situation; there is the problem of *motivation*, which is known to play an important role in the learning process, and there is the support given when learners are discouraged, which the teacher often considers as one of his most important tasks.

Motivation

In traditional courses, one of the teacher's roles was to provide learners with external motivation by doing activities they enjoyed, so as to make learning attractive. [...]

The situation is different, though, where adults are concerned: most of the time they are not obliged to follow the course or even to learn anything. None the less, in the evening classes, the teacher continues to try to stimulate his learners: first, simply by offering a regular course at fixed times, but also by being friendly with them, by organizing activities which they enjoy, and so on. In self-directed group learning, the teacher may also stimulate learners' motivation by means of the materials and exercises which he suggests, but motivation comes more from the group itself. In the autonomous learning scheme, the teacher's role in stimulating external motivation is reduced to a minimum, since it is up to the learners to contact their helper when they need him: there is no longer anyone physically present to make them work, so if they are to continue at all they need a high degree of internal motivation. It is here that the teacher can help prepare the learner psychologically, by showing him that a learning programme has to be constructed and that this is an activity in which he, the learner, has a crucial role to play.

A further psychological factor is related to the fact that a teaching/ learning situation is one where individuals establish relationships with one another. The effects of these contacts as far as learning is concerned may be either positive or negative. In those structures where a teacher is present, every participant either has or would like to have some sort of privileged relationship with him. If the impression the teacher makes on the learner is not a good one, however, instead of stimulating learning he actually becomes an obstacle to it. If an evening class group does not like its teacher, it will learn less or even nothing at all. In the autonomous learning scheme, on the other hand, if the learner and the helper do not get on particularly well, it does not really matter since clashes of personality have less direct influence on the learning programme: the work and acquisition is done far away from the helper, while in a traditional group the learner is more or less condemned to learn in the teacher's presence.

Similarly, an individual learner's motivation may be either stimulated or inhibited by the other members of the group. Some learners refuse to join the autonomous learning scheme because they like the company of other people. Some like to study without having to follow along with others or to talk with them. To satisfy these different requirements, the institution has to make different learning systems available.

Support

Observation of almost any kind of learning session will show that a good part of the teacher's time is taken up with 'supporting' the learner – congratulating him on his performance or his progress, for example. Learners tend to be rather sensitive at such times for two main reasons: the first is the inequality which exists between the one who knows and the one who doesn't know. The second reason is that the learner is reorganizing his cognitive system and it is known that during such periods the assimilation of new elements can have an upsetting effect on the individual, he even seems to lose part of the knowledge he had previously acquired, and this phenomenon of regression is often accompanied by periods of depression. The other members of the group may increase or decrease the individual's degree of discouragement. The learner may find his own performance inadequate when compared to other members of the group, or he may find that they are not getting along any faster than he is, a discovery which encourages him. In any case, the teacher is continually trying to upgrade learners' opinions of themselves by complimenting them on their performances and so on.

We have not yet been able to identify who provides support in self-directed learning groups.

In the autonomous learning scheme, as our recordings of the interviews between learners and helpers clearly show, this was one of the helpers' most frequent tasks. The helper does not automatically praise the learner's performance, but when the learner's self-assessment is a negative one, he tries to reassure him by stressing the positive aspects. He does this not by saying 'What you are doing is fine', but by getting the learner to compare his present state with what he was like earlier, as well as by helping him find ways of altering his programme so that he feels he is making progress.

Organizing a group

Another of the teacher's roles, and a preponderant one, is that he is the leader of the group: he is the one who is responsible for its cohesion, the one who sees to it that everyone is at their ease, who smoothes over the differences between the members, who sees that the course is properly organized and who distributes speaking turns.

The Troisième Age groups usually choose a leader, sometimes several, who take it in turn.

In the autonomous learning scheme the task of leader also occurs, but in a slightly different form, during the interviews between learner and helper. Very often, it is the helper who plays the role of leader, organizing the interview by introducing the different topics for discussion and changing from one topic to another. The recordings of these conversations are important to us because they bring out the learner's attitudes to the teacher as well as enabling us to study their respective roles in the conversation. We have observed that these roles vary from interview to interview and even within the same interview. At times the learners seem to take the initiative, and if in fact this is the case it seems reasonable to hypothesize that they can take the initiative in their learning programme.

This leads to the conclusion that the role of leader is not necessarily attached to the teacher, and that any learner can play this role, provided the teacher gives him a chance.

CONCLUSION

Our purpose in listing the tasks which are necessary in any learning programme was to show that these tasks are not obligatorily and exclusively the province of either the teacher or the learner in their mutual interactions. It can be seen that the tasks which were traditionally carried out by the teacher can just as well be done by the learner. The teacher is no longer the one who does things, but the one who helps other people to do them. [. . .]

These two types of responsibility – doing and helping to do – are not mutually exclusive. They are the two poles of a range of possibilities – possibilities which determine a variety of teaching/learning systems. What is important, in our view, is the fact that this analysis allows both teacher and learner to become aware of just what sort of learner and teacher they are and of their pedagogical personality, and to decide just what sort of system suits them best and what roles they are willing to undertake within that system.

REFERENCES

Holec, H. (1980) *Autonomy and Foreign Language Learning*, Oxford: Pergamon Press.
Riley, P. (1977) 'Discourse networks in classroom interaction: some problems in communicative methodology', in *Mélanges Pédagogiques*, Nancy: CRAPEL.

Chapter 13

Developing learning skills in vocational learning

Sylvia Downs

THE NEED FOR LEARNING THROUGHOUT LIFE

That change is happening and that the rate of change is accelerating has been accepted for some time. This is mirrored in many of the jobs around us; much work that was previously done manually or by basic machines has now been automated and computerized. Therefore, methods such as Taylorism – the analysis of manual movements to determine the most efficient way of doing a job – have become largely obsolete.

As part of research into helping adults become better learners (Downs 1985) a number of people and organizations in industries that were subject to change, or who were concerned with a number of industries across a broad spectrum, were approached. All were asked what changes had occurred or were occurring and the effect these changes had on training. The replies, summarized in Table 13.1, show the increasing importance of conceptual thinking and understanding in jobs which are changing from rote tasks to monitoring what is going on, fault finding, understanding the system and taking immediate remedial action if problems occur.

Allied to the changes in the nature of jobs is the fact that instead of people staying in one kind of job for their whole working life, they are now likely to need to learn different job skills to ensure continuing employment. This is apart from the interest that mental activity affords the individual. But why the emphasis on learning and not training? The answer is summarized in these two statements: *People do not have to be trained in order to learn. People often learn in spite of the training they receive.*

Training, in those situations where it is necessary, is essentially a means to an end – that is, to bring about learning. However, it is evident from many sources that training does not always bring about the right kind of learning, indeed that some people learn *in spite* of the training they receive rather than because of it. The dazzling potential of the new technologies in training and the excitement that is generated may distract attention away from achieving the right kind of learning, and substitute a preoccu-

Table 13.1 Changes and implications for learning and training

Previous	Present	Implications
Labour intensive	Capital intensive	More value added by people
Mechanical systems	Micro-electronic systems	More conceptual learning
Training in physical skills and procedures	Learning of systems; learning of social skills	More conceptual ideas, less procedural and manual learning
Faults easily diagnosed but often lengthy to repair	Fault diagnosis difficult, repair often speedy	Cost effective attitude to fault finding; importance of diagnostic skills
Established machinery	Prototypes	Experts must become trainers
Time-served training	Training to standards	Modular training to specified objectives with measures; systematic training

Source: Derived from Sylvia Downs, 'Retraining for new skills', *Ergonomics* 28(8), 1985, pp. 1205–11.

pation with the efficiency of the new technologies of training. The hardware and the software should be subordinate to the need to achieve the right kind of learning, and not the other way round. It is sometimes said that we should start with the training need and not with the technology. We should, in fact, start further back. We should start with the learning needs.

What is meant by developing skilled learners? The concept and the techniques for developing more skilful learners described here come out of research – first at the Industrial Training Research Unit at Cambridge, and subsequently at the Occupational Research Unit of the University of Wales Institute of Science and Technology (UWIST). The early research was funded by the Department of Education and Science (DES) and later by the then Manpower Services Commission (MSC). Both bodies were interested in finding ways of making learning processes more effective – not by concentrating on training methodology but on what trainers *actually* do when training, and on the ways in which people actually learn. One of the early findings in the research was that there is a wide variety of ways to learn, but that many people use only a very small number of them. It was found that poor learners were not only passive and put the responsibility for learning onto others, but also had few and sometimes inappropriate strategies for learning (Downs and Perry 1982). Skilled learners tend to use a greater number of methods than less skilled learners, and are able to choose a method that is suited to the type of material to be learned; be it memorizing a telephone number or understanding how tides occur. Part of the reason why poor learners found learning to be a stressful activity was because of this confusion over the distinction between facts and concepts. The research showed that people could, through appropriate exercises, increase the number of methods of learning open to them and choose appropriately between them. Experimental studies showed that, as a result, they could transfer learning more effectively to new situations than had previously been the case. By becoming more conscious of the processes of learning, and by understanding that it is not a homogeneous activity, the trainees became more skilled learners.

A simple model was designed to distinguish the different learning requirements of:

1 Facts which need to be memorized (M).
2 Concepts which need to be understood (U).
3 Physical actions which need to be practised ('doing') (D).

Each of the three aspects of the resultant mnemonic, MUD, was amplified to show the kinds of strategies involved. (In a later section, we look at how ICI implemented this model in their training.) Of the three aspects, 'concepts which need to be understood' is of growing importance because of the changing nature of organizations and everyday life.

WHAT PREVENTS US LEARNING?

One often hears remarks such as 'I was never any good at maths' or 'that is a closed book to me'. Both sentences show an attitudinal problem to learning, which may or may not be a self-imposed blockage. Sometimes, there is an air of almost self-congratulation about aspects of non-learning. Some men, for example, seem incapable in a kitchen and some women claim not to know the rudiments of engines. This could well be owing to stereotyping; if one has a sense of pride or distinction in not knowing, believing that this gives social acceptance, then the learning blockage is very difficult to overcome. Many blockages, however, are caused by fears and worries which, if one can allay them, allows learning to take place.

In research into adult learning (Downs and Perry 1987), a list of learning difficulties was compiled from critical incident interviews with long-term unemployed people and with participants in two different series of courses on learning, one of which was in a large company and the other in a Skill Centre; from relevant literature; and from the researchers' past experience. These learning difficulties were used to provide the basis of a conceptual model of blockages to learning (see Figure 13.1). As the figure illustrates, blockages were first divided into those that learners can influence (or have more control over) and those they cannot. Even in this latter case, an acceptance of what is lacking or obtrusive is a first step towards dealing with these problems. Often there is an emotional reaction to difficulties,

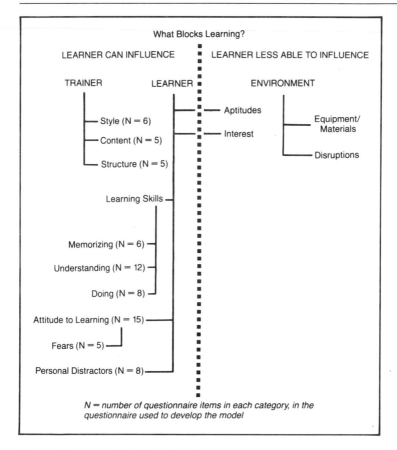

Figure 13.1 A model of learning blockages

which transfers the blame for not learning on to extraneous factors, rather than dealing with the question, 'Do I want to learn or not, and if I do, how do I proceed by overcoming the problems?'

There are three major categories which the learner can influence:

- learning skills (represented by MUD);
- attitudes (fears and worries);
- distractions.

A further aspect that the model suggests the learner should be able to influence is that of training style, content, and structure. This strikes at the heart of the trainer-learner relationship. Traditionally, the learner is seen in a subordinate and dependent relationship to a trainer, not in a dominant role. But a trainer, in effect, only exists so that the learner can learn. If learners cannot do so, they have every right to insist that the training should change so that they can learn.

Passivity towards learning and transferring responsibility for the learning on to someone else are interrelated and can often be the major blockage. The effects are often exacerbated by teachers or trainers being protective or impatient of poorer learners. In the research the poor learners found learning a more stressful activity than did other students and being taught an irksome experience. Frustration builds up towards a rebellion and resentment against learning and, by extension, those they hold responsible for the learning.

In a study of learning blockages, Timmer (1984) found that 65 per cent of a group of unemployed people believed that the trainer was responsible for learning. Timmer found strong inter-correlations among various kinds of blockages in this group, notably between the perception of responsibility for learning and negative aspects of the style used by trainers, such as going too fast, not explaining things properly, being impatient and using jargon. Timmer described a 'communication vacuum' where learners do not ask questions or give the trainer feedback because of their belief that they are not responsible for learning.

The starting point, therefore, may well be a failure from an early age to be shown or develop effective learning strategies. This could well lead to attitudinal blockages which prevent a re-evaluation of learning skills or strategies, and the wholesale transfer of responsibility on to someone who was assumed could make sense of learning.

PRODUCT AND PROCESS

The comparative failure of some groups in terms of learning, and the effects this often has in the form of learning blockages, might well be avoided if parents and teachers were aware of different ways of learning and were able to encourage them. If, however, these people do not themselves know what helps learners to learn, obviously an enormous task of re-education is necessary. The questions needing answering are:

1 To what extent is a conscious awareness of learning methods encouraged by teachers/trainers?
2 To what extent is any failure to encourage the development of these methods due to a lack of knowledge on the part of the teacher/trainer?
3 Where there is such a failure, would training in how to develop ways of learning help teachers/trainers?

A research (Downs and Perry 1984) was commissioned by the then MSC to answer precisely those questions. The Youth Training Scheme (YTS) was faced with the problem of developing the potential of a large number of young people, often described as 'low achievers', in a work-based learning environment. They were instructed by supervisors whose main experience of teaching was having been traditionally taught, often some years ago.

The scheme aimed to provide learning opportunities in six broad areas, one of which involved learning to learn, skill transfer and skill ownership. All these required learners to take responsibility for their own learning and to increase the number of ways they knew how to learn so as to select the most relevant for a particular learning need. In order for trainers to be able to help learners in this, they naturally must know how to be selective about learning processes themselves.

The research began by observing a number of supervisors training their trainees. (The intention was to observe forty, but – as often happens in research – it was eventually only possible to study nine.) The results of the observations are given in Table 13.2, and it was felt that:

1 the instructor behaviour described in columns 1–3 helps develop learning skills while also teaching about the product;
2 the methods described in columns 4–6 also teach about the product and impart some learning skills;
3 the instructors who base their training on the methods described in columns 7–9 are likely to promote passive learning behaviour and are most unlikely to help develop learning skills.

One supervisor in particular used training methods which helped trainees to develop learning skills. The majority, however, used methods that promoted product-oriented, task-learning behaviours, and were only marginally helpful in developing learning skills. Furthermore, four out of nine supervisors used methods which actually inhibited the development of learning skills; two of them used these methods sometimes, and the others used them all the time.

Apart from the sewing supervisor, the rest all too often used show-and-tell as a predominant training method. They decided when and how to give help, corrected trainees' mistakes, did the complicated parts for the trainees, and finished off the task to the desired standard. All this behaviour takes away decision and responsibility from the trainees and makes them dependent, passive and subordinate – characteristics directly contrary to the perceived needs of industry.

It may well be that the supervisor in YTS had no idea about methods which would help trainees develop their learning skills while at the same time learning about their product. If this were so, a short familiarization might be all that was needed to help supervisors use those methods which would allow trainees to improve their learning skills and by so doing, be better able to learn other things: in other words, to improve their transferable process skills of learning.

To test this out, a number of managers, training officers and senior supervisors were asked to think of a supervisor who they thought was

Table 13.2 Incidences of behaviour observed between supervisors and trainees during half-hour periods

Craft	Super-visor	1 Trainees correct own mistakes	2 Thought provoking questioning	3 Trainees work from model sample alone with guidance	4 Trainees work on task after being shown it	5 Trainees left alone without guidance	6 Supervisors do task or part of task – especially crucial parts	7 Supervisors correct trainees' mistakes	8 Supervisors ask checking questions	9 Supervisors write on blackboard and trainees copy
Sewing	A	2	5	3						
Machine shop	B				1	1	2			
Upholstery	C				4		7	2		
Bricklaying theory	D									1*
Cooking	E				2	1	5			
First aid	F								3	1*
Upholstery	G				4		5			
Machine repair	H₁			3	3		6		3	
Manufacturing	H₂				1					

Key: *Continuous behaviour lasting over half an hour.
H₁ and H₂ refer to one supervisor who was observed on two occasions.

good at helping trainees learn for themselves. The sample group was then asked to give incidents of behaviour to justify the choices. These were combined where statements were very similar and listed for frequency. Those with a very low frequency were omitted and finally a list of eighteen behavioural statements was obtained:

1 Supervisor tries to avoid letting the trainee make mistakes.
2 If trainee suggests there is another way to do a task, the supervisor asks him or her to try the new way out.
3 When trainees make mistakes the supervisor tells them what caused them.
4 Supervisor repeats things many times.
5 Supervisor leaves trainee alone if trainee is trying to work something out.
6 Supervisor gives the trainee a project to design and when it is finished the supervisor marks it right or wrong.
7 When the trainees ask a question the supervisor does not answer directly, but gives them hints so they can find the answer themselves.
8 Supervisor gives help to trainee when trainee is puzzling over a task.
9 Supervisor tells the trainees in great depth the skill they will have to learn.
10 Supervisor praises every step that a trainee completes even if sometimes it is not up to standard.
11 Supervisor begins to demonstrate a task and asks trainees to say how they think it ought to be done.
12 Supervisor always tells trainees what is wrong with a machine so they know how to mend it.
13 Supervisor continually helps trainee when trainee is trying to do something.
14 Supervisor explains in detail to avoid trainees having to ask questions.
15 The supervisor asks trainees to try things out for themselves and to ask questions when they need help.
16 Supervisor sometimes deliberately lets the trainees make mistakes so that the trainees themselves can correct them.
17 Supervisor ignores some mistakes the trainee makes if they are not considered very important.
18 When trainees make mistakes the supervisor corrects them so they can carry on with the task.

Each statement was put on to a card and supervisors and trainees in training workshops were each given a pack, from which they were asked to select eight which, in their opinion, were most effective in helping the trainees to learn for themselves.

Table 13.3 shows the results for trainees and supervisors. Although there was a fairly high level of agreement between the two on what are

Table 13.3 The cards chosen by the trainees and supervisors

Card no.*	Chosen by trainees (%)	Chosen by supervisors (%)	Trainees' most often chosen cards	Supervisors' most often chosen cards	Trainees' least often chosen cards	Supervisors' least often chosen cards
1	27	25				*
2	61	88	*	*		
3	68	75	*	*		
4	18	31			*	
5	64	75	*	*		
6	20	25			*	*
7	59	50	*	*		
8	56	88		*		
9	43	19				*
10	23	50		*	*	
11	61	38	*			
12	52	19			*	*
13	20	6			*	*
14	11	6			*	*
15	75	62	*	*		
16	39	41				
17	16	6			*	*
18	43	25				*

Note: The sample involved 16 supervisors and 44 trainees.
*As listed on page 214.

effective methods of teaching, there were some interesting cases where the views diverged. The supervisors felt that they should praise every step that a trainee completes even if it is not up to standard; the trainees, on the other hand, generally considered this a worthless approach. Whereas the trainees approved of the supervisor beginning to demonstrate a task and asking trainees to say how they think it ought to be done, the supervisors did not see that with the same degree of importance.

Some cards were not often chosen; the trainees tended not to like the supervisor repeating things many times, and most supervisors did not entirely approve of telling the trainees in great depth the skill they would have to learn.

Overall, what variation there was seemed to have arisen from an over-protectiveness on the part of the supervisors, who wished to praise in order, as they saw it, to encourage, and not to overload with information. Apart from this, the main message was that both trainees and supervisors recognized behaviour which would help the development of learning skills, but both accepted the absence of such behaviour in the training. It seems that both the groups shared a perception that training was about being taught a product and had nothing to do with the processes of learning. This view is widely documented by, among many others, such observers as Knowles (1980), Smith (1982), Cheren (1983), and Harri-Augstein and Smith (1982).

Most, if not all such writers concerned with learning autonomy, point out that many problems are caused by the effects of learned behaviour. What is pertinent for one situation, such as school, may or may not be pertinent for another, such as work. It may be that school environments and behaviours should be modified towards the next environment, whether that is, hopefully, academic pursuit or employment. If they are not, it is left up to the individual to be capable of perceiving the differences and adapting rapidly to any new environment and its demands.

Accordingly, a questionnaire was developed to find out if people have the capacity to perceive the needs of different environments, or indeed if their previous school experience had already prepared them for the work environment (see Figure 13.2). The impetus behind this research was a large number of complaints by managers in industry that young entrants were either stupid or lazy because they sat around until told what to do; they did not ask questions when they did not understand something; they did not check their work; and they were quite happy with a degree of error. It seemed that the school behaviours identified in the 1982 report (Downs & Perry 1982) were being carried over into the work environment; young people still saw learning as someone else's responsibility and that the role of learner was to accept passively being told what to do and when and how to do it. These attitudes and assumptions made unlikely any decisive action either by employers or employees to change views and behaviours.

Most of those who co-operated in answering the questionnaire found it helpful, stimulating and interesting. It was of less use where discussion, for a variety of reasons, could not take place. The questionnaire stimulates initial discussion, and could be a useful adjunct or introduction to other activity. Many young people entering work find the change of environment and attitudes bewildering. Where error has in the past been expected of them, they now have to learn that error of understanding, fact, or procedure could have disastrous effects. Where they expected to learn by themselves, they are now often part of a work team in which knowledge and learning must be shared. Where they lacked responsibility for anything outside attending school, they may well now be expected to take action on their own initiative if they see something needs doing.

Preparing for these changes is an important preliminary to work and a problem area is where teachers and trainers reinforce, however unwittingly, those attitudes that are fitted to learning at school. It is likely that the more these are reinforced, the harder it could be for young people to adapt to learning in a work environment.

A number of recent school-leavers were asked what differences they saw in learning at school from learning at work. The following are some examples from their large response:

- At school you are hardly asked for your opinions and ways of doing things.
- At school there is a social gap between teachers and pupils.
- At school you can get away with not listening.
- School loads the emphasis on getting a good mark.
- Higher standards and self-discipline are expected at work and you have to push yourself a lot more.
- At work your job depends on learning, not just passing.
- At school you are treated like children and manipulated like puppets.

The emotional and mainly unfavourable response these learners had to school could well be a reflection of the difficulty they had in adjusting between two very different environments. It seems that a beneficial role that schools could play would be to introduce students to the different environment school-learners will eventually face.

The 'learning at school and work' questionnaire aims, in this respect, to act as a starting point, first – where necessary – for teachers to understand for themselves the difference in environment, and second, for them to reinforce the message embedded in the questionnaire by preparing learners for the work environment they will face in the future.

Finally, it must be repeated that the questionnaire is intended to help young people change their concepts, which can only happen if their ideas

	Agree	Disagree	School or work
1 Asking questions means we have not been listening			
2 We need to grasp the total picture as well as learning the parts			
3 Learning is aimed at increasing our capabilites			
4 Teachers and trainers are responsible for assessment and feedback			
5 When we do something wrong we can always correct it or do it again			
6 We learn only from teachers and trainers			
7 Thinking about our own experience is an important part of understanding			
8 When there is a lot to learn, it is sensible to focus on what we might be tested on			
9 The best way to understand something is to memorize it			
10 What we learn is of value to us as individuals			
11 It is important to ensure that we cover everything that needs to be learned			
12 If something is learned incorrectly the results can be costly and dangerous			
13 Teachers and trainers provide the discipline for learning			
14 Learning takes place everywhere			
15 We cannot do anything about the content and style of the tuition			
16 Asking questions disrupts the group			
17 We should find ways of getting feedback on what we have done			
18 Asking questions is helpful and important and often helps other people to learn			
19 We learn from everyone			
20 Asking questions is a good way of checking			
21 Teachers and trainers are responsible for what, how, and when we learn			
22 Sharing knowledge is cheating			
23 The effect of learning incorrectly is that we get less marks or fail exams			
24 We must all share our knowledge			
25 The main purpose of learning is to obtain qualifications			
26 We judge the value of learning something against whether we can use it			
27 Asking questions shows we are stupid and people might laugh at us			
28 We are responsible for our own learning			
29 The sensible way of learning is to break it down by subject, such as geography, history, mechanics, and electronics			
30 We should assess our own work or arrange for someone else to assess us			

Total school score _____

Total work score _____

Total   30 _____

Figure 13.2 Readiness to change in response to changes in the environment: the 'learning at school and work' questionnaire

about the individual statements are discussed, ideally in a group of peers. The questionnaire will have little or no value if it is merely used as a test and scored without any discussion taking place. This would do nothing but reinforce what many view as 'school behaviour'.

DEVELOPING LEARNING SKILLS

Self-help

The research on learning blockages indicates that learners have, sometimes, to accept that instruction will be imperfect and it is up to the learner to make the best of it. Thus, trainers can be questioned and even told that they need to explain something more clearly, or go a little slower, or let the learners try to puzzle things out for themselves.

A great deal of learning, however, lies outside formal teaching or training. Research in 1988 looked at the ways effective learners – judged by success in their jobs – learnt, and the resources they used in cases where they were not being formally taught or trained.

To obtain the information, thirty-eight interviews were conducted with three groups as follows:

Group A: People such as researchers, consultants and senior civil servants who are constantly having to cope with new learning in their jobs (N = 14).

Group B: People who not only have to cope with new learning but also are in jobs for which no formal training is normally given. This group includes broadcasters, professors, head teachers and editors (N = 12).

Group C: People in jobs where they are expected to learn for themselves with a minimum of help, such as supervisors and founders of small businesses (N = 12).

A draft interview structure was designed and piloted, covering questions on each person's background history, as well as why they learned and how they went about their learning.

At the start of each interview the following points were made:

• We are interested in anything you have learned for yourself, such as a sport, a language or a hobby as well as things within work.

• We are particularly interested in *how* you went about learning something rather than *what* you actually learned.

• Confidentially will be maintained for individuals and their organizations.

• The purpose of the interview is to glean ideas which will help other people to learn.

Those interviewed included 25 men and 13 women. The mean age was 42 years with a scatter from 28 to 62 years. Of the 38 people, 12 did not have a degree, 14 graduated at around the age of 21, and 12 graduated as mature students (see Table 13.4).

Table 13.4 Characteristics of groups

Groups	A	B	C
Male (numbers)	9	9	7
Female (numbers)	5	3	5
Mean age (years)	46	42	38
Youngest (years)	30	28	28
Oldest (years)	62	52	54

General points which emerged from the interviews included the following:

1 There were 72 common ways of learning mentioned across all three groups, despite the scatter of academic achievement and the very different level of jobs people did. These ranged from a hairdresser who had established his own salon and a person who carried out a home ironing service on the one hand, and on the other, an editor of a well-known journal and a senior professor at the London School of Economics. Some of these approaches are shown in Table 13.5 as an indication of the range.

2 Effective learners have a great range of ways of learning at their disposal and each has a preferred order of using these ways when approaching something new. Some, for example, immediately seek people in order to talk through their learning, while others have to formulate ideas to an advanced stage before they will discuss them. This appears to relate to other people's work on learning styles (Honey and Mumford 1982), and reinforces previous research conclusions that it is necessary to introduce people to a wide range of ways of learning so that they can select those which suit them best.

3 While all respondents could readily identify periods in their lives when they had learned a lot, none had consciously thought about his or her own ways of learning and all had great initial difficulty in articulating their learning processes. This was equally true, both of academics and those with lesser qualifications.

4 Most of these learners pointed out that they rarely set out to learn things and they stressed the need for some important external happening to force them to begin learning, such as having children, buying one's first house, promotion and starting a new job.

5 Learning arises from an awareness of one's own shortcomings, or an awareness that others can see one's shortcomings or from others pointing them out.

6 Some suffered fears and inhibitions about asking questions which often needed strong motivation to overcome; self-confidence engendered by practice was quoted as a major help in overcoming inhibitions, which otherwise acted as a significant barrier to learning. This was particularly true of the reluctance to ask supplementary questions of people.
7 There was a wide degree of agreement about certain important areas, such as learning from mistakes, getting realistic rather than comforting feedback from people, or reducing the pain of this by assessing oneself before checking this out with another person.
8 Learning is largely a social activity. There were virtually twice as many responses about how people were used as there were about the use of any other resources. The people being turned to were often not experts, but sympathetic, trustworthy persons who were available, such as members of one's family, friends or colleagues at work.

Table 13.5 How do you get started?

	A	B	C*
1 Collecting small bits of information – break into parts	✓	✓	✓
2 Follow a model, using actual words or actions before modifying for oneself	✓	✓	✓
3 Start with simple concepts, or easy explanations, before building on them (e.g. start with simple text books)	✓		✓
4 Experiment with drawing on past experience	✓	✓	✓
5 Hang on to what you know and try out new bits	✓	✓	✓
6 Setting deadlines	✓	✓	✓
7 Setting priorities for what has to be learned and developing a programme. Working out what, when, where and how you will learn it	✓		✓
8 Recognize gradual assimilation and plan for it by lists	✓	✓	✓
9 Learn the meaning of jargon/technical terms	✓	✓	✓
10 Discipline through rewards (if no intrinsic reward)	✓		
11 Observe initially without making value judgements	✓	✓	
12 Be prepared for discomfort	✓	✓	✓
13 By actions other than reading	✓		✓
14 Ask very simple questions even if they look stupid	✓		✓
15 Make sure you understand as you go along	✓		✓
16 Assess who can best help you	✓	✓	✓
17 Experiment with new equipment so that you can make mistakes when it does not matter			✓
18 Do not get feedback too early	✓		
TOTAL	17	10	15

*Occupational groups listed on p. 219.

It is possible that effective learners have radically different ways of going about things which account for their success and the absence of which account for the lack of success in low achievers. However, comparing these three groups of effective learners with people in previous research, it appears there are no such radical differences. What differences there were centred on a general approach to practice in learning and their use of many different ways and resources.

It is probable that what made members of the sample effective learners was their constant need to learn in their jobs, which included research, senior management, consultancy and setting up new businesses. All were practising conceptual skills such as comparing, associating, relating, deducing and judging. They used a variety of ways or strategies of learning, but most of these had been recognized in total within groups of less effective learners. The major distinction therefore lay in the assiduity of the practice of learning skills. The distinction would be immediately recognized by, for example, skilled golfers who need constantly to practise a combination of physical and conceptual skills.

Belbin and Belbin (1972) pointed out the importance of practising skills when they said 'the boiler operators who had participated in any form of education or training since leaving school, did better in their theoretical examinations than those who had not, even though they were no better in their practical work'.

Helping others

It is obviously very helpful if the conditions of learning, where this involves teachers or trainers, can be shaped from the point of view of the learner, rather than, as often happens, learners having to do the best they can in circumstances not all that conducive to learning: The research done with supervisors shows how ingrained are traditional approaches to training. If social, industrial, and market changes are slow there may be an argument that traditional methods can adapt gradually and thus keep in step. Where change is rapid, variable or accelerating, traditional methods become more and more out of step with what is needed. At the same time, the desire to cling on to what is known and well-practised makes people take up entrenched positions. Where a gulf is small, adjustments may be easily made; where a gulf becomes significant, the changes needed are fundamental and often unacceptable to those entrenched. At this point, artificial distinctions are often thought up to defend positions. In industries, for example, technological changes have affected many organizations:

- Job delineations are blurring and job contents frequently changing.
- There is more need for the formation of teams and teamwork.

- Individuals are taking more responsibility for their own safety, quality of work, planning and self-discipline.
- Hierarchical structures are breaking down, leaving less levels.
- Formal training is being modified towards an emphasis on learning on the job from experts, peers and line management.

When such changes are taking place, many activities in organizations that were previously often separated now become merged. Trainers, for example, are now often consultants to line managers, whereas before they often used to perform a discrete function. Part of their advice is about how to carry out training which encourages the responsible, proactive work-force needed, rather than training methods which tend to cause a passive, subordinate learning climate. This often requires a re-education of both trainers and line managers, not because they are necessarily adamantly against the changes, but usually because they are trained in a traditional form of teaching and training. The following example of ICI and its application of developing skilled learners shows this re-education in action.

ICI and Developing Skilled Learners

The process began when a personnel specialist at ICI came across Developing Skilled Learners (DSL) at a conference. The approach was discussed and subsequently a trial workshop was run for a small number of divisional managers. The workshop was necessary as it had been discovered that unless the processes of DSL were experienced, many managers confused what they thought of as good training practice with Developing Skilled Learners. It was a shock to some of them to realize that a great deal of good training actually prevented the development of skilled learners, even though it was efficient in getting people to learn specific things. The ICI Agricultural Division had decided that the changes it needed to make depended on the work-force transforming itself into adept flexible learners and that DSL fitted into their model of change.

A further workshop was organized for twelve selected trainers so that they could experience the DSL techniques. The twelve would then be charged with disseminating the concepts and methods throughout the division. The novelty of the DSL approach lies in both method and in content. The changes in content stem from paying as much attention to how we go about learning (that is, the processes) as to what we learn (the product). Traditional training concentrates mainly, and sometimes solely, on the product.

DSL introduces the simple mnemonic MUD (mentioned briefly at the beginning of this chapter), which divides learning material according to different ways we use to learn it. Exercises are introduced so that learners discover different ways of memorizing (represented as the M of MUD).

Gaining understanding (U) is helped by thinking of reasons or purposes in what one is trying to understand; beginning with a definition of the subject matter; thinking of things which could go wrong, of causes and effect, prevention and cure; looking at things from other viewpoints; and comparing and contrasting with similar and dissimilar things with which one is familiar. This technique is called the 'Keys to Understanding'. Another technique used was the 'Questioning Demonstration' in which a task is silently demonstrated and the learners are invited to ask any question they like both prior to the demonstration and during it. The questions are answered fully and are recorded on a flip chart. After the demonstration is over, and the learners have performed the task for themselves (the 'D' of MUD), the questions are examined to identify which ones were most helpful to learning the task. In this way, the learner not only learns how to perform the task, but also that certain kinds of questions are far more helpful than others. In this and other exercises, the learner, when learning about a product, also learns about identifying and correcting mistakes, the value of errors in increasing understanding, the need to avoid early errors when memorizing or learning to do something, how to develop standards, how to get feedback, and how to observe, listen and record.

Learners are also often asked to work in pairs using worksheets. This is less threatening to the individual and the learners discover the benefits of shared learning, including stimulating each other, and the impressive range of ideas that can be generated within the groups as a whole. Pondering sessions are introduced during which learners consider the purposes of a training session, what they think they have learned, and how they might apply this. As far as possible, concepts are developed by the learners rather than supplied by the trainer. Formal talks and lectures are replaced with prepared exercises, which are used to develop concepts in the learners. Another session helps learners identify what blocks learning and to develop ideas for overcoming the blocks. Many of the blockages identified stem from trainers themselves, or at least from poor and inexperienced trainers. As an increasing amount of training in the future will be done by non-specialist trainers, the ability to learn from supervisors or product experts who are not necessarily skilled trainers becomes increasingly important. The whole emphasis of the DSL approach is to make the learner actively responsible for learning, and to break out of the traditionally passive role so often found in trainees.

Evaluating the impact of DSL at ICI

Evaluating the effects of an intervention in a complex organization is always difficult. In the agricultural division it was decided that the evaluation would take the form of seeing if the concepts that were introduced in the workshop survived over a period of time, and assessing the extent to which DSL was being introduced and the plans to implement it in the future. Three months after the original workshop, the participants' action plans were on schedule. After five months a DSL course run by some of the original participants was observed. The material had been redesigned to meet the needs of ICI and it was judged by the researchers that the concepts and specific content were true to the principles of DSL. After twelve months, 8 of the original 12 participants and 8 second generation DSL trainers had applied DSL in around 30 different ways. This included courses on DSL, the redesign of an induction course, supervisor training, training of trainers, management familiarization, interviewing techniques, computer-based training packages, and also on youth training schemes. The ideas and techniques had spread beyond the division and had been applied in local schools, church groups, and in the trainers' own homes.

A basic shift had occurred away from good training practice used to teach product or content only, towards the DSL approach of helping learners be responsible, adaptable and versatile in their approach to learning. The lessons from ICI were that the ideas had been introduced and disseminated gradually, so that they did not appear to be 'flavour of the month' – here today and gone tomorrow. Instead, an awareness was built up and a demand created which was then satisfied. In short, the development of skilled learners was stitched firmly into the prevailing culture of facilitating and fostering meaningful change. The only intervention of any substance by the researchers was the five-day workshop for the twelve disciples. The right seeds had been sown on well-prepared soil.

CONCLUSION

What this chapter has attempted to do is describe relevant parts of research which began in the Industrial Training Research Unit, Cambridge, in 1979; were developed with the Occupational Research Unit, UWIST, funded by the then Manpower Services Commission, and are continuing.

The descriptions have therefore concentrated on this work and its application to a number of industries (Pearn and Downs 1988). Apologies are due to many creative and original writers that have not been referred to, but from whom we learned a great deal about the large body of work on autonomous learning and creating learning cultures.

A central point in such approaches is to enable the learner to initiate, outline, and assess his or her learning. This requires a confidence and assertiveness which are both helped by a knowledge and awareness of the different pertinent learning strategies or skills one might use. This links to the areas of research on causal attribution (Hewstone 1989) and perceived self-efficacy (Bandura 1989). As one young woman attending a workshop on learning put it, 'when we came we was rubbish but now we know we ain't'. The work on developing learning skills was experimentally shown to be beneficial to a wide range of abilities and circumstances. In New Zealand, for example, the work was used to help women returning to work and disadvantaged groups. In South Africa, training was remodelled to incorporate the work and methods appropriate for groups of managers, trainers and apprentices – both black and white. Similarly, in the UK the work has been integrated into many training courses in such organizations as British Airways, Barclays Bank, Glass Training, Glaxo, ICI, Shell, and the Skill Centres.

The purposes to which the work has been put include designing training, developing open learning material, and developing learning skills. In addition it has been applied to areas where increased understanding is important for changes in behaviour. Among these topics are safety, quality, work restructuring, quality assurance, appraisals, staff development and induction.

The research began in Further Education and was carried on under the MSC. As such, the emphasis was on the influence developing learning skills might have in the area of industry, commerce and employment. The research team found the results of its experiments added to its conviction that developing skills helped a number of people to deal with material to be learned in a more confident, effective, and proactive way.

Two final points should be mentioned. First, although the work has been described in terms of industry and employment, it has, as stated earlier, a wider application in terms of helping some people gain in confidence and independence. Second, the research and its applications are a very small part of a movement towards considering learners and their needs, which echoes the shift from largely rote learning to forming concepts.

Some examples of this are the changes of name in many companies. For instance, 'training centre' has become 'learning centre', and 'correspondence course' or 'home study' has become 'open learning'. People are recognizing that constant change means constant learning. This in turn means practice in learning, which builds up confidence in the ability to learn.

REFERENCES

Bandura, A. (1989) 'Perceived self-efficacy in the exercise of personal agency', *The Psychologist* 2 (10), 411–24.

Belbin, E. and Belbin, R. M. (1972) *Problems in Adult Retraining*, London: Heinemann.

Cheren, M. (1983) 'Helping learners achieve greater self-direction', in R. M. Smith (ed.), *Helping Adults Learn How to Learn*, NDCE, Series 19, San Francisco: Jossey-Bass.

Downs, S. (1985) 'Retraining for new skills', *Ergonomics* 28 (8), 1205–11.

_____ and Perry, P. (1982) 'How Do I Learn?', *Journal of European Industrial Training* 6 (6), 27–32.

_____ (1984) 'Developing Learning Skills', *Journal of European Industrial Training* 8 (1), 21–6.

_____ (1987) *Developing Skilled Learners: Helping Adults to Become Better Learners*, MSC Research and Development No. 40, Sheffield: Manpower Services Commission.

Harri-Augstein, E. S. and Smith, M. (1982) *Reading to Learn*, London: Methuen.

Hewstone, M. (1989) *Causal Attribution*, Oxford: Basil Blackwell.

Honey, P. and Mumford, A. (1982) *Using your Learning Styles*, Maidenhead: Peter Honey.

Knowles, M. S. (1980) 'How do you get people to be self-directed learners?', *Training and Development Journal*, May, pp. 96–9.

Pearn, M. and Downs, S. (1988) 'Developing Skilled Learners: a strategy for coping with new technology', *Media in Education and Development*, vol. 21, 7–12.

Smith, R. M. (1982) *Learning How to Learn: Applied Theory for Adults*, New York: Cambridge.

Timmer, P. (1984) 'A statistical study of the distribution of learning blockages in the long term unemployed', Unpublished paper, University of Warwick.

Chapter 14

The interpersonal relationship in the facilitation of learning

Carl R. Rogers

Source: This is an edited version of a chapter which appeared in C. R. Rogers, *Freedom to Learn for the 80s*, Ohio, Charles E. Merrill, 1983. It first appeared in R. Leeper (ed.), *Humanizing Education*, ASCD, NEA, 1967. (Copyright © by the Association for Supervision and Curriculum Development, NEA.)

[. . .] I wish to begin this chapter with a statement that may seem surprising to some and perhaps offensive to others. It is simply this: Teaching, in my estimation, is a vastly over-rated function.

Having made such a statement, I scurry to the dictionary to see if I really mean what I say. *Teaching* means 'to instruct'. Personally, I am not much interested in instructing another in what she should know or think, though others seem to love to do this. 'To impart knowledge or skill'. My reaction is, why not be more efficient, using a book or programmed learning? 'To make to know'. Here my hackles rise. I have no wish to *make* anyone know something. 'To show, guide, direct'. As I see it, too many people have been shown, guided, directed. So I come to the conclusion that I *do* mean what I said. Teaching is, for me, a relatively unimportant and vastly overvalued activity.

But there is more in my attitude than this. I have a negative reaction to teaching. Why? I think it is because it raises all the wrong questions. As soon as we focus on teaching, the question arises, what shall we teach? What, from our superior vantage point, does the other person need to know? I wonder if, in this modern world, we are justified in the presumption that we are wise about the future and the young are foolish. Are we *really* sure as to what they should know? Then there is the ridiculous question of coverage. What shall the course cover? This notion of coverage is based on the assumption that what is taught is what is learned; what is presented is what is assimilated. I know of no assumption so obviously untrue. One does not need research to provide evidence that this is false. One needs only to talk with a few students.

But I ask myself, 'Am I so prejudiced against teaching that I find no situation in which it is worthwhile?' I immediately think of my experiences in Australia long ago. I became much interested in the Australian

Aborigines. Here is a group that for more than 20,000 years has managed to live and exist in a desolate environment in which modern man would perish within a few days. The secret of the Aboriginal's survival has been teaching. He has passed on to the young every shred of knowledge about how to find water, about how to track game, about how to kill the kangaroo, about how to find his way through the trackless desert. Such knowledge is conveyed to the young as being *the* way to behave, and any innovation is frowned upon. It is clear that teaching has provided him the way to survive in a hostile and relatively unchanging environment.

Now I am closer to the nub of the question that excites me. Teaching and the imparting of knowledge makes sense in an unchanging environment. This is why it has been an unquestioned function for centuries. But if there is one truth about modern man, it is that he lives in an environment that is *continually changing*. The one thing I can be sure of is that the physics that is taught to the present-day student will be outdated in a decade. The teaching in psychology will certainly be out of date in twenty years. The so-called 'facts of history' depend very largely upon the current mood and temper of the culture. Chemistry, biology, genetics, and sociology are in such flux that a firm statement made today will almost certainly be modified by the time the student gets around to using the knowledge.

We are, in my view, faced with an entirely new situation in education where the goal of education, if we are to survive, is the *facilitation of change and learning*. The only man who is educated is the man who has learned how to learn; the man who has learned how to adapt and change; the man who has realized that no knowledge is secure, that only the process of *seeking* knowledge gives a basis for security. Changingness, a reliance on *process* rather than upon static knowledge, is the only thing that makes any sense as a goal for education in the modern world.

So now with some relief I turn to an activity, a purpose, which really warms me – the facilitation of learning. When I have been able to transform a group – and here I mean all the members of a group, myself included – into a community of *learners*, then the excitement has been almost beyond belief. To free curiosity; to permit individuals to go charging off in new directions dictated by their own interests; to unleash the sense of inquiry; to open everything to questioning and exploration; to recognize that everything is in process of change – here is an experience I can never forget. I cannot always achieve it in groups with which I am associated, but when it is partially or largely achieved, then it becomes a never-to-be forgotten group experience. Out of such a context arise true students, real learners, creative scientists and scholars, and practitioners, the kind of individuals who can live in a delicate but ever-changing balance between what is presently known and the flowing, moving, altering problems and facts of the future. [. . .]

But do we know how to achieve this new goal in education or is it a will-o'-the-wisp that sometimes occurs, sometimes fails to occur, and thus offers little real hope? My answer is that we possess a very considerable knowledge of the conditions that encourage self-initiated, significant, experiential, 'gut-level' learning by the whole person. We do not frequently see these conditions put into effect because they mean a real revolution in our approach to education and revolutions are not for the timid. But we do [...] find examples of this revolution in action.

We know – and I will briefly mention some of the evidence – that the initiation of such learning rests not upon the teaching skills of the leader, not upon scholarly knowledge of the field, not upon curricular planning, not upon use of audiovisual aids, not upon the programmed learning used, not upon lectures and presentations, not upon an abundance of books, though each of these might at one time or another be utilized as an important resource. No, the facilitation of significant learning rests upon certain attudinal qualities that exist in the personal *relationship* between the facilitator and the learner.

We came upon such findings first in the field of psychotherapy, but now there is evidence that shows these findings apply in the classroom as well. We find it easier to think that the intensive relationship between therapist and client might possess these qualities, but we are also finding that they *may* exist in the countless interpersonal interactions between the teacher and pupils.

QUALITIES THAT FACILITATE LEARNING

What are these qualities, these attitudes, that facilitate learning? Let me describe them very briefly, drawing illustrations from the teaching field.

Realness in the facilitator of learning

Perhaps the most basic of these essential attitudes is realness or genuineness. When the facilitator is a real person, being what she is, entering into a relationship with the learner without presenting a front or a façade, she is much more likely to be effective. This means that the feelings that she is experiencing are available to her, available to her awareness, that she is able to live these feelings, be them, and able to communicate them if appropriate. It means that she comes into a direct personal encounter with the learner, meeting her on a person-to-person basis. It means that she is *being* herself, not denying herself.

Seen from this point of view it is suggested that the teacher can be a real person in her relationship with her students. She can be enthusiastic, can be bored, can be interested in students, can be angry, can be sensitive and sympathetic. Because she accepts these feelings as her own, she has no need to impose them on her students. She can like or dislike a student product without implying that it is objectively good or bad or that the student is good or bad. She is simply expressing a feeling for the product, a feeling that exists within herself. Thus, she is a person to her students, not a faceless embodiment of a curricular requirement nor a sterile tube through which knowledge is passed from one generation to the next.

It is obvious that this attitudinal set, found to be effective in psycho-therapy, is sharply in contrast with the tendency of most teachers to show themselves to their pupils simply as roles. It is quite customary for teachers rather consciously to put on the mask, the role, the façade of being a teacher and to wear this façade all day, removing it only when they have left the school at night.

But not all teachers are like this. [. . .] Take Barbara Shiel [. . .] She gave her pupils a great deal of responsible freedom, and I will mention some of the reactions of her students later. But here is an example of the way she shared herself with her pupils – not just sharing feelings of sweetness and light, but anger and frustration. She had made art materials freely available, and students often used these in creative ways, but the room frequently looked like a picture of chaos. Here is her report of her feelings and what she did with them.

> I find it maddening to live with the mess – with a capital M! No one seems to care except me. Finally, one day I told the children . . . that I am a neat, orderly person by nature and that the mess was driving me to distraction. Did they have a solution? It was suggested there were some volunteers who could clean up . . . I said it didn't seem fair to me to have the same people clean up all the time for others – but it would solve it for me. 'Well, some people like to clean,' they replied. So that's the way it is.
>
> (Shiel 1966)

I hope this example puts some lively meaning into the phrases I used earlier, that the facilitator 'is able to live these feelings, be them, and able to communicate them if appropriate'. I have chosen an example of negative feelings because I think it is more difficult for most of us to visualize what this would mean. In this instance, Miss Shiel is taking the risk of being transparent in her angry frustrations about the mess. And what happens? The same thing that, in my experience, nearly always happens. These young people accept and respect her feelings, take them into account, and work out a novel solution that none of us, I believe, would have suggested. Miss Shiel wisely comments, 'I used to get upset and feel guilty when I became angry. I finally realized the children could accept *my* feelings too. And it is important for them to know when they've "pushed me". I have my limits, too.' (Shiel 1966).

Just to show that positive feelings, when they are real, are equally effective, let me quote briefly a college student's reaction, in a different course:

> Your sense of humour in the class was cheering; we all felt relaxed because you showed us your human self, not a mechanical teacher image. I feel as if I have more understanding and faith in my teachers now. I feel closer to the students too.

Another says:

> You conducted the class on a personal level and therefore in my mind I was able to formulate a picture of you as a person and not as merely a walking textbook.

Another student in the same course:

> It wasn't as if there was a teacher in the class, but rather someone whom we could trust and identify as a 'sharer.' You were so perceptive and sensitive to our thoughts, and this made it all the more 'authentic' for me. It was an 'authentic' *experience*, not just a class.

(Bull 1966)

I trust I am making it clear that to be real is not always easy, nor is it achieved all at once, but it is basic to the person who wants to become that revolutionary individual, a facilitator of learning.

Prizing, acceptance, trust

There is another attitude that stands out in those who are successful in facilitating learning. I have observed this attitude. I have experienced it. Yet, it is hard to know what term to put to it so I shall use several. I think of it as prizing the learner, prizing her feelings, her opinions, her person. It is a caring for the learner, but a nonpossessive caring. It is an acceptance of this other individual as a separate person, having worth in her own right. It is a basic trust – a belief that this other person is somehow fundamentally trustworthy. Whether we call it prizing, acceptance, trust, or by some other term, it shows up in a variety of observable ways. The facilitator who has a considerable degree of this attitude can be fully acceptant of the fear and hesitation of the student as she approaches a new problem as well as acceptant of the pupil's satisfaction in achievement. Such a teacher can accept the student's occasional apathy, her erratic desires to explore byroads of knowledge, as well as her disciplined efforts to achieve major goals. She can accept personal feelings that both disturb and promote learning – rivalry with a sibling, hatred of authority, concern about personal adequacy. What we are describing is a prizing of the learner as an imperfect human being with many feelings, many potentialities. The facilitator's prizing or acceptance of the learner is an operational expression of her essential confidence and trust in the capacity of the human organism.

I would like to give some examples of this attitude from the classroom situation. Here any teacher statements would be properly suspect since many of us would like to feel we hold such attitudes and might have a biased perception of our qualities. But let me indicate how this attitude of prizing, of accepting, of trusting appears to the student who is fortunate enough to experience it.

Here is a statement from a college student in a class with Dr Morey Appell:

> Your way of being with us is a revelation to me. In your class I feel important, mature, and capable of doings things on my own. I want to think for myself and this need cannot be accomplished through textbooks and lectures alone, but through living. I think you see me as a person with real feelings and needs, an individual. What I say and do are significant expressions from me, and you recognize this.
>
> (Appell 1959)

[. . .] the facilitator who cares, who prizes, who trusts the learner creates a climate for learning so different from the ordinary classroom that any resemblance is purely coincidental.

Empathic understanding

A further element that establishes a climate for self-initiated, experiential learning is empathic understanding. When the teacher has the ability to understand the student's reactions from the inside, has a sensitive awareness of the way the process of education and learning seems *to the student*, then again the likelihood of significant learning is increased.

This kind of understanding is sharply different from the usual evaluative understanding, which follows the pattern of 'I understand what is wrong with you.' When there is a sensitive empathy, however, the reaction in the learner follows something of this pattern, 'At last someone understands how it feels and seems to be *me* without wanting to analyse me or judge me. Now I can blossom and grow and learn.'

This attitude of standing in the other's shoes, of viewing the world through the student's eyes, is almost unheard of in the classroom. One could listen to thousands of ordinary classroom interactions without coming across one instance of clearly communicated, sensitively accurate, emphatic understanding. But it has a tremendously releasing effect when it occurs.

Let me take an illustration from Virginia Axline, dealing with a second grade boy. Jay, age 7, has been aggressive, a trouble-maker, slow of speech and learning. Because of his 'cussing', he was taken to the principal, who paddled him, unknown to Miss Axline. During a free work period, Jay fashioned very carefully a man of clay down to a hat and a handkerchief in his pocket. 'Who is that?' asked Miss Axline. 'Dunno,' replied Jay. 'Maybe it is the principal. He has a handkerchief in his pocket like that.' Jay glared at the clay figure. 'Yes,' he said. Then he began to tear the head off and looked up and smiled. Miss Axline said, 'You sometimes feel like twisting his head off, don't you? You get so mad at him.' Jay tore off one arm, another, then beat the figure to a pulp with his fists. Another boy, with the perception of the young, explained, 'Jay is mad at Mr X because he licked him this noon.' 'Then you must feel lots better now,' Miss Axline commented. Jay grinned and began to rebuild Mr X (Axline 1944).

The other examples I have cited also indicate how deeply appreciative students feel when they are simply *understood* – not evaluated, not judged, simply understood from their *own* point of view, not the teacher's. If any teacher set herself the task of endeavouring to make one non-evaluative, acceptant, empathic response per day to a student's demonstrated or verbalized feeling, I believe she would discover the potency of this currently almost nonexistent kind of understanding.

WHAT ARE THE BASES OF FACILITATIVE ATTITUDES?

A 'puzzlement'

It is natural that we do not always have the attitudes I have been describing. Some teachers raise the question, 'But what if I am *not* feeling empathic, do *not*, at this moment, prize or accept or like my students. What then?' My response is that realness is the most important of the attitudes mentioned, and it is not accidental that this attitude was described first. So if one has little understanding of the student's inner world and a dislike for the students or their behaviour, it is almost certainly more constructive to be *real* than to be pseudoempathic or to put on a façade of caring.

But this is not nearly as simple as it sounds. To be genuine, or honest, or congruent, or real means to be this way about *oneself*. I cannot be real about another because I do not *know* what is real for him. I can only tell, if I wish to be truly honest, what is going on in me.

Let me take an example. Early in this chapter I reported Miss Shiel's feelings about the 'mess' created by the art work. Essentially she said, 'I find it maddening to live with the mess! I'm neat and orderly and it is driving me to distraction.' But suppose her feelings had come out somewhat differently in the disguised way that is much more common in classrooms at all levels. She might have said, 'You are the messiest children I've ever seen! You don't care about tidiness or cleanliness. You are just terrible!' This is most definitely *not* an example of genuineness or realness, in the sense in which I am using these terms. There is a profound distinction between the two statements, which I should like to spell out.

In the second statement she is telling nothing of herself, sharing none of her feelings. Doubtless the children will *sense* that she is angry, but because children are perceptively shrewd, they may be uncertain as to whether she is angry at them or has just come from an argument with the principal. It has none of the honesty of the first statement in which she tells of her *own* upsetness, of her *own* feeling of being driven to distraction.

Another aspect of the second statement is that it is all made up of judgements or evaluations, and like most judgements, they are all arguable. Are these children messy, or are they simply excited and involved in what they are doing? Are they *all* messy, or are some as disturbed by the chaos as she? Do they care nothing about tidiness, or is it simply that they don't care about it every day? If a group of visitors were coming, would their attitude be different? Are they terrible, or simply children? I trust it is evident that when we make judgements, they are almost never fully accurate and hence cause resentment and anger as well as guilt and apprehension. Had she used the second statement, the response of the class would have been entirely different.

I am going to some lengths to clarify this point because I have found from experience that to stress the value of being real, of *being* one's feelings, is taken by some as a licence to pass judgements on others, to project on others all the feelings that one should be 'owning'. Nothing could be further from my meaning.

Actually the achievement of realness is most difficult, and even when one wishes to be truly genuine, it occurs but rarely. Certainly it is not simply a matter of the *words* used, and if one is feeling judgemental, the use of a verbal formula that sounds like the sharing of feelings will not help. It is just another instance of a façade, of a lack of genuineness. Only slowly can we learn to be truly real. For first of all, one must be close to one's feelings, capable of being aware of them. Then one must be willing to take the risk of sharing them as they are, inside, not disguising them as judgements, or attributing them to other people. This is why I so admire Miss Shiel's sharing of her anger and frustration, without in any way disguising it.

A trust in the human organism

It would be most unlikely that one could hold the three attitudes I have described, or could commit herself to being a facilitator of learning unless she has come to have a profound trust in the human organism and its potentialities. If I distrust the human being, then I *must* cram her with information of my own choosing lest she go her own mistaken way. But if I trust the capacity of the human individual for developing her own potentiality, then I can provide her with many opportunities and permit her to choose her own way and her own direction in her learning.

It is clear, I believe, that the teachers [...] rely basically upon the tendency towards fulfilment, towards actualization, in their students. They are basing their work on the hypothesis that students who are in real contact with problems that are relevant to them wish to learn, want to grow, seek to discover, endeavour to master, desire to create, move towards self-discipline. The teacher is attempting to develop a quality of climate in the classroom and a quality of personal relationship with students that will permit these natural tendencies to come to their fruition.

Living the uncertainty of discovery

I believe it should be said that this basically confident view of the human being and the attitudes toward students that I have described do not appear suddenly, in some miraculous manner, in the facilitator of learning. Instead, they come about through taking risks, through *acting* on tentative hypotheses. [...] I can only state that I started my career with the firm view that individuals must be manipulated for their own good; I only came to the attitudes I have described and the trust in the individual that is implicit in them because I found that these attitudes were so much more potent in producing learning and constructive change. Hence, I believe that it is only by risking herself in these new ways that the teacher can *discover*, for herself, whether or not they are effective, whether or not they are for her.

I will then draw a conclusion, based on the experiences of the several facilitators and their students that have been included up to this point: When a facilitator creates, even to a modest degree, a classroom climate characterized by all that she can achieve of realness, prizing, and empathy; when she trusts the constructive tendency of the individual and the group; then she discovers that she has inaugurated an educational revolution. Learning of a different quality, proceeding at a different pace, with a greater degree of pervasiveness, occurs. Feelings – positive, negative, confused – become a part of the classroom experience. Learning becomes life and a very vital life at that. The student is on the way, sometimes excitedly, sometimes reluctantly, to becoming a learning, changing being. [...]

EVIDENCE FROM STUDENTS

Certainly before the research evidence was in, students were making it clear by their reactions to student-centred or person-centred classrooms that an educational revolution was underway. This kind of evidence persists to the present day.

The most striking learnings of students exposed to such a climate are by no means restricted to greater achievement in the three Rs. The significant learnings are the more personal ones – independence, self-initiated and responsible learning, release of creativity, a tendency to become more of a person. I can only illustrate this by picking, almost at random, statements from students whose teachers have endeavoured to create a climate of trust, of prizing, of realness, of understanding, and above all, of freedom [. . .] here is one of a number of statements made by students in a course on poetry led (not taught) by Dr Samuel Moon.

> In retrospect, I find that I have actually enjoyed this course, both as a class and as an experiment, although it had me quite unsettled at times. This, in itself, made the course worthwhile since the majority of my courses this semester merely had me bored with them and the whole process of 'higher education.' Quite aside from anything else, due mostly to this course, I found myself devoting more time to writing poetry than to writing short stories, which temporarily interfered with my writing class.
>
>   . . . I should like to point out one very definite thing which I have gained from the course; this is an increased readiness on my part to listen to and to seriously consider the opinions of my fellow students. In view of my past attitude, this alone makes the course valuable. I suppose the real result of any course can be expressed in answer to the question, 'Would you take it over again?' My answer would be an unqualified 'Yes.'
>
> (Moon 1966: 227)

I should like to add to this several comments from Dr Bull's sophomore students in a class in adolescent psychology. The first two are midsemester comments.

> This course is proving to be a vital and profound experience for me . . . This unique learning situation is giving me a whole new conception of just what learning is . . . I am experiencing a real growth in this atmosphere of constructive freedom . . . the whole experience is challenging.

> I feel that the course had been of great value to me . . . I'm glad to have had this experience because it has made me think . . . I've never been so personally involved with a course before, especially *outside* the classroom. It has been frustrating, rewarding, enjoyable, and tiring!

The other comments are from the end of the course:

> This course is not ending with the close of the semester for me, but

continuing . . . I don't know of any greater benefit which can be gained from a course than this desire for further knowledge.

I feel as though this type of class situation has stimulated me more in making me realize where my responsibilities lie, especially as far as doing required work on my own. I no longer feel as though a test date is the criterion for reading a book. I feel as though my future work will be done for what *I* will get out of it, not just for a test mark.

I think that now I am acutely aware of the breakdown in communications that does exist in our society from seeing what happened in our class . . . I've grown immensely. I know that I am a different person than I was when I came into that class . . . It has done a great deal in helping me understand myself better . . . thank you for contributing to my growth.

My idea of education has been to gain information from the teacher by attending lectures. The emphasis and focus were on the teacher . . . One of the biggest changes that I experienced in this class was my outlook on education. Learning is something more than a grade on a report card. No one can measure what you have learned because it's a personal thing. I was very confused between learning and memorization. I could memorize very well, but I doubt if I ever learned as much as I could have. I believe my attitude toward learning has changed from a grade-centred outlook to a more personal one.

If you wish to know what this type of course seems like to a sixth grader, let me give you a sampling of the reactions of Miss Shiel's youngsters, misspellings and all.

I feel that I am learning self ability [*sic*]. I am learning not only school work but I am learning that you can learn on your own as well as someone can teach you.

I like this plan because there is a lot of freedom. I also learn more this way than the other way you don't have to wate [*sic*] for others you can go at your own speed rate and it also takes a lot of responsibility.

(Shiel 1966)

Or let me take two more, from Dr Appell's graduate class:

I have been thinking about what happened through this experience. The only conclusion I come to is that if I try to measure what is going on, or what I was at the beginning, I have got to know what I was when I started – and I don't . . . so many things I did and feel are just lost . . . scrambled up inside . . . They don't seem to come out in a nice little pattern or organization I can say and write . . . There are so many things left unsaid. I know I have only scratched the surface, I guess. I can feel so many things almost ready to come out ... maybe that's enough. *It seems all kinds of things have so much more meaning now than ever before* ... This experience has had meaning, has done things to me and I am not sure how much or how far just yet. I think I am going to be a better me in the fall. *That's one thing I am sure of.*

(Appell 1863)

You follow no play, yet I'm learning. Since the term began I seem to feel more alive, more real to myself. I enjoy being alone as well as with other people. My relationships with children and other adults are becoming more emotional and involved. Eating an orange last week, I peeled the skin off each separate orange section and liked it better with the transparent shell off. It was juicier and fresher tasting that way. I began to think, that's how I feel sometimes, without a transparent wall around me, really communicating my feelings. I feel that I'm growing, how much, I don't know. I'm thinking, considering, pondering and learning.

(Appell 1959)

I can't read these student statements – sixth grade, college, graduate level – without being deeply moved. Here are teachers, risking themselves, *being* themselves, *trusting* their students, adventuring into the existential unknown, taking the subjective leap. And what happens? Exciting, incredible *human* events. You can sense persons being created, learnings being initiated, future citizens rising to meet the challenge of unknown worlds. If only one teacher out of 100 dared to risk, dared to be, dared to trust, dared to understand, we would have an infusion of a living spirit into education that would, in my estimation, be priceless.

THE EFFECT UPON THE INSTRUCTOR

Let me turn to another dimension that excites me. I have spoken of the effect upon the *student* of a climate that encourages significant, self-reliant, personal learning. But I have said nothing about the reciprocal effect upon the instructor. When she has been the agent for the release of such self-initiated learning, the faculty member finds herself changed as well as her student. One such says:

To say that I am overwhelmed by what happened only faintly reflects my feelings. I have taught for many years but I have never experienced anything remotely resembling what occurred. I, for my part, never found in a classroom so much of the whole person coming forth, so deeply involved, so deeply stirred. Further, I question if in the traditional setup, with its emphasis on subject matter, examinations, grades, there is, or there can be a place for the 'becoming' person with his deep and manifold needs as he struggles to fulfill himself. But this is going far afield. I can only report to you what happened and to say that I am grateful and that I am also humbled by the experience. I would like you to know this for it has enriched my life and being.

(Rogers 1961: 313)

Another faculty member reports as follows:

Rogers has said that relationships conducted on these assumptions mean 'turning present day education upside down.' I have found this to be true as I have tried to implement this way of living with students. The experiences I have had have plunged me into relationships which have been significant and challenging and beyond compare for me. They have inspired me and stimulated me and left me at times shaken and awed with their consequences for both me and the students. They have led me to the fact of what I can only call . . . the tragedy of education in our time – student after student who reports this to be his first experience with total trust, with freedom to be and to move in ways most consistent for the enhancement and maintenance of the core of dignity which somehow has survived humiliation, distortion, and corrosive cynicism.

(Appell 1959)

TOO IDEALISTIC?

Some readers may feel that the whole approach of this chapter – the belief that teachers can relate as persons to their students – is hopelessly unrealistic and idealistic. They may see that in essence it is encouraging both teachers and students to be creative in their relationship to each other and in their relationship to subject matter, and feel that such a goal is quite impossible. They are not alone in this. I have heard scientists at leading schools of science and scholars in leading universities arguing that it is absurd to try to encourage all students to be creative – we need hosts of mediocre technicians and workers, and if a few creative scientists and artists and leaders emerge, that will be enough. That may be enough for them. It may be enough to suit you. I want to go on record as saying it is *not* enough to suit me. When I realize the incredible potential in the ordinary student, I want to try to release it. We are working hard to release the incredible energy in the atom and the nucleus of the atom. If we do not devote equal energy – yes, and equal money – to the release of the potential of the individual person then the enormous discrepancy between our level of physical energy resources and human energy resources will doom us to a deserved and universal destruction.

I am sorry I can't be coolly scientific about this. The issue is too urgent. I can only be passionate in my statement that people count, that interpersonal relationships *are* important, that we know something about releasing human potential, that we could learn much more, and that unless we give strong positive attention to the human interpersonal side of our educational dilemma, our civilization is on its way down the drain. Better courses, better curricula, better coverage, better teaching machines will never resolve our dilemma in a basic way. Only persons acting like persons in their relationships with their students can even begin to make a dent on this most urgent problem of modern education.

SUMMARY

Let me try to state, somewhat more calmly and soberly, what I have said with such feeling and passion.

I have said that it is most unfortunate that educators and the public think about, and focus on, *teaching*. It leads them into a host of questions that are either irrelevant or absurd so far as real education is concerned.

I have said that if we focused on the facilitation of *learning* – how, why, and when the student learns, and how learning seems and feels from the inside – we might be on a much more profitable track.

I have said that we have some knowledge, and could gain more, about the conditions that facilitate learning, and that one of the most important of these conditions is the attitudinal quality of the interpersonal relationship between facilitator and learner.

Those attitudes that appear effective in promoting learning can be described. First of all is a transparent realness in the facilitator, a willingness to be a person, to be and live the feelings and thoughts of the moment. When this realness includes a prizing, caring, a trust and respect for the learner, the climate for learning is enhanced. When it includes a sensitive and accurate emphatic listening, then indeed a freeing climate, stimulative of self-initiated learning and growth, exists. The student is *trusted* to develop.

I have tried to make plain that individuals who hold such attitudes, and are bold enough to act on them, do not simply modify classroom methods – they revolutionize them. They perform almost none of the functions of teachers. It is no longer accurate to call them *teachers*. They are catalysers, facilitators, giving freedom and life and the opportunity to learn, to students.

I have brought in the cumulating research evidence that suggests that individuals who hold such attitudes are regarded as effective in the classroom; that the problems that concern them have to do with the release of potential, not the deficiencies of their students; that they seem to create classroom situations in which there are not admired children and disliked children, but in which affection and liking are part of the life of every child; that in classrooms approaching such a psychological climate, children learn more of the conventional subjects.

But I have intentionally gone beyond the empirical findings to try to take you into the inner life of the student – elementary, college, and graduate – who is fortunate enough to live and learn in such an interpersonal relationship with a facilitator, in order to let you see what learning feels like when it is free, self-initiated and spontaneous. I have tried to indicate how it even changes the student–student relationship – making it more aware, more caring, more sensitive, as well as increasing the self-related learning of significant material. I have spoken of the change it brings about in the faculty member.

Throughout, I have tried to indicate that if we are to have citizens who can live constructively in this kaleidoscopically changing world, we can *only* have them if we are willing for them to become self-starting, self-initiating learners. Finally, it has been my purpose to show that this kind of learner develops best, so far as we now know, in a growth-promoting, facilitative relationship with a *person*.

REFERENCES

Appell, Morey L. (1959) 'Selected student reactions to student-centered courses', Unpublished manuscript, Indiana State University.
_____ (1963) 'Self-understanding for the guidance counselor', *Personnel & Guidance Journal*, October, pp. 143–8.
Axline, Virginia M. (1944) 'Morale on the school front', *Journal of Educational Research*, pp. 521–33.
Bull, Patricia (1966) 'Student reactions, Fall, 1965', Unpublished manuscript, New York State University College.
Moon, Samuel F. (1966) 'Teaching the self', *Improving College and University Teaching*, 14 Autumn, pp. 213–29.
Rogers, Carl R. (1961) *On Becoming a Person*, Boston: Houghton Mifflin.
Shiel, Barbara J. (1966) 'Evaluation: a self-directed curriculum, 1965', Unpublished manuscript. n.p.

Chapter 15

The utilization of learning objectives – a behavioural approach[1]

L. B. Curzon

Source: This is an edited version of a chapter in L. B. Curzon, *Teaching in Further Education, An Outline of Principles and Practice* (4th edn), London, Cassell, 1990.

AIMS, GOALS AND OBJECTIVES

A perusal of many of the texts relating to learning objectives (or, as they are alternatively named, behavioural or performance objectives) indicates that there is now a standardized nomenclature which differentiates sharply the three concepts of aims, goals and objectives.

1 *Aims* are general statements representing ideals or aspirations. Thus, the Schools Council defined the aim of humanities teaching as 'to forward understanding, discrimination and judgement in the human field'. The Business and Technician Education Council (BTEC) described its fundamental aim as ensuring 'that students on BTEC courses develop the necessary competence in their careers in their own, employers' and the national interest'. The National Research Council (USA), in its 1989 report[2] on mathematics education, hoped to achieve the aims of 'making mathematics education significant for all Americans' and 'improving significantly students' mathematical achievement'.
2 *Goals* described the actual 'destination' of learning, in general terms. Thus the goal of BTEC (in relation to its aim outlined above) is the provision of a series of appropriate courses leading to BTEC awards.
3 *Objectives* are statements, often of a quantifiable, operational nature, indicating events from which mastery of desired activities may be correctly inferred. An objective is defined by Mager as 'an intent communicated by a statement describing a proposed change in a learner – a statement of what the learner is to be like when he has successfully completed a learning experience. It is a description of a pattern of behaviour we want the learner to be able to demonstrate'.[3]

The essence of learning objectives

How ought a learning objective to be defined?[4] [...] a learning event may be said to culminate in *a change in the learner's behaviour*. The result of that change may be observed (and learning may be inferred) by noting what the learner can *do*, as compared with what he was unable to do before the learning event. *A statement which describes what a learner will be able to do on the completion of an instructional process is known as a behavioural (or learning) objective.* In Bloom's words: 'An objective states an attempt by the teacher to clarify within his own mind or communicate to others the sought-for changes in the learner'. Thus we could state that: following an introductory lesson concerning the carburettor, the learner 'will name correctly the different components of the carburettor'; or, that, following a unit of instruction relating to the industrial trade cycle, the learner 'will *describe* in their correct sequence the events which make up a trade cycle'. The naming and describing refer to types, or to forms, of *behaviour* from which one can observe whether the objectives of the lessons have been attained, or not.

Lesson notes prepared by student teachers may be required to contain statements of the 'object of the lesson'. Often, however, the 'object' is couched in very wide terms ('to teach the use of the micrometer'), or in a style which makes its attainment incapable of assessment ('to instil an appreciation of management techniques'), or in a manner so terse as to render impossible any interpretation of the teacher's real aims ('Ohm's Law'). This latter statement – 'Ohm's Law' – is no more than an indication of lesson content. The other examples of statements of 'the object of the lesson' are really means to ends, rather than ends in themselves. The method of defining and stating objectives which is outlined below is rigorous, precise and based on considering those objectives in terms of student performance ('the learner will describe . . .'), rather than in terms of teacher performance ('to teach the use of . . . ').

Two types of learning objectives will be considered:

1 The *general* objective: this is usually stated in terms of that section of the general syllabus which forms the unit of instruction.
2 The *specific* objective: this states the observable behaviour of the student which is expected at the end of the period of instruction.

An example, based on a course in elementary economics, might read as follows:

• *General objective*: At the end of this period of instruction the student shall apply correctly the basic principles of the theory of rent to a consideration of a variety of other economic phenomena.
• *Specific objectives*: The student shall:
(a) state the theory of rent in his own words;

(b) distinguish correct and incorrect applications of the theory;

(c) outline the concepts of profit and wages in terms of economic rent.

[. . .]

The teaching functions of learning objectives

There are three principal teaching functions of behavioural objectives, based on their construction, enunciation and use in the context of classroom teaching. First, they impose on the teacher the discipline of selecting and formulating the steps which he or she considers necessary in the process of instruction. Second, they provide him or her with an overall view of the structure of his instructional task. Third, they present him or her with the basis of a suitable assessment procedure.

A statement of objectives presupposes a planned series of instructional steps. Each step has to be seen as a link in a process; each should be considered as starting from an ascertained level of student performance; each should be planned so as to contribute to a movement of that performance to a higher level. This is not an easy task since it involves the teacher posing and answering repeatedly many questions, including: 'What is the student able to *do* before the instruction commences?' 'What do I want him to be able to *do* after the period of instruction?' 'What resources will be available to the class?' and 'What are the constraints (for example, time available for instruction)?' Without answers to questions of this kind, the defining of learning objectives will be less than precise.

From the pattern of steps formulated in terms of objectives should emerge the structure of the lesson designed to achieve the defined instructional ends. The 'total view' of the lesson, or series of lessons, in terms of ends, of the means to achieve those ends and of the modes of recognition of their attainment, is important because it gives the teacher a 'general line of advance' – a prerequisite for the control of instruction.

A further prerequisite for that control is assessment of the student's progress. Such an assessment is built into the very process of formulating learning objectives. Attainment of the learning objective can be recognized and, therefore, assessed and evaluated in terms of student behaviour.[5]

The defining and stating of learning objectives in terms of student attainment

Consider a teacher's statement of his lesson objective in the following terms: 'to show students that no loss of matter accompanies chemical change'. Couched in these terms, the objective presents difficulties of interpretation. It views the outcome of the lesson solely in terms of the *teacher's* activities ('to *show* students . . .'). It does not provide a statement of the desirable outcome of those activities in terms of what *the students* will have learned. A teacher could, in fact, 'show students' an experiment designed to illustrate the indestructibility of matter without their learning anything. As a 'declaration of intent' the statement is of some interest; as a formulation of direction and outcome it is of little value.

Consider next a teacher's statement formulated in terms of *lesson outcome* and viewed from the point of *student attainment*. Assume that the section of the general science syllabus on which the lesson or series of lessons will be based reads, simply: 'indestructibility of matter: simple experiments'. The teacher must interpret this phrase and decide on the appropriate teaching method. He should then state the objectives *in terms of the outcome he would wish to see as the result of his teaching*. Next, the teacher should specify how that outcome can be satisfactorily demonstrated and evaluated. The teacher's objectives are therefore stated in terms of an *instructional product* which can be assessed, thus:

- *General objective*: Following the series of lessons, the student will:
  (a) understand the meaning of the term 'indestructibility of matter'; and
  (b) evaluate correctly the three experiments to be undertaken together with their results.
- *Specific objectives*: The student will, within a period of one hour, and without the use of books or notes:
  (a) recall and define the term 'indestructibility of matter';
  (b) illustrate in essay form the concept, 'all chemical changes take place without loss of matter';
  (c) analyse in essay form the results of the experiment involving the burning of phosphorus in a closed flask;
  (d) analyse in note form the results of the experiment involving . . . ;
  (e) analyse in note form the results of the experiment involving . . .

It will be noted that the teacher's general objective as stated above is 'understanding' and 'correct evaluation'. The product of instruction is stated in the form of a group of specific objectives – that is, certain types of behaviour which will demonstrate to the teacher that the students understand and are able to evaluate correctly. That demonstration allows him to assess their progress in relation to his overall objective. In sum, objectives ought to be defined and stated in terms of learning outcomes – that is, student attainment. In that way their use may contribute to the control of the learning event; that is their real significance.[6] [. . .]

Tyler's 'general objectives'

Tyler[7] advocates, in contrast to those who support the writing and use of specific objectives, a concentration on the design and use of *general objectives* [. . .] The most useful way of defining an objective is, according to

Tyler, to consider two 'dimensions' – behaviour and content. 'Behaviour' is described by Tyler as 'the kind of behaviour to be developed in the student'. 'Content' means 'the content or area of life in which the behaviour is to operate'. An object requires, additionally, context. What, asks Tyler, is the precise significance of a behavioural objective requiring a student to 'think rationally'? About what ought he to be thinking? What is the point of content devoid of context? What is the learner supposed to *do* with the law of diminishing returns or the calculus? Tyler insists on objectives based on behaviour *and* content.

Mere lists of objectives provide, according to Tyler, no real indication of the very structure of knowledge, with which their compiler ought to be concerned. A useful statement of objectives involves the utilization of a graphic two-dimensional chart so as to discover 'concise sets of specifications'.[8] Along one axis is 'behaviour'; along the other is 'content'. Intersections of vertical and horizontal columns are marked where they suggest a direct relationship between content area and behavioural aspect; absence of a mark suggests absence of such a relationship or the presence of a trivial, immaterial relationship. The marked relationships can be used as the basis for a formulation of course objectives. Tyler suggests that, in general, one year's work in a subject area necessitates seven to fifteen behavioural categories and ten to thirty content categories.

THE CONTROVERSY ON LEARNING OBJECTIVES

The principles and use of learning objectives (also known as behavioural objectives) in the classroom have attracted the severe criticism which is levelled against perceived manifestations of behaviourism, such as programmed instruction. Education, the anti-behaviourists emphasize, is a process, the outcome of which can be neither defined nor measured in strict behavioural terms. (Objection has been taken, also, to the 'input-output' formulations of some advocates of learning objectives; it has been stated, for example, that 'the terminology of the production line is inappropriate to describe the process of instruction'.) To suggest that overt behaviour is the sole criterion of a learner's cognitive attainment is to miss, it is argued, the 'real point' of education. Further, it is claimed that the learning outcome, by its very nature, defies the precise, quantitative analysis upon which the theory and use of learning objectives rest. To attempt to formulate this outcome in exact terms is, it is claimed, to trivialize the really important ends of instruction. How does one 'measure' emotional development or personal enrichment? There is a fear, too, that the minimum requirements of a learning objective may become the maximum level of attainment, so that innovation and exploration could be discouraged.

Eisner,[9] a trenchant critic of the use of educational objectives, makes four significant points. He claims that the outcomes of instruction are too complex and numerous for educational objectives to encompass. The quality of learning which stems from student interaction is very difficult to predict, so that the teacher cannot specify behavioural goals in advance. Next, there are some subject areas in which the specification of learning objectives is impossible – even if it were desirable. In the arts, for example, how can one state criteria and objectives? And ought not instruction in these areas to yield behaviour which may be unpredictable and which, therefore, comes as a surprise to teacher and learner alike? Further, he argues, most of the outcomes of instruction need not be specified in advance. The teacher ought not to ask: 'What am I trying to accomplish?' Rather ought he to ask: 'What am I going to *do*?' From his doing will stem the accomplishment. ('We can only know what we wanted to accomplish after the fact.')

Hogben[10] has drawn attention to the practical problems of drawing up objectives. He refers to the sheer number of statements and the considerable expenditure of time which would be involved in translating a curriculum into behavioural terms and emphasizes that the type and quality of much classroom learning is largely unpredictable, so that objectives cannot always be stated realistically in advance of the lesson. There is more to education, he argues, than objectives that can be stated unambiguously in terms of student behaviour. In particular, 'responsive diversity' must be encouraged. He makes five suggestions: first, that although some course objectives can be stated, they need not be framed in specific, behavioural terms; second, that long-term objectives (which may not become apparent to students until long after the end of a course) ought to be stated; third, that unexpected and unintended outcomes ought not to be ignored; fourth, that the objectives in their totality ought to mirror the goals which generated them; finally, that objectives which cannot be easily assessed ought not to be ignored in the building of a curriculum.

Popham[11] advances the following arguments against the validity of behavioural objectives. First, because trivial learner behaviour is the easiest to cast in objective form, the really important outcomes of education may not receive appropriate emphasis. The stating of explicit goals prevents advantage being taken of those opportunities unexpectedly occurring during a lesson. Behavioural changes are not the only type of important educational outcome. Further, in some subject areas (the fine arts, for example) it is very difficult to identify measurable student behaviour. Measurability generally implies accountability, and teachers might be judged on ability to change behaviour alone.

Macdonald-Ross[12] emphasizes the following objections to behavioural objectives. First, there are no well-defined prescriptions for their derivation. Defining objectives before the event often conflicts with the exploration which should characterize the learning process. Unpredicted classroom events (often important) cannot be utilized fully in the context of pre-specified goals. In some disciplines appropriate criteria can be applied only after the event. Finally, lists of behaviours are not an adequate reflection of the real structure of knowledge.[13]

The case against the use of learning objectives may be summed up in metaphoric terms thus:

Education is an exciting journey, the precise destination of which cannot be known in advance. It recognises no bounds, it cannot be constrained by paths and marked roads. It needs no compass, no guide other than the sun, moon and stars. Maps and milestones rob the journey of its real meaning. Those who make the journey must be allowed to wander as they will, to use roads only when they wish, to walk into unknown territory if they so desire. It is better to journey hopefully than to arrive and the exciting prospects of discovery must be allowed to every traveller.

In answer, it has been emphasized that the basic rationale of learning objectives is the effective utilization of scarce human and other resources so as to achieve desired ends; this is impossible to attain save by reference to standards and criteria of achievement. It is arguably more interesting to travel hopefully than to arrive, but it is vital to know one's destination and necessary to be able to recognize it. It is also of importance that travellers should not be exposed unnecessarily to the hazards of falling by the wayside and never completing the journey. Nor may we ignore the fact that most educational travellers have a very limited time in which to complete a very arduous journey. The lesson viewed as a planned, exciting journey, with instructional objectives used as milestones along the route, in no way removes the wonder of learning and the satisfaction which comes with achievement. Further, the use of objectives does not necessarily destroy the spontaneity of class response which can enrich a lesson. Nor does it prevent a teacher effectively utilizing the side winds, the unexpected issues which often arise during a lesson.

Macdonald-Ross[14] stresses the following advantages claimed for behavioural objectives. First, they encourage teachers to think and plan in a detailed fashion and to make explicit previously unstated values. They provide a rational foundation for evaluation and provide a basis of a self-improving system which can achieve internal consistency and realize in practice aims set in theory.

In answer to the criticism that the principles of behavioural objectives are derived from the principles of behaviourist psychology, it has been pointed out that this is based on a confusion, since cognitive psychologists may also infer a student's learning from his or her behaviour. The use of the adjective 'behavioural' in relation to objectives, or other aspects of educational practice, should not be taken as evidence of the user's total adherence to behaviourist, non-cognitive, theories of learning.

If a lesson is viewed as an unprepared activity, with no discernible objective, if its content is to be determined by whim and its course by improvization on the spur of the moment, learning goals may be irrelevant. If, however, the efficiency of the instructional process is to be tested by its success in leading students to desired goals, then those goals ought to be stated as accurately as possible and the paths of their attainment ought to be charted with precision. The use of learning objectives may contribute to that end.

LEARNING OBJECTIVES IN THE CLASSROOM: SOME PRACTICAL MATTERS

The following points relating to the use of objectives in the classroom are among those reiterated frequently by teachers in further education who have experimented with the design of curricula.

1　The use of learning objectives in the classroom may involve a complete break with some traditional views of teaching; it necessitates a highly structured and carefully planned instructional activity in which the teacher plays a clearly predominant role.
2　Planning a scheme of objectives is all-important. The objectives – which must never be of a trivial nature – must be planned and listed in schematic, sequential form on the basis of perhaps two to five per lesson. To have as few objectives as possible, given the specific demands of the unit of instruction, is a useful practice. (Note the view of Gage[15] that it is not necessary to specify *every* student behaviour that is required, just as roadmaps, to be useful, need not specify every town and stream between points A and B.)
3　The use of time must be planned carefully. Periods of at least 45 minutes seem to be needed where objectives are in use.
4　Gagné[16] emphasizes that the designer of a pattern of objectives must take decisions on whether the *purpose* of the lesson has been kept in mind, whether the planned lesson displays an appropriate *balance* of expected outcomes, and whether the types of objective are *matched* correctly to the selected approach to instruction.
5　Complete records of student achievement in relation to tests arising from the use of objectives must be kept.
6　Students should be informed carefully of the purpose of this type of instruction. Where it is possible to issue lists of learning objectives at the beginning of a session, motivation can be heightened; the objectives can act as a useful reference point, checklist and self-test material for students.

7 Instruction by the use of detailed learning objectives may make unusually heavy demands on a class. Concentrated effort is required from students for extended periods, and control of the class may throw a heavy burden on the teacher. It is advisable that a lesson based on the use of learning objectives be 'broken up' by short 'buzz groups', for example.

8 Failure to attain an objective is not to be viewed by teacher or students as a catastrophe. The aphorism suggesting that an unattained objective is an incorrectly drawn objective is unhelpful: it does not take into account, for example, the phenomenon of 'noise' in communication channels.[17]

9 Consider carefully the concept of learning objectives as providing indicators of progress along roads to travel rather than as terminal points.

NOTES

1 See generally for this chapter: *Development and Evolution of Behavioural Objectives* by R. J. Armstrong *et al.* (Brown, 1970); 'Formulating and selecting educational objectives' by B. S. Bloom in *Evaluation to Improve Learning* (Maidenhead: McGraw-Hill, 1981); *Objectives in Curriculum Design* by I. K. Davies (Maidenhead: McGraw-Hill, 1976); 'Preparing instructional objectives' by N. Gronlund in *Measurement and Evaluation in Teaching* (Ontario: Collier-Macmillan, 1981); *Writing Worthwhile Behavioural Objectives* by J. Vargas (London: Harper & Row, 1972).

2 *Notices of the American Mathematical Society* 36 (3).

3 See, e.g. *Preparing Instructional Objectives* by R. F. Mager (London: Pitman, 1984).

4 Ibid.

5 See *Writing Behavioural Objectives – A New Approach* by H. McAshan (McKay, 1970); 'Which objectives are most worthwhile?' by D. Rowntree in *Aspects of Educational Technology* (London: Pitman, 1973).

6 See *Mathematics Behavioural Objectives* by J. C. Flanagan *et al.* (Westinghouse, 1971).

7 R. W. Tyler, *Basic Principles of Curriculum and Instruction* (Chicago UP, 1949); 'Some persistent questions on the defining of objectives', in C. Lindvall (ed.), *Defining Educational Objectives*, (Pittsburgh UP, 1964).

8 See Tyler 1964, *op. cit.*

9 E. W. Eisner, 'Educational objectives: help or hindrance', in *The School Review*, vol. 75, pp. 250–60, 1967.

10 Hogben, 'The behavioural objectives approach: some problems and some dangers', in *Journal of Curriculum Studies* 4, 1972.

11 'Probing the validity of arguments against behavioural objectives', in *Behavioral Objectives and Instruction* by R. Kibler *et al.* (Allyn & Bacon, 1970).

12 M. I. Macdonald-Ross, 'Behavioural objectives – a critical review', in *Instructional Science*, vol. 2, pp. 1–52 (Amsterdam: Elsevier, 1973).

13 Ibid. see also, e.g. 'Some limitations on the use of objectives in curriculum research and planning' by L. Stenhouse in *Paedogogica Europaea*, vol. 6, pp. 73–83, 1970; 'Behavioural objectives? No!' by G. Keller in *Educational Leadership* (1972).

14 In Macdonald-Ross 1973, *op. cit.*
15 See *Educational Psychology* by N. J. Gage and D. C. Berliner (Huddersfield: Rand McNally, 1979).
16 R. M. Gagné, *The Conditions of Learning* (New York: Holt, Rinehart & Winston, 1977).
17 The fidelity of the message communicated in a classroom is always affected in some measure by a variety of 'interference' known as 'noise'. The causes of this type of 'interference' in the teaching–learning process are varied, including deficiencies in the physical environment and social factors such as the attitudes and styles of both learners and teachers. (Eds.)

Chapter 16

What is skill and how is it acquired?

John Sloboda

Source: This is an edited version of two chapters in A. Gellatly (ed.), *The Skilful Mind*, Milton Keynes, Open University Press, 1986.

There are two rooms in my house that have recently been repainted, one by a professional decorator, the other by me. The decorator was skilled at his job. I was not. By what marks might one detect the difference? Well, the end product certainly tells something. If you look closely at the walls that I painted you will find unevenness of texture; too much paint here, barely enough to cover there. You will find faint vertical streaks where the paint has run, and you will find small overshoots and under-shoots at the edges. The walls painted by the professional are even in texture, and the edges are beautifully straight.

Notwithstanding these differences, I actually managed to cover my tracks quite well. Unless you gave my walls a very close examination you would not find any obvious faults. The most dramatic differences between myself and the professional would have been apparent had you actually stood and watched us at work.

To begin with, the professional finished the job in about half the time it took me. Not only were his individual strokes faster, but he stopped less often, I was stopping very regularly, not through laziness, but because I continually needed to assess what I had done, and decide what needed doing next. Other delays occurred too. For instance, I ran out of paint with only three-quarters of the job done, and had to go to the shop for more.

Second, the professional made his job appear easy. The paint just seemed to flow onto the wall in a relaxed and co-ordinated sequence of movements. My own movement sequence was jerky and effortful. For instance, one brushful would have too much paint on it, the next too little; once I would start with an upstroke, next with a down; I would constantly be attending to minor 'bugs', such as spillages and drips.

Finally, the professional's sequencing was impeccable. He arranged things so that he was not constantly having to move apparatus around. He always ended up in the right place at the right time (for example, returning to put on the second coat just at the time when the first coat was dry enough), and was completely systematic in the way each wall was tackled. I worked haphazardly, treating each wall in a different way, leaving odd patches unpainted when, for example, a ladder was not conveniently placed. I was constantly having to stop painting in order to get something I needed or to move obstacles out of the way.

THE CHARACTERISTICS OF SKILL

For a long time, psychologists have wanted to specify exactly what the characteristics of skilled activities are. My painting example informally includes many of the major characteristics, but I would like to deal with them in a more systematic way under five principal headings; fluency, rapidity, automaticity, simultaneity, and knowledge. The first-letter mnemonic FRASK may be helpful in keeping these in mind.

Fluency

An activity is fluent if the components of it run together in an integrated and uninterrupted sequence. The term 'fluency' is usually applied to the microstructure of a task (elements occurring over a span of a few seconds) rather than to its long-term structure. Thus we speak of a fluent translator as one who can provide an appropriate translation with a minimum of pauses or hesitations. A fluent typist is one who can maintain a relatively even and continuous output of key presses.

It seems likely that fluency is brought about by two things. One is the overlapping in time of a sequence of movements. That is to say, preparatory movements for action B are begun whilst action A is still being completed. The other is the building of a set of actions into a single 'chunk', which can be controlled and run off as a single unit of behaviour.

The existence of chunking in skilled typists has been elegantly demonstrated by Shaffer (1976). In this study, typists saw a computer console on which was displayed a single line of text. The console was linked to a keyboard in such a way that every time a key was pressed the text moved one space to the left. This meant that the leftmost character (or space) 'fell off' the screen and a new character appeared on the right.

Shaffer was able to vary both the window size (that is, length of line displayed) and also the amount of preview (that is, how far from the right a letter had moved before the subject was required to type it). With no preview, a subject had to type a character as soon as it appeared on the right of the screen. With preview, the subject typed a character as it arrived at a preordained position towards the middle of the screen. Typists were given three different varieties of text to work on:

1 normal English prose;

2 jumbled prose in which English words were printed in random order;
3 jumbled words, where letter order was randomized.

These three conditions are illustrated in Figure 16.1.

The vertical line indicates the position of the letter to be typed under 8-character preview

(a) in Ayrshire. I told John about the meeting, and also

(b) meeting told. About, John also in the Ayrshire I and

(c) metegni ldto. Atoub, nJoh slao ni eht sirAeyha I dna

Figure 16.1 Types of text used in Shaffer's typing study

Shaffer found that typists required about eight characters of preview to obtain their fastest speeds. Increasing preview beyond eight characters did not result in further improvements in speed or accuracy. Fastest consistent speeds were about 10 characters per second (100 words per minute) in conditions (a) and (b), but were only two characters per second in condition (c). It seems that skilled typists can deal with familiar English words much better than with strings of nonsense letters. We can get a better insight into *why* words are typed faster when we look at what happened when Shaffer reduced preview below eight characters. In condition (c), reducing preview to zero had no effect whatsoever on speed, which remained at two characters per second. However, such reduction had a dramatic effect in the other two conditions which dropped right down to two characters per second as well.

It seems that fluent typing depends on the typist being able to see the whole of an average English word (six characters) before beginning to type it. Only then can the full set of finger movements required to type the word be assembled into a single performance unit. Such a unit can be 'rattled off' at speed. When there is no preview, or when the letters do not make up familiar words, such chunking is not possible, and the job must be done letter by letter.

The lack of difference between conditions (a) and (b) is also of interest. It shows that these typists were not forming chunks bigger than individual words. If they had been then we would have expected condition (a) to be even faster than condition (b). It looks as though in general any given pair of adjacent words occurs too infrequently to be chunked in the way that individual words are. It is, however, likely that word sequences such as 'Dear Sir' or 'Yours sincerely' could attain the status of chunks for some secretaries.

There are, of course, two levels of chunking occurring in fluent typing. There is what one might call *input* chunking – the perceptual act of grouping letters into units such as words; and there is also *output* chunking

– the assembling of co-ordinated movement sequences. Perhaps the best way of appreciating the nature of output fluency is to experience the loss of it. One effective way of disrupting fluency is to upset the sensory feedback we normally receive from motor behaviour. This interferes with the ability to dovetail separate movements with one another. For instance, suppose you were wearing a set of headphones and speaking into a microphone which fed into the headphones. Under these conditions it is possible to introduce a delay, so that instead of hearing your own voice as you speak you hear it a little while later. Delaying the auditory feedback from one's own voice by about 0.2 second usually causes severe speech disruption. It induces stuttering, repetition of sounds, and excessive pausing between words and syllables. Fluent behaviour is crucially dependent upon normal feedback arriving at the normal time. More commonly, loss of fluency is experienced when we are nervous. We trip over our feet and stumble on our words. Fluency is usually the last feature of skill to be acquired and its loss the first sign of disruption due to disease, intoxication, or fear.

Rapidity

Most skills involve the ability to make an appropriate response quickly. The skilled tennis player must not only get to the right place on the court and choose an appropriate stroke, he or she must do these things in an incredibly short time. It is the ability to make the right response almost immediately that is so characteristic of all skills.

One of the most widely quoted and influential studies which demonstrates the speed of skilled performance is a study of chess players carried out by Chase and Simon (1973). They took subjects at differing levels of expertise from novice up to grandmaster and showed them chessboards on which were placed some pieces copied from the middle of an actual game between experts. Subjects were allowed to view the board for five seconds. It was then removed and they were asked to reconstruct the positions of the pieces on a blank board. A novice was able, on average, to replace about four out of 20 pieces correctly. A master, in contrast, replaced about 18 out of 20 correctly.

Since the subjects viewed the board for the same period of time, these results show that a master is able to deal with the same amount of information much more rapidly than a novice. A second part of the study shed substantial light on the mechanisms involved. In this, the boards shown to subjects contained pieces placed on them at random, in a way that could not have occurred in any rational game. Faced with such boards, a novice performed exactly the same as in the first experiment, getting about four out of 20 pieces correct. The master, however, showed a dramatic drop in performance, from 18 down to four out of 20. On these random boards the master was no better than the novice.

This shows us that the master's skill does not rest simply on superior perception or memory, it is linked to the detection of familiar and game-relevant patterns in the stimulus. The master immediately 'understands' what is seen in meaningful terms so that, for instance, one group of four pieces becomes a 'castled king', another a 'knight fork' and so on. This view is confirmed by the way in which the master carries out the reconstruction, tending to put down linked groups of pieces together, with longer pauses between groups. The ability of the knowledgeable player to perceive meaningful patterns on the board is analogous to the ability of a knowledgeable football spectator to recognize carefully rehearsed moves amidst the frantic activity on the pitch.

Automaticity

One of the most universal characteristics of skill is the way in which it becomes 'easy' to its practitioners. We no longer experience any effort when carrying out some well-learned skill such as walking. It 'just happens' without us having to think about it. If this were not the case, our ability to act upon the world would be drastically limited. Our whole time would be spent attending to the simplest things.

The sight-reading of piano music is a complex skill. In a study of professional sight-readers, Wolf (1976) interviewed several practitioners and asked them what were the principal problems in sight-reading. One pianist answered: 'for me, personally, there are none'. This is not arrogance, but an honest answer about a highly automated skill. It is the kind of answer that most of us would have to give if asked about the problems we had in walking. Yet that is a skill of comparable complexity to piano sight-reading, and one that takes infants a long time to learn.

One of the ways of testing whether a skill is automatic is to see whether the practitioner can deal appropriately with a situation, even when not concentrating or expecting it. So, for instance, a skilled driver is able to brake rapidly at a potential hazard, even if the mind were on something else in the immediately preceding moments. [. . .]

Another characteristic of automatic skills seems to be that they are, in some sense, mandatory. That is to say, a stimulus triggers its automatic response regardless of whether we wish it to or not. When we look at a familiar printed word we usually cannot help experiencing its meaning. We find it almost impossible to experience it just as a set of letters. Similarly, we find it almost impossible not to recognize a familiar face as a person we know and to see it instead as a set of individual features.

The tendency of automatic skills to be called into play 'despite ourselves' can sometimes lead to embarrassing and amusing occurrences which have been studied in the context of 'absent-mindedness' (for example, Reason and Mycielska 1982). The mother of a large family tells of the time when she was at a dinner party and found herself cutting into small pieces the dinner of her surprised neighbour while holding a conversation with someone else. If we laugh then we should laugh with rather than at the unfortunate mother since diary studies have shown that most people are able to record large numbers of slips of this kind in their everyday lives. The outcomes need not always be as embarrassing but the principle is the same. Slips of this nature seem to be an inevitable consequence of the automatization of skilled behaviour.

Simultaneity

I still remember with horror my first driving lesson. My instructor was trying to teach me how to change gear. This involved a complicated sequence of movements involving clutch, accelerator, and gear lever simultaneously. If this was not enough, my instructor kept shouting 'keep your eyes on the road, keep steering'. The multiple demands on my attention seemed impossible to fulfil. Now, some 20 years later, it all seems so trivially easy. Changing gear is a fluent and co-ordinated movement sequence which I can do without losing any of my attention on the road. I can do all these things whilst maintaining an intellectually demanding argument with my passenger on some unrelated topic.

Simultaneity is a characteristic of skill in two senses. First, the components of a skilled activity can be executed simultaneously (as in conjoint movements of hands and feet for gear changing). Second, because of the high degree of automaticity, it is often possible to carry out an unrelated activity at the same time as performing a skilled activity. One way that psychologists test how automatic a skill has become is to measure the effect on performance of adding a second, simultaneous task for the subject to perform.

One of the most strikingly counterintuitive demonstrations of simultaneity was provided by Allport et al. (1972), in an experiment where they examined performance on two skills: sight-reading of piano music and prose 'shadowing'. Subjects were experienced sight-readers. They were first asked to perform each task alone. For the sight-reading test, an unfamiliar piano piece was placed in front of the subject who was required to perform it on the piano without rehearsal. In the shadowing test the subject heard a prose passage through headphones and was required to speak it out as it was being heard. The two tasks were then combined. A subject was asked to continue as best she could with both tasks together.

After a very small amount of practice, subjects were able to perform the two tasks together. They did not break down in either of them. Even more surprising was the fact that the two tasks did not seriously affect one another. Each task was performed in the dual condition almost as well as each task was performed alone.

There has been a lengthy debate in psychology about whether or not it is possible to attend to two things at once. Some theorists have proposed that attention is like an indivisible beam which can only be pointed at one thing at a time. Dual task performance must then be explained in terms of rapid switching of attention between the two tasks (Broadbent 1982). Others have seen it more as a *quantity* of resource which can be devoted entirely to one task or split up between several. Proponents of both views broadly agree that automatic tasks require little or no attention to be allocated to them. Therefore, when at least one of a pair of simultaneous activities is automatic, then there is enough attentional capacity to maintain both tasks. In the above experiment it seems likely that sight-reading had attained a high degree of automaticity.

Knowledge

When I get into a dispute about some topic close to my heart, I don't always win. As I nurse my wounds afterwards I often come up with the perfect response that I *should* have made to my opponent's apparently devastating blow. In the heat of the debate, however, I was just unable to gain access to the appropriate piece of knowledge, the argument I wanted to bring out. In a similar manner, examination candidates often realize what they *should* have written minutes after walking out of the examination room.

I use these examples to make the point that skill is not simply a matter of having knowledge. It involves this knowledge being readily available at the appropriate time, in response to the situation that demands its use. For instance, what is important for driving is that I should immediately slow down when I see green traffic lights turning to amber. It is no use having the conceptual knowledge that amber means 'stop' unless I can apply it in the driving situation. Recently, cognitive psychologists have paid increasing attention to the possible role in skilled behaviour of what are called *associative pattern-action pairs*. Such associations are like rules which an organism can apply to particular situations. They have the form: '*If Condition X Applies Then Carry Out Action Y*'. They look rather like the stimulus-response bonds which have had a venerable history in behaviourist explanations of animal learning. However, in these so called 'production rules', X need not be a simple external stimulus, and Y need not be an overt behaviour. We can include such things as internal mental states and goals as well. So the rule, 'If you see a police patrol car in your rear-view mirror, then feel panic' is a production rule, though one we would perhaps like to be without.

A set of production rules sufficient for carrying out some coherent task can be incorporated in a *production system*. One of the major reasons why psychologists have begun to think about skills in terms of production systems is the fact that such systems can be very easily simulated on a computer. [. . .]

Production system theory provides a useful way of understanding how knowledge may be organized in the service of skill at several different levels. First is the level of individual actions. Particular environmental patterns can trigger immediate knowledge about the right thing to do in that circumstance. In driving, for instance, a green light turning to amber triggers an immediate application of the brakes. Two significant facts about such knowledge stand out. One is that the knowledge may be completely inaccessible (or 'out of mind') until the circumstances which demand its use occur. Do you know without trying, for instance, which muscle you would use first when standing up from a seated position? The second fact is that our capacity to acquire new pattern-action pairs seems limitless.

The point about accessibility is made nicely by a study on taxi-drivers (Chase 1983). Experienced Pittsburgh taxi-drivers were called into the laboratory and asked to describe the best routes between pairs of points in the city. This they were able to do. It turned out, however, that their routes were not always the best routes or the routes that the drivers would actually take. This was shown by repeating the study in real life; actually asking drivers to *drive* from A to B. When this happened the drivers would often remember better short cuts than the ones they had produced in the lab. These short cuts seemed to be triggered by the experience of arriving at particular locations. A driver would realize 'of course, if I turn left here I can cut round such and such a bottleneck'. This is, of course, completely adaptive. Taxi-drivers need to find good routes when on the job, not when thinking about it.

A complex cognitive skill such as chess playing is also amenable to production system analysis. We may suppose that the chess master has many thousands of production rules which link each commonly occurring pattern or chunk to a good move associated with the pattern. In this way, masters experience good moves 'just springing off the board' at them. Poor players have to work through the consequences of many bad moves before stumbling on a good move.

THE STRUCTURE OF SKILLS

We can also use the notion of a production system to elucidate the nature of planning and structuring in skill, and the ability to keep track of where one is at. For this, in addition to production rules, we must postulate a working memory-system in which a goal stack may be held. A simple example of a common skill much quoted in this context is the ability to travel around an industrialized country. If I am in a rural location and need to get to a big city quite quickly then I could set the goal of, for instance, 'getting to London'. This goal can act as the X condition of a production rule which might be, *'If The Goal Is To Get To London Then Set The Goal Of Getting To The Nearest Railway Station'*. So the goal of getting to London is 'pushed down' the stack and the second goal of 'get to the station' sits on top as the current goal. You can imagine a goal stack to be rather like the spring-loaded plate racks found in canteens. Now the operative goal is 'get to station'. This may well call up a further rule which ways, *'If The Goal Is To Get To The Station Then Set The Goal To Call a Taxi'*. So now 'call a taxi' becomes the current goal, with two unachieved goals stacked beneath it. This may call up further goals such as 'look up telephone number'. At some point there will be a goal which calls into play a production rule involving behaviour which achieves the topmost goal. When this happens, this goal can be jettisoned from the stack and the previous goal becomes current. This can then be achieved, and so on through the stack until there are no further goals left. The goal stack gives structure and direction to the total behaviour.

Without the structuring of a goal stack behaviour would tend to be uncoordinated and entirely driven by the current situation. Indeed, when the retention of goals in the stack is inadequate a partial breakdown of behaviour occurs. We can observe this through a particular class of absent-minded error. This occurs to most of us. You walk into a shop, and then stand there foolishly, trying to remember why you came in. The goal of 'buying X' led to the new goal of 'go to the shop', but on your way you started to think of other things and this intervening mental activity led to the loss of the original goal from the stack.

In real life, most of us are not pursuing just one set of goals, such as described above, but many disparate goals. It is sometimes hard to keep them all in mind, and we can never be directly working on more than one or two of them. It follows that the ability to remember what one's multiple goals are, and where one has got to in achieving each of them, is an important skill in its own right. We all know people who always seem to be forgetting to do things, whilst others seem to be able efficiently to keep on top of a wide variety of different but complex commitments. The role of external memory aids seems very important here. These are such things as diaries, knots in handkerchiefs, lists of things to do, and notes to oneself. We can see the mobilization of these aids as an explicit recognition of the fact that external stimuli are the best and most reliable triggers for action. Skill in fulfilling multiple commitments seems to be skill in engineering one's own environment to provide the necessary reminders at the right place and time.

ACQUIRING SKILL

[. . .] We now turn to a related question: what does one have to do to become skilled? The human animal is unique in the number of skills that are acquired through learning. We are also unique in the diversity of our skills. Some of us are skilled mathematicians, others are skilled musicians, yet others are skilled mechanics. How is it that people can be so different in their skill profile?

Many animals appear extremely skilful. Observe, for example, how a cat stalks a bird. It crouches low so as to be concealed by ground cover; takes care to move slowly and quietly towards its prey. Then, when it becomes difficult to remain unobserved, it springs forward with claws outstretched to give the prey minimum time to react. My cat's skill at this operation is evidenced by the number of dead birds and mice that are proudly deposited on my kitchen floor. I could learn quite a lot about hunting techniques from carefully observing my cat.

Where did the cat's skill come from? As far as we know, most animal skills are inherited rather than learned. Kittens reared in isolation still show an appropriate repertoire of stalking and hunting behaviours (Hinde 1966). They appear to be instinctual. Moreover, all individuals of a given species appear to inherit roughly the same set of skills.

Is it possible that human skills are inherited? In the next section we shall examine the view of skill acquisition that attributes it to 'talent' or 'innate potential'. We will then go on to contrast it with the view that talent is less important than opportunity and practice. We will conclude by looking at a case study of an exceptional skill, which shows that we really need both views to understand properly the acquisition of skill.

Talent and skill acquisition

It is indisputable that gifted parents tend to have gifted children. Sometimes specific talents such as musical talent seem to run in families for several generations. Unfortunately, it has long been realized that this finding, in itself, tells us very little about how the skill was acquired. It could be that the son of a musician has inherited some special propensity for musical achievement. Equally, it could be the case that a musical parent provides more opportunity and encouragement for a child to learn musical skills than does a non-musician. In real life, the influences of heredity and environment are inextricably mixed together, and it is very hard to establish that a particular influence is decisive.

Much of the serious psychological research in this area has centred around the notion of intelligence, and has been the subject of great controversy. One controversy concerns the question of whether there is some unitary capacity or faculty that comprises the basis for intelligent action, or whether intelligence is simply the conjunction of several distinct and independent skills. Supporters of the first view point to the fact that people who are good at one type of thing tend to be good at a whole range of other things. This fact forms the basis of intelligence testing. It is precisely because many skills correlate with one another that we can obtain a useful picture of a person's ability by just sampling a few skills. But the correlation is not perfect, and we find in almost every person areas of skill that are either much better or much worse than one might predict on the basis of intelligence measures. A good example of this is the dyslexic, who reads less well than his other intellectual achievements would predict. Gardner (1983) provides an accessible overview of the issues surrounding this general controversy.

A second controversy concerns the degree to which we can find reliable ways of measuring the separate effects of environment and heredity. This topic is fraught with methodological and theoretical difficulties. It is also a political and ideological minefield, since it is frequently linked to the issue of putative racial differences (Eysenck versus Kamin 1981). Very few people come to the issue with an open mind. None the less, I will stick my neck out and say that there are probably three ways in which inherited characteristics might have a significant effect on skill acquisition:

1 There are some genetically transmitted conditions that cause largely irreversible mental retardation, presumably as a result of abnormal development of the brain or nervous system (for example, Down's Syndrome). These conditions may destroy capacities that are essential for some skills. All such conditions unfortunately, tend to handicap their possessors. There are no known conditions of this sort that confer significant advantage.

2 Inherited physical characteristics are undoubtedly a factor in determining achievement in some skills. It will depend largely on the shape of your vocal cavities as to whether you have a chance of becoming an opera singer. It will depend largely on your size and the shape of your skeleton as to whether you could become a ballerina, and so on. Inherited physical characteristics of the nervous system are also likely to be of importance.

3 There are a whole set of what one might call dispositional or motivational factors that could have an indirect effect on skill acquisition. From very early in life, infants seem to differ from one another in their degree of activity, the amount of sleep they require, their primary mood, and so on. Research on adult personality shows significant individual differences in such factors as ability to concentrate on boring tasks for long periods of time. There is also evidence for stable preferences for certain domains of activity. Some people seem to be biased toward visual activities, others towards verbal. These preferences may be linked to very early infancy, where significant differences in developmental profile may be observed (Kagan et al. 1978). Some children develop early language skill but lag behind in physical development. Others show the reverse trend. All of

these factors could have a strong influence on both the type and level of skill acquired. We can imagine the physically precocious extrovert as being more likely to acquire football skill, whilst the verbal introvert might be more likely to develop skill at poetry. This is not so much a question of *capacity*. Rather, it represents the amount of effort that a person is likely to want to devote to particular types of activity. Some activities seem to 'go against the grain', others seem intrinsically rewarding.

Practice and skill acquisition

Paul Tortelier was one of the world's foremost professional cellists. He was born to poor working-class parents who had no particular background of musical accomplishment. Before he was born they decided that their child should achieve great things in the world, and that they were going to have him trained as a cellist. By hard work, saving, and self-sacrifice, they were able to buy instruments, lessons, and other forms of support; and their son achieved their intentions for him.

Such rags to riches stories strike a deep chord in many of us, and prompt the following question. Suppose the young Tortelier had been snatched from his cradle at birth and replaced by another baby, chosen at random from the population at large? Suppose further that his parents were unaware of the switch, and treated the substitute in exactly the same way. Would they have turned *anyone* into that world-class cellist?

To the extent that we are inclined to answer 'yes' to that question we are basing our answer on the assumption that skills are not acquired by virtue of what you *are* but by what you *do*. Anyone can acquire a skill if only he or she does the right things.

It is impossible in practice to run the hypothesized substitution experiment. What we can do, however, is look at people in the process of acquiring skills and ask whether there is anything that seems to be linked with successful acquisition for a wide variety of skills and for a wide range of people. It will not come as a great surprise to be told that the single most important factor that psychologists know about is practice. Just as practice is the ingredient most emphasized by sports coaches and piano teachers.

A great deal of research has looked at the effects of practice on simple perceptual-motor skills. A frequently used task is one in which the reaction time is measured for pressing a button in response to a light turning on. Sometimes there is only a single light and a single button, while in other experiments there may be several of each, with subjects having to respond perhaps to one light at a time or to various patterns of lights coming on together. A study of Siebel (1963) is representative. Subjects viewed ten lights arranged in a horizontal row. Below the lights were ten buttons, one for each light. The subjects rested their fingers on the keys and

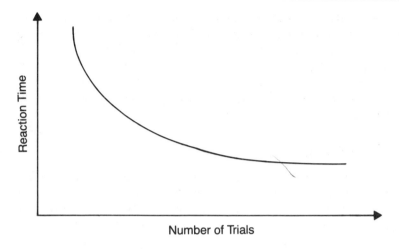

Figure 16.2 A typical graph of reaction time plotted against numbers of trials

watched the lights. After a signal, a random subset of the lights would go on. Subjects were required to depress the keys corresponding to the illuminated lights (and no others). Individual subjects repeated this task for upwards of 40,000 trials.

Siebel measured mean reaction-time to depress the correct combination of keys. Rapidity of response is a crucial characteristic of skill, which is why many researchers have used reaction time as a primary measure of skill level. The faster you can respond, the more skilled you are (given, of course, that your response remains accurate). Siebel found that reaction time dropped from an initial level of about two seconds down to 0.4 seconds with this large amount of practice. One can hardly imagine that this task had any interest for the subjects, yet sheer, dogged repetition caused continued improvement right through the 40,000 trials.

More detailed information can be gained by plotting reaction time (RT) against trial number, and Figure 16.2 shows the typical result of doing this. It illustrates what is sometimes called the 'law of diminishing returns'. Early practice results in quite large gains in speed, but equivalent amounts of practice later on yield only small gains. Sometimes this flattening-out of the acquisition curve occurs because one is coming up against physiological limits – for example, the fixed speed at which your nerves will conduct impulses. More often, though the flattening out begins to occur long before any such limits are being approached.

Why do we get diminishing returns with practice? One possibility could be that people concentrate less and less as they repeat a task, becoming unable to benefit from late trials to the extent of early ones. This might be a plausible explanation for decline in a single session. It would hardly account for a smooth decline over 40,000 trials spread over many days.

If learning were entirely dependent on concentration, one should see many fluctuations up and down as concentration waxed and waned. [...]

Explaining the 'law of diminishing returns'

A line of explanation for diminishing returns has been suggested by Newell and Rosenbloom (1981) and is built directly on the notions of chunking and pattern-action production rules that we have already explored. They propose that, as a subject carries out some task such as Siebel's, continuous attempts are made to chunk the lights into patterns. Each such chunk will be associated with a particular finger pattern of response. To begin with, the display will be processed as ten separate lights, and a response must be made to each individually. As time passes, the subject will come to respond, say, to *pairs* of lights as single units, then to triplets, and so on, until some theoretical ceiling is reached when the complete ten-light array is seen as a single pattern. [...] If we assume, for simplicity's sake, that it takes a constant time to perceive and respond to a single chunk, then we can see that the larger the chunks are, the less time it will take to respond to the whole display.

It is quite easy to see intuitively that the more chunks a person learns the quicker will be the response to any particular set of lights, because there is more possibility of detecting a familiar pattern in it. Thus, practice will increase task speed. What is less easy to see is why this notion also predicts the law of diminishing returns, but in fact it does do so. This is because a given small chunk will occur in the array more frequently than a large one, and so can be learned and put to use more quickly.

To see why this should be important, consider first the effects of chunking the display into five pairs of two adjacent lights. Each pair can take on one of four configurations (off-off, off-on, on-off, and on-on). There are five pairs, so in all there are five times four configurations, which is 20. All of these need to be learned, together with their 20 associated response patterns. If on any trial of the experiment a random half of the lights come on, then any given configuration of a pair is likely to appear once in every four trials on average. So since each of the 20 chunks appears frequently, there is a lot of opportunity to notice and learn to respond to each one. Given our assumption that it takes a constant time to respond to any chunk, then a person who has learned these 20 pair-patterns wil be able to halve the response time, always seeing the display as five chunks rather than as ten individual lights. This is the reason that the early stages of practice can result in large performance gains.

Now consider what would be involved in learning to respond to the display as two chunks each containing five items. There are 32 different configurations of on and off that a set of five lights can take up. There are two chunks in the display of ten, so there are 64 configurations in all that need to be learned (32 times two). If on any trial a random half of the lights come on then each configuration of a chunk will only appear once in every 32 trials. There are more patterns to learn, and much less frequent opportunities to observe any given pattern. Thus it will take a subject a great deal longer to move from processing the display as five chunks to processing it as two chunks than it will have done to move from ten to five. The first move reduces reaction time by a half, say from two seconds to one second. The second move reduces reaction time by three-fifths, from one second to 0.4 of a second. Not only will it have taken longer to bring about the second move, but this will also have yielded a smaller absolute increase in speed. This explains the phenomenon of diminishing returns, and its approximation to a logarithmic function.

Studies such as Siebel's, and the theorizing built round them, offer opportunities for mathematically precise thinking about skill. They show in a particularly elegant way why it takes so long to become really good at something. And yet such studies are lacking in several respects. First, the skills studied are very simple. They involve a single response to a stimulus rather than a co-ordinated sequence. Second, the stimuli themselves lack natural pattern and structure. It is very rarely in the real world that the material we deal with is so unpredictable. There are similarities between new situations and old ones that we already know about. We can make informed guesses and plans. Some patterns crop up much more often than one would expect by chance, and so on. Third, we normally have the opportunity to decide *how* we will practise a skill. In Siebel's task, subjects had to respond to all ten lights on every trial. It might be that a better strategy would be to learn the responses for each hand separately.

This leads to the fourth criticism. In such experiments as Siebel's, the subjects usually work entirely on their own, the skill is wholly without a social context. This is not true of real-life skills. These are usually learnt with the aid of some form of coaching. The coaching may be from an older practitioner, it may come from a book, it may amount to no more than trying to copy what you once saw someone else do. Nevertheless, there is normally available some source of comment and suggestion. For all these reasons, the rate of improvement on a task such as Siebel's probably represents a pessimistic estimate of our ability to acquire real-life skills.

ENHANCING THE EFFECTS OF PRACTICE

In this section, we will look briefly at some things which have been shown to help many types of practice become more effective. These are features of practice around which any coaching programme must be constructed. The first and most important of them is *feedback*.

Feedback

Feedback is, quite simply, knowledge of what your actions have achieved. It can come in two forms, intrinsic and extrinsic. Intrinsic feedback is that provided as a direct consequence of bodily movement and sensation. If you move your arm, you can both feel the result through *kinaesthesis*, and you can see where the arm is through vision. Extrinsic feedback is that provided by some external source or agent, frequently a coach or teacher. Being told whether an answer you supply is right or wrong is a type of extrinsic feedback. Feedback of one sort or another is essential to all skill acquisition. One cannot improve unless one has ways of judging how good present performance is, and in what direction change must occur.

There are several ways in which one may harness feedback to achieve more successful skill acquisition. The first is actually to pay attention to existing feedback. This can be something as simple as checking over what one has written when writing a letter or an essay. Many students and others omit to do this, and suffer as a result. The second is to make sure that the feedback is immediate. Comments on an essay returned after several weeks are of little use because the author has probably forgotten the precise steps taken in preparing the essay. It is no longer possible to link feedback to specific aspects of behaviour. In an ideal world the tutor would supervise every step of the essay-writing process, offering suitable comments at each stage. This means that the two persons would have to be in close and prolonged contact, with the likelihood of an intense relationship developing. And intense relationships are familiar in contexts where there is a master and an apprentice, a trainer and an athlete, or a drama coach and a student. An example from literature is the relationship between Svengali and the young singer, Trilby, in Du Maurier's novel of that name.

More exotic than ordinary feedback, are ways of helping people to become aware of internal sensations of which they are not normally conscious. By making use of a visual display which monitors some aspect of body state (such as heartbeat or galvanic skin response) one can learn to identify the bodily sensations which accompany changes in these states, and some people are able to control these states even when the augmented feedback (often known as *biofeedback*) is removed.

Sometimes feedback seems to have primarily a motivating effect. It provides information which is not strictly essential but which seems to increase involvement in the task. For instance, Smode (1958) asked subjects to practise what is known as a 'tracking task', in which a randomly moving

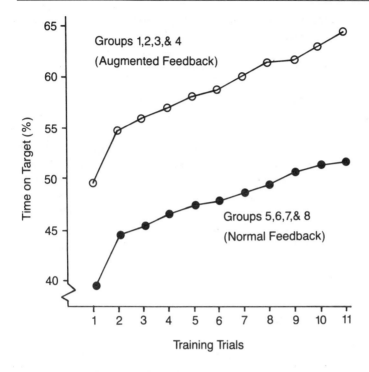

Figure 16.3 The effects of giving different kinds of feedback

needle could be kept on a central mark by rotating a dial in compensatory movement. After each trial all subjects were given 'normal' feedback in the form of the length of time that they had managed to keep the needle centred during that trial. In addition, one group of subjects were given 'augmented' feedback in the form of a counter on which their total score over trials was accumulated. This augmented feedback had a dramatic effect on performance, as Figure 16.3 shows. The advantage also persisted after the augmented feedback had been removed. In a second day of learning where all subjects just received normal feedback, those subjects who had received augmented feedback on day 1 continued to do better.

Spacing

If you are able to devote six hours to practising a given skill should you do six solid hours of work, or six separate hours on different days? In general, it seems that it is better to *space* practice over several sessions than to *mass* it all together (Welford 1968). There are several reasons why this might be so. One is that fatigue and lowering of attention tend to occur as a repetitive task is continued. As a result bad habits may be formed, with further practice strengthening this undesirable behaviour.

Frequent rests can allow the fatigue and the bad habits to dissipate. On the other hand, when motivation is high, it is quite possible to become totally immersed in a task for many hours without any noticeable loss of attention, so the prescription to space one's practice is by no means a universally beneficial one.

Attitude

A third issue relates to the question of what mental attitude or activity should accompany practice. Should you repeat a task fairly mechanically with an essentially passive mind, intending, as it were, to stamp the skill in by sheer repetition; or should you be actively structuring the task, looking for patterns and similarities, guessing what might come next? This is a somewhat vexed question, and psychologists have not been able to supply any definite answers. It is very clear that sheer dogged repetition does have beneficial effects (see the Siebel study described earlier). There is also a lot of talk in such areas as the psychology of sport about the importance of stopping being too cerebral and letting one's body 'take over'. There is certainly plenty of evidence that we do things better if we can get them to the level of automatic control, sitting back and letting the system 'get on with it'; and it is possible that where physical movements are concerned part of such a process may be the retrieving of early, partly instinctive movement patterns which have become overlaid by maladaptive attempts to control them (Tinbergen 1974).

Even at a more complex cognitive level, a lot of skill learning seems to be largely incidental and unintended. It sometimes seems that if you are interested enough in an activity, your involvement will, in itself, result in the acquisition of some degree of skill. It is when you attempt to acquire a skill that relates to an activity which does not intrinsically interest you that a substitute for interest must be manufactured. Educational researchers have clarified the nature of effective study strategies and skills, and the teaching strategies needed to support them. It can be helpful to see these strategies as ways of getting the unmotivated learner to do what, with motivation, would come naturally. If you think that this seems like a poor substitute for letting people study what actually interests them, and some kind of indictment of our educational system, then you would not be alone (Illich 1973). But this view is incomplete on its own. For even when we are interested to master a particular skill, we can still benefit from advice and feedback. In the acquisition of skills, it is the function of a coach to provide these.

AN EXCEPTIONAL TALENT – A CASE STUDY

I would like to conclude this chapter by describing a quite extraordinary skill, which I have recently been involved in studying (Sloboda *et al.* 1985). The subject of this study, who will be referred to as NP, is an autistic man in his early twenties. Like many autistic people, he is severely mentally retarded. He has almost no spontaneous language, shows social withdrawal and other bizarre behaviour patterns, and he requires the total care of a specialist residential institution. What makes him different from the majority of autistic people is the fact that in one small area of his life he is anything but retarded. He has an amazing capacity to memorize piano music.

In tests that we carried out, NP was able to memorize a classical piano piece (Grieg Opus 47, no. 3) lasting over two minutes, almost note-perfectly in 12 minutes. He did this simply by listening to sections of a tape-recording of a piece and copying what he heard on the piano. A day later, with no intervening opportunity for rehearsal, he was still able to reproduce the piece almost perfectly. At no stage did he observe the printed music, see anyone else demonstrating the fingering, or receive any other extrinsic feedback. He was not told what key the piece was in, but was instantly able to choose the right notes and play them with the right combinations of fingers, even though he had probably never heard the piece before, and certainly had never attempted to learn it.

This level of memory skill is very rare, even among musicians of above-average intelligence. It is probably equalled only by the legendary accomplishments of a handful of prodigies, such as Mozart or Erwin Nyerghihazi (Revesz 1925). NP provides an ideal test case for some of the questions about skill acquisition that we have raised in this chapter.

First, we can ask whether the skill fits the notions of inherited talent that we discussed at the beginning of the chapter. There is certainly little evidence of musical accomplishment in NP's immediate family background, which is one of quite severe social deprivation. He did, however, show early precocity in music, without a great deal in the way of family encouragement. Recordings which survive from the age of six show a level of skill much above that of a normal 6-year-old. It is reported that although he had no piano at home, he made a coherent performance on his very first public exposure to the instrument. Given what is known about his circumstances, the possibility of secret coaching can almost certainly be ruled out. Even today, there is a real sense in which NP cannot actually be taught. His 'lessons' consist of his teacher playing him new pieces to memorize. No one has taught him how to memorize as he does. No one *knows* how he does it, and he is not able to explain himself. Opportunities have been put in his way, but NP must be one of the purest examples of a self-taught expert that exists.

On the face of it, NP looks like providing very strong evidence for the existence of an inherited gift for music. His lack of achievement in any other area of skill makes it look like a quite *specific* gift for music. But appearances can be deceptive, and we would do well to examine this 'gift' a little more closely. The first thing to notice is that the measure of the gift is equalled by the measure of what one can only call NP's obsession with music. Whenever he has a free choice of activity, he almost always chooses either to listen to music (on radio, record, etc.) or to play it. It also seems that when not doing either of these things, he is turning music over in his mind. It would not be unreasonable to suppose that his mind is engaged with music, in an intensely concentrated way, for five or six hours each day. Like Mozart, music is his life and his love. It is hard to know where this obsessive fascination with music came from. It could be a genuinely inherited disposition, or it could come from some crucial early experience. One general aspect of the autistic personality seems to be obsessiveness, and there are in existence people who have similar exceptional skills in other areas, such as mental calculation. Maybe the autistic mind is primed to latch onto an obsession, but the particular obsession may be determined entirely by circumstance.

A second argument against treating NP's skill as a specifically *musical* gift comes from a closer analysis of the way he memorizes music. As well as playing him some classical pieces such as the Grieg, we tried him on a piece which broke many of the rules of 'normal' music. This was an atonal piece by Bartok. Although this Bartok piece (Mikrokosmos, Whole Tone Scales from Book 5) had many fewer notes than the piece composed by Grieg, NP found it almost impossible to memorize. We interpret this as showing that NP's memory skill is based on the ability to chunk conventional musical input into higher-order patterns. When, as in the Bartok, these patterns are absent, performance is severely disrupted. This is just like the chess studies reported earlier, where the master player's memory for the positions of pieces was superior only when the board was taken from an actual game, not randomly constructed. This is confirmed by an analysis of the few errors NP made on the Grieg piece. They were nearly all structurally plausible errors, in which one musically appropriate chunk was replaced by something similar and equally appropriate (much as one might misremember a sentence by substituting synonymous expressions).

All the evidence we have is that extensive practice is the only and inevitable route to the formation of chunks which can make such impressive skills possible. But, as Siebel's random light data show, this chunking process operates on any material whatsoever, and seems not to be essentially different for music or any other specialized material. NP provides strong corroboration for the general equation that *Motivation* + *Practice* = *Skill*. The roots of specific motivations are almost entirely mysterious, but could easily have an inherited component. Practice can be accomplished, however, without any particularly strong motivation, and it seems that our cognitive system will respond by chunking both the inputs and outputs of any task that we practise enough. None the less, amounts of practice of the sort required to attain expertise are almost always unsustainable without strong motivation. Given the most supportive and enriched environment in the world, most of us would fail to acquire many skills, not because we are, in some ultimate sense, incapable of doing so, but rather because, to us, they just don't seem to matter that much.

REFERENCES

Allport, D. A., Antonis, B. and Reynolds, P. (1972) 'On the division of attention: a disproof of the single channel hypothesis', *Quarterly Journal of Experimental Psychology*, 24, 225–35.
Broadbent, D. E. (1982) 'Task combination and selective intake of information', *Acta Psychologica*, 50, 253–90.
Chase, W. G. (1983) 'Spatial representations of taxi-drivers', in D. R. Rogers and J. A. Sloboda (eds), *Acquisition of Symbolic Skills*, New York: Plenum.
_____ and Simon, H. A. (1973) 'The mind's eye in chess', in W. G. Chase (ed.), *Visual Information Processing*, New York: Academic Press.
Eysenck, H. J. versus Kamin, L. (1981) *Intelligence Controversy*, New York: John Wiley.
Gardner, H. (1983) *Frames of Mind*, London: Heinemann.
Hinde, R. A. (1966) *Animal Behaviour*, New York: McGraw-Hill.
Illich, I. D. (1973) *Deschooling Society*, London: Penguin.
Kagan, J., Lapidus, D. R. and Moore, N. (1978) 'Infant antecedents of cognitive functioning: a longitudinal study', *Child Development*, 49, 1005–23.
Newell, A. and Rosenbloom, P. S. (1981) 'Mechanisms of skill acquisition and the law of practice', in J. R. Anderson (ed.), *Cognitive Skills and their Acquisition*, Hillsdale, N.J.: Erlbaum.
Reason, J. and Mycielska, K. (1982) *Absent Minded? The Psychology of Mental Lapses and Everyday Errors*, New York: Prentice-Hall.
Revesz, G. (1925) *The Psychology of a Musical Prodigy*, London: Kegan Paul, Trench & Trubner.
Shaffer, L. H. (1976) 'Intention and performance', *Psychological Review*, 83, 375–93.
Siebel, R. (1963) 'Discrimination reaction time for a 1023 alternative task', *Journal of Experimental Psychology*, 66, 1005–23.
Sloboda, J. A., Hermelin, B. and O'Connor, N. (1985) 'An exceptional musical memory', *Music Perception*, 3, 155–69. University of California Press Berkeley, California.
Smode, A. (1958) 'Learning and performance in a tracking task under two levels of achievement information feedback', *Journal of Experimental Psychology*, 56, 297–304.
Tinbergen, N. (1974) 'Ethology and stress disease', *Science*, 185, 20–7.
Welford, A. T. (1968) *Fundamentals of Skill*, London: Methuen.
Wolf, T. (1976) 'A cognitive model of musical sight-reading', *Journal of Psycholinguistic Research*, 5, 143–71.

Author index

Subject index

ability 88–9
Aborigines 228–9
absent-minded errors 258, 261
abstract conceptualization abilities 148
'academic drift' 106
acceptance 232–3
access 8–10, 159–76; black students
  178–80, *see also* black students;
  courses for women returners 82–3;
  disjunction 161–3, 164, 173–4;
  integration 163–4; learning in relation
  174–5; personal stance 165–8;
  recognising and respecting
  differences 168–70; as stigma 192–3;
  unlearning to not speak 170–3
accommodation 141–2
accreditation: experiential learning
  104–5; unpaid home work 79–82
action research 139–40
active experimentation abilities 148
adaptation to the world 146–50, 151
adaptive mechanisms, hierarchy of 124,
  131
adaptive techniques 185–6
adult development 6–7, 118–35; adult
  education and 119–22; as dialectical
  process 133–5; life cycle tasks
  119–21; methodological difficulties
  122–6; models 95–7; social and
  historical bias 126–33
adult education 87–106; and adult
  development 119–22; adulthood and
  adults 90–7; defining 106; defining
  adults 87; formal, non-formal and
  informal 102–5; individuals and
  groups 97–101
adulthood 5–8, 90–7

aims 243; see also learning objectives;
  objectives
Allende, S. 51
andragogy 6, 92, 109–16; assumptions
  110–11; controversy 111–13;
  'eldergogy' 111; 'gerogogy' 111;
  history 109–10; redefining 114–15
animal skills 262
apprenticeship 41
assimilation 141–2
associations 99, 101 see also groups
attainment 245–6
attitudes 2–3; facilitation of learning
  230–6, 241–2; to gender 31, 33–4;
  and practice 270; teachers' and access
  166
Australia 228–9
automaticity 257–8, 270
autonomous (independent) learners
  195, 200, 203; leadership of groups
  206; motivation 204; preparation for
  learning 197–8; selection of
  materials/methods 201; support 205
Aylwin, P. 63

'banking' concept of education 144–5
barrios 52–3, 54, 55, 58, 64
behaviour 2–3; content and 247; holistic
  theories 148–9; school and work
  216–19; and vocational education 4,
  46–7
behavioural learning theories 138,
  143–4, 151–2
behavioural objectives *see* learning
  objectives
biofeedback 268
black students 9–10, 178–93; access and
  race as stigmas 192–3; adaptive

techniques 185–6; anger 9–10,
179–80, 181, 187; development of
access 178–80; group support 190–2;
hidden curriculum 181–2;
institutional racism 188–9; masks
182–5; personal change 186–7;
personal tutoring 189–90; positive
discrimination 188; remedying
racism 190; unlearning to not speak
171–3
budgets, planning 74
Business Administration qualifications
79
business interests 44
business management 68, 82–3
Business and Technical Education
Council (BTEC) 243

cash flow 74
Catholic Church 53, 62
CENECA 58, 58–9
Centre de Recherches et d'Applications
pédagogiques en Langues
(CRAPEL) 10, 194–206
Chartists 21, 22
chess players 256–7, 260
children: cognitive development 141–3;
development profiles 263–4;
pedagogy 92, 110, 111, 114, 115
Chile 4–5, 51–64; breaking the culture
of silence 61–4; new literacy 56–60;
popular movement 52–5
Christianity 17
chunking 254–6, 266–7, 272
City and East London College of
Further Education 178
coaching 267–70
cognitive development 141–3
cognitive styles 94
collectivism 97–101
common sense 155
communication 200; teachers' skills
167–8
community groups 99–100, 101
community work 67, 68
compensatory education 102
competence 66; unpaid home work 5,
77–82; vocational education 4, 12,
39–40, 47–8
concrete experience abilities 148
concrete operational stage 142
confidence-building 169–71, 225–6

conflict resolution 146–8
constructive feminist challenge 30, 34–8
content 247
continuing education 88, 106
continuity of experience 145–6
coping strategies 185–6
'corporate classrooms' 103–4
Council for Adult and Experiential
Learning (CAEL) 104–5
creativity 150, 151
credit sources 74
critical feminist challenge 30–4
cross-sectional research 122–3
culture 1–2, 88–9; of silence in Chile
51–2, 61–4
curriculum: adult education 88–90,
105–6; feminist challenge to design
30–8

decision-making: experiential learning
150, 151; teaching learning 196–7,
197–8
democracy 64–5
descriptive inventories 127, 128
developing skilled learners (DSL)
219–26; helping others 222–3; ICI
and 223–5; self-help 219–22
development: adult see adult
development; cognitive 141–3;
different profiles 263–4; learning as
adaptation 150; personal 186–7,
237–9, 242
developmental psychology 152
Dewey's model of learning 140–1, 146
dialectical operations 92–4
dialectical process, development as
133–5
differences, recognising/respecting
168–70
diminishing returns, law of 265–7
'disappeared', the 53, 64
disjunction 160–1, 161–3, 163–4
mediating 173–4
domestic workplace see home work,
unpaid

economic analysis, radical 25
economic exchange value 76
education: in adult education 87–8;
'banking' concept 144–5;
compensatory 102; conservative view
of 32; continuing 88, 106; formal,